An Actor
and a
Gentleman

LOUIS GOSSETT JR.
AND PHYLLIS KARAS

FOREWORD BY
CHRISTOPHER LAWFORD

WILEY

John Wiley & Sons, Inc.

Published by John Wiley & Sons, Inc., Hoboken, New Jersey
Published simultaneously in Canada

Design by Forty-five Degree Design LLC

Photo credits appear on page 299 and constitute an extension of the copyright page.

For general information about our other products and services, please contact our Customer Care Department within the United States at (800) 762–2974, outside the United States at (317) 572–3993 or fax (317) 572–4002.

Wiley also publishes its books in a variety of electronic formats. Some content that appears in print may not be available in electronic books. For more information about Wiley products, visit our web site at www.wiley.com.

Library of Congress Cataloging-in-Publication Data:
Gossett, Louis, date.
  An actor and a gentleman / Louis Gossett Jr. and Phyllis Karas.
       p. cm.
  Includes index.
ISBN 978-0-470-57471-3 (cloth : alk. paper); ISBN 978-0-470-62087-8 (ebk);
ISBN 978-0-470-62093-9 (ebk); ISBN 978-0-470-62094-6 (ebk)
1. Gossett, Louis, 1936- 2. Actors—United States—Biography. 3. African American actors—Biography. I. Karas, Phyllis. II. Title.
  PN2287.G65A3 2010
  792.02'3092—dc22
  [B]

                                                                        2009049266

Printed in the United States of America

10 9 8 7 6 5 4 3 2 1

To my two sons, Satie and Sharron. Don't forget who is in charge. It is definitely not you or me or anybody else on the planet.

—Lou Gossett Jr.

To Jason, Belle, and Danny, the loves of my life.

—Phyllis Karas

CONTENTS

Foreword by Christopher Lawford   vii

Acknowledgments   xi

1	The Bubble Burst: Hollywood, 1968	1
2	Twice as Good: 1936–1952	19
3	The Beatnik Years: 1954–1959	55
4	Hooked on Theater: 1959–1963	81
5	Finding My Place: 1964–1967	110
6	More Like Home: 1967–1970	133
7	A Rock and a Hard Place: 1970–1974	149
8	Fatherhood: 1974–1980	170
9	*An Officer and a Gentleman*: 1981–1983	184
10	The Eyes of a Lizard: 1983–1985	196
11	Losing Love: 1985–1992	214
12	Dodging the Bullet: 1992–1993	235
13	Six Months to Live: 1993–2001	247
14	No, Thanks: 2001–2004	255
15	Putting the Demons to Rest: July 4, 2004	263
16	Eracism: January 5, 2006	271

CONTENTS

Photo Credits   299
Index   301

Photo galleries begin on pages 106, 210, and 290.

FOREWORD
by Christopher Lawford

I met Lou Gossett Jr. fifteen years ago when I walked into his production office to sell him on a movie I wanted to produce with him for Showtime. Lou liked the idea, and we worked on the pitch for weeks. The network passed, but a friendship was born. Lou was one of Hollywood's biggest stars; he took a chance on someone with an idea who wasn't afraid to knock on his door. He treated me as an equal, and in Tinseltown that's a rarity. No matter how many awards he has won, and there have been many, Lou has never changed—he's always willing to help when he can and believes it is the right thing to do.

It takes guts to write a book this honest, this revealing, with this level of detail and care. I know—I did it. It's scary to put your life out there like this for all to see. It is clear when you read this book why it has never been in Lou Gossett's nature to shy away from revealing any aspect of his story, no matter how controversial it might be. For his entire life, Lou has never been able to keep quiet. He always had to demand what was rightfully his and say what needed to be said. The gift of having someone like Lou in our world is that there are people out there who don't even know him but will benefit because he will not be quiet. Because he has experienced discrimination and addiction firsthand, he can speak to these issues, and people who hear him know he is speaking the truth.

Reading this book today, in an America where Barack Obama is the forty-fifth president, it is painful to remember what Lou Gossett and other African Americans had to endure to realize their dreams. This book reminds us that it wasn't just people in the South or those marching in Selma who confronted hatred and faced discrimination.

Although I admire Lou Gossett Jr. for myriad reasons, it is our recovery from the disease of addiction that has joined the two of us. We both have a profound commitment to recovery and to our belief that by sharing our stories publicly we will make a difference in someone's life. When I asked Lou to be interviewed for my book about recovery, *Moments of Clarity*, he never hesitated. He revealed a piece of himself that was so vulnerable and so personal. He has done it again in *An Actor and a Gentleman* because he knows that by telling the story about his own descent into addiction and the rebirth into a life beyond his wildest dreams, he is making a difference in a world where this conversation is usually avoided because of fear and misunderstanding.

But more than being an actor or a man in recovery, Lou is a man who cares about humanity, not unlike one of his heroes, Nelson Mandela, a man who feels another human being's pain and struggle and is unconditionally committed to a life of love and service to his fellows. I come from a family where it was never enough to worry about your own well-being or success, but rather it was important to affect change in the world and help others less fortunate. Growing up in Coney Island, Lou developed that same ethic, thanks to his mother, who never stopped caring for children less fortunate than her son. Living in a community filled with teachers and neighbors ostracized during the McCarthy era because of their beliefs not only ignited a passion in Lou for the arts and for telling the truth, but also inspired his deep need to change the world.

Above all, however, there is also great joy in this story about a tall, lanky teenager who loved to shoot hoops in Brooklyn, took Broadway by storm, and beat Hollywood's long odds by winning an Academy Award. It is this enormous wealth of human experiences that makes this book so inspirational and entertaining to read.

Personally, I am most grateful to Lou Gossett Jr. for his friendship and his decency. This is a man you can count on to give a giant performance and bring a character to life, a man who will struggle to do what is right, who will be there when it is easier to turn away. I am certain this book will make a difference in the lives of those who read it, in the same way that this fine, brilliant, and decent man has made a difference in the world.

ACKNOWLEDGMENTS

First, I want to acknowledge God, under whose canopy we all exist. Next, I must offer my heartfelt thanks to my great-grandmother Bertha Wray, who managed to live past 110 and taught me who was always in charge; to my mother and father, who worked tirelessly to make sure that I did not suffer; to my beautiful sons, Satie and Sharron, and their equally beautiful wives, Clemence and Deanna; to Satie and Sharron's exquisite children, Malcolm, Olivia, Brionne, and Mycah, along with Sharron's new family, which now belongs to all of us; to my cousin Yvonne, whose light has always shone brightly in my life; to all the men and women of my family, the Gossetts, the Wrays, the Haygoods, the Hallums, the Baltziglers and the Greens; to my best friend, the late Ed Bondy; to the good Bill W.; and to Cousin Brucie, Ted, Bobby, Stu, Liz, Hubert, and especially Azime.

There are so many more whom I could name that the list would stretch for pages and pages. But for each of those special people, who must know who they are, I thank you with all my heart, wish you every success in your life, and promise that my love for you is unconditional.

Thank you and God bless.

—Louis Gossett Jr.

How could I ever write a single word without the support of my family: my dearest Jack, Adam and Amy, Josh and Chalese? Along with my husband and children, I thank Toby and Larry Bondy, Mel and Eddie Karas, Sheryl Perlow and Dana Bondy, Julie Hoffman and Beth Speciale, Tom and Sherry Bowman, and Joy and Tom Glennon, who never stopped asking and caring. Their understanding and love enable me to work, knowing they will be there when I put down my pen. And my friends— how I treasure each one of them: Sheila Braun, Barbara Ellerin, Karen Feldman, Ali Freedman, Barbara Gilefsky, Sharda Jain, Arlene Leventhal, Karen Madorsky, Barbara Schectman, Risa Sontz, and Sarah Woolf.

I offer my gratitude to fellow writers, Melissa, Anne, Judy, Caryl, and Florence, who listen patiently and offer such wise advice.

And, finally, my heartfelt thanks to the indefatigable and brilliant Helen Rees, who makes everything happen, and Colette Phillips, who made the connection.

—Phyllis Karas

1

The Bubble Burst

HOLLYWOOD, 1968

It was my second trip to Hollywood. The first one, seven years earlier to make the film version of *A Raisin in the Sun*, had been far from perfect. Only twenty-five years old at the time, I had arrived in Hollywood for my first movie full of confidence, buoyed by the critical acclaim for my role in the Broadway production of *A Raisin in the Sun*, and had been caught off guard by any problems. So much had changed in my career since then that I was certain I would now be welcomed far more warmly than I had been received in 1961.

Since my first Hollywood movie, I'd gone on to become a star on Broadway, replacing Billy Daniels in *Golden Boy* with Sammy Davis Jr. I'd hung out with James Dean and studied with Marilyn Monroe, Marty Landau, Steve McQueen, and other up-and-coming stars in an offshoot of the Actors Studio taught by Frank Silvera. I'd learned during those seven years that the only way I could afford my true loves—Broadway, off-Broadway, and summer stock—would be to shuttle back and forth from the East to the West Coast for episodic TV, which could pay a minimum of $2,500 per episode. The time was now right for me to begin this lifestyle, and the show for which I had come to Hollywood was *Companions in Nightmare*. The first NBC Movie of the Week, *Companions* was paying even more than the minimum, more money than I had ever seen as an actor.

Now that I was being paid more, I was certain I would be treated with more respect than I'd found in 1961. Not only had I changed, but surely Hollywood had as well. During the filming of *Raisin*, I'd been forced to stay in a fleabag motel on Washington Boulevard, one of the very few places that admitted blacks. It had the appearance of a true Hollywood edifice, all fluffy pink and aqua and orange, the way they love to make buildings in Miami and Texas and all tropical places. But the clientele of this establishment had been pure black, and the interior was infested with an army of flying cockroaches. When I arrived, I had no idea where the rest of the cast, including Sidney Poitier and Ruby Dee, were staying, but this crummy, dirty motel was my temporary home in 1961. Meeting Bobbie Cote, Sidney Poitier's beautiful, bald-headed leading lady in *Something of Value*, was the only bright light in this dingy hole in the wall. I didn't sleep a wink while I was there, waiting for the cockroaches to land on my prematurely bald head, although I did get a lot of batting practice trying to knock them out. After a few weeks, some of the other actors I knew from New York realized where I was staying and moved me to the Montecito Hotel on Hollywood Boulevard. That's where the rest of the cast were staying—along with a crowd of New Yorkers that included Yaphet Kotto. Ironically, he would be my brilliant understudy three years later in *Zulu and Zayda*.

Now, as I flew to Hollywood in 1968 for NBC's first made-for-TV movie, I was coming back as one of the top clients of the William Morris Talent Agency. Thirty-two years old, I was sitting in first class of the propeller plane, whose engines would continue to vibrate in my ears for days after the flight ended. How those stewardesses treated us first-class passengers! Top-of-the-line restaurant waitresses, they tossed the salad in front of me and made sure that I was entertained, fed, and rested during the seven-hour flight from New York to L.A. Everything was elegantly prepared and served, with real knives and forks and thick cloth napkins, and the food included potatoes with sour cream and chives, rich coffees, and ice cream. There were no in-flight movies then, but I was never bored. This might not be the way airlines are run today, but it certainly was forty years ago.

In any case, I wouldn't have had much time to watch a movie because I spent most of the flight studying the script. I felt overwhelmed by the thought of working with all of those famous people who would be part of *Companions in Nightmare*. I knew from the first moment that I saw the script that movie mogul Lew Wasserman had taken a giant step. He must have personally given the okay for me to play Lieutenant Adam McKay, the chief inspector of the homicide squad. I could hear him saying, "Give the kid a shot. He's good." Both Lew and my agent, Ed Bondy, along with the brilliant director Norman Lloyd, had understood from the get-go that putting a black man in this role in the first NBC Movie of the Week was no small deal. In all of my former roles, such as in *The Desk Set*, where I'd played a mail clerk, I had played subservient or supporting characters. But not in *Companions*. Here, my character would be a peer, a police chief telling the great stars Melvyn Douglas, Anne Baxter, and Patrick O'Neal what to do, when to speak, when to come, when to leave. It might not sound like a big deal today, but in 1968, it was.

I could think of few films and plays during my time, and before, where the African American actor was considered an equal to his white counterpart. There were exceptions, but, for the most part, we were psychologically and subtlely given roles secondary to the white star, not allowed to confront a white actor as his equal. I'd seen Canada Lee do that to a small degree as a sailor in *Lifeboat* with Anne Baxter and as a boxer with John Garfield in *Body and Soul*, but that was it.

Of course, I would never forget *Blackboard Jungle* in 1955, when Sidney Poitier played the tough high school kid who saves Richard Kiley's life when Vic Morrow tries to kill him. Ironically, at age eighteen, I'd been in consideration for that same role, but MGM decided to use established mature actors who could play young for the students' roles. Sidney, who was twenty-eight at the time, turned in an extraordinary and flawless portrayal of Gregory Miller. Yet despite the fact that Sidney saves a white man's life in the film, his role as a juvenile delinquent was far different from my role as the homicide chief. Sidney had just played a Philadelphia homicide detective in *In the Heat of the Night*, where the significance of his role came close to that of my role in *companions*.

I cannot credit Lew Wasserman enough for all that he did for me in entrusting me with the role of Adam McKay. Lew, the last of the creative heads of studios, was raised in the tough city of Cleveland, where he'd always held his own as a Jewish kid. He was also a businessman, a tough man you'd never want to cross. He was the creative mind behind the Universal Studio Tour, along with the Universal Studios theme park. When Lew retired in the late 1990s, that innovative artistic dimension left with him. He was one of the last to hold out before the computer whizzes took over. He died in 2002 at age eighty-nine, but if he were still in charge today, the whole industry would be different.

Lew and my agent had arrived in Hollywood via New York. I believe it was a conscious decision on both of their parts to change history when they made up their minds to have a black man play a character who is equal to, if not more important and powerful than, the established superstars in the film. I have always seen this act as a tribute that should not be left unspoken.

From the moment I got that role, I wanted to be certain that I proved myself worthy of this opportunity. If I was going to shout down the superstar who played the psychiatrist, I would make my voice heard clearly and firmly. There would be no hesitation in my step as I loosened the knot around this doctor who wanted to keep his records sequestered. I would act strongly and with no signs of self-consciousness as I investigated all of his psychotic patients and found the killer in any way I could.

But before I could even begin to try to deal with these concerns in front of the cameras, I had to get to the studio itself, a journey I had never expected to be a nightmare of its own. As with the first-class plane ticket, the journey had begun in style, for this time—unlike in 1961—I was registered at the glamorous Beverly Hills Hotel in a bungalow that was equal to the presidential suite. I was the first black man, other than a diplomat, ever to stay in that suite. To make the pot even sweeter, Universal had rented a white Ford 500 Galaxie hard-top convertible for me. As soon as I checked into the hotel, a magnificent pink castle gleaming like a fairy-tale mountain of luxury, I put on my sexy, colorful Hawaiian shirt and, feeling like a million dollars, grabbed a cab for the short ride to the nearest Budget Rent-a-Car, where my car awaited me.

"This is yours," the guy at Budget told me, as he handed me the keys to the white convertible. "Watch this." Then he pressed some buttons, and the hard top disappeared into the back of the car. Feeling fabulous, my head all puffed up, I turned on my favorite R&B radio station and blasted the music, as I would have done in New York. With one elbow out the window, leaning back into the bright red interior and beaming for all to see as the music pumped away, I headed proudly onto Sunset Boulevard. I had no idea there was something wrong with this picture of a large black man, dressed fashionably, swaying to the music in a shiny white convertible with the top down. So I just began to drive, slowly, eager for everyone out there to see who was behind the wheel of this magnificent automobile. I was sure I was the only other black actor, besides Sidney Poitier, to be treated like this. I had made it. I just had to make the performance perfect to prove I was worthy of all this attention.

But things did not work out the way I had planned. When the first policeman stopped me, it was almost funny. "Where do you think you are going, boy?" he asked me. He was not chewing tobacco, but he could have been the twin brother of Rod Steiger's bigoted police chief in *In the Heat of the Night*. For a second I almost laughed, but when I noticed the deadly serious look in the man's eye, I quickly changed my mind. I read on his badge that he was a sheriff of L.A. County and got a little more worried. "You turn that radio down and put up your roof," he ordered me. Then, taking what seemed like an inordinate amount of time, he checked my license and registration. Finally, after giving me the standard response that black drivers who are pulled over hear all the time, "You answer the description of someone we're looking for," he let me go. No ticket. No warning. I let out a sigh of relief and drove really slowly, roof up, radio off, arms inside the car, grateful the ordeal had ended.

But it didn't take me long to realize that my troubles were just beginning. My "welcome wagon" policeman must have radioed ahead: "He's coming down Sunset Boulevard between LaCienega Boulevard and Doheny Drive. He's passing in front of Ben Frank's in a rented white Ford with red interior." Within minutes, eight of LAPD's finest flew out of the woodwork. Each would repeat the same routine: tell me to lean against my car or the curb, make me open up the trunk, call the car rental office, pretend they were checking me out on the radio, matching my description against the guy they were supposedly looking for, and finally, having pulled me down one more notch, let me go. This army of sheriffs turned what should have been a twenty-minute ride from the car rental agency into a four-hour ordeal.

As I endured the phalanx of nasty policemen who got their jollies from putting me down, I had a sudden memory of a confrontation I'd had years earlier with my great-grandmother Bertha. I'd been no more than sixteen at the time, but I'd been all puffed up that day, too. Thanks to my role in *Take a Giant Step*, I'd been making more money than any other black man in our Brooklyn neighborhood. Dressed in my Thom McAn shoes and my Robert Hall suit, I spent way too much time strutting down the streets, a girl on each arm, reveling in my newfound position as the center of attention.

When I walked into the house one night, Bertha called me over. "You sit down here, Junior," she said in her no-nonsense tone, wagging the remaining half of her right index finger in my face. I'd never forgotten the story of that misshapen finger. She'd been around six when the accident happened. She was walking down the road on the plantation in Georgia, where she'd been born into slavery. Suddenly, out of nowhere, a horse-drawn wagon filled with slaves who'd just learned they'd all been freed hurtled toward her. Terrified that the wagon would run her over, Bertha raced along the road and fell down. One of the wagon wheels struck her hand. Luckily, only one finger on her right hand was smashed. To me, that finger was her badge of honor, proof of the life she had led as a slave.

"And let me tell you something," she continued. "God was here before you got here. He is going to be here while you are here. And he is going to be here long after you're gone. So you might as well calm down and let Him handle things now." I had never forgotten those wise words, which had taken me down a notch or two that night. When Bertha wagged what was left of a finger at you, she might as well have been Sergeant Emil Foley, whom I was to play years later in *An Officer and a Gentleman*. But somehow, that Hollywood afternoon, the memory of her words soothed my deteriorating spirits and helped me endure this maddening experience.

Still, there was no way I could make any sense at all out of what was happening to me that day. Though I understood that I had no choice but to put up with this abuse, it was a terrible way to be treated, a humiliating way to feel. Each policeman seemed adept at finding a new way to demean me, to make me feel violated. I realized this was happening because I was black and had been showing off with a fancy car—which, in their view, I had no right to be driving. I quickly understood that I could not do anything else to draw attention to myself. I had to put up with it. I heard my mother's words loud and clear: "Be careful, son. Don't make any waves."

By the time I arrived back at the hotel, I was struggling to remind myself that it was the city of L.A., not Universal Studios, that had humiliated me. But I was not about to give up. I was here to do a movie. I was a Broadway star and was on my way to becoming a Hollywood star. So I handed the car keys to the hotel valet and walked into the hotel's fancy dining room for dinner—and what a meal it was! Prime rib, sliced at my table, with mouth-watering horseradish condiments, freshly baked bread, delicious asparagus, and strawberry shortcake. It was equal to the most perfect meals I had ever eaten, the dinner I always ordered at Sardi's on opening night, what I call "my favorite rich man's meal." And, most important, the frustration and anger I felt about the car ride had dissipated into a confused and silly memory.

My appetite sated, it was now time to get some exercise, to explore this famous Beverly Hills. It was ten o'clock, and I was not the least bit sleepy. I walked up the street into the canyon, passing the most beautiful and sumptuous homes I had ever seen, all of the movie stars' homes. I had not walked more than a block away from the hotel when the first policeman found me, and I was thrust back into the same scenario I had experienced that afternoon. He was only the first one. These policemen might not have been from the crew who had verbally assaulted me when I'd been sitting behind the wheel of my white chariot, but, despite their air of sophistication, they were cut from the identical cloth as the L.A. sheriffs who had taken such good care of me on their beat.

"Who the hell do you think you are, boy, walking around loose in this neighborhood!?" the first one shouted at me. After I exhibited my license and hotel reservation receipt, he got out of his car, told me to stay where I was, and made a call. As I stood there, I wondered whether I should just run back to the hotel to protect myself from any mistreatment I was going to face.

"Officer," I asked politely, "should I call someone who will identify me?"

"You stay right there," he told me. "Don't you move."

"I am a registered guest at the hotel," I tried to explain.

"We know you are not," he said. "Now just shut up. You match the description of someone who stole a car in this neighborhood. Now you tell me how come you don't have a California license."

"I'm from New York," I said, getting more nervous by the second. "I have a New York driver's license. And I'd be glad to call . . ."

"I told you to be quiet," he said and went back to his car.

Convincing myself that this was yet another weird Hollywood custom, I forced myself to remain calm and keep smiling. Before I knew what was happening, a second car pulled up. A policeman got out and pushed me into the backseat as the first policeman took the passenger seat. I tried to make small talk, assuming this was all a ridiculous mistake, but there was silence in the car as we drove around the area. A few minutes later, the car stopped and the first policeman pushed me out. "Hug the tree," he ordered, shoving me again, this time toward a giant tree on the sidewalk.

Maybe I'm being welcomed to the neighborhood this way, I told myself, struggling to keep calm, to try and make a joke out of this. Maybe the police do this to all newcomers, make them look at the local vegetation.

"There's a law that says you're not supposed to be walking around residential Beverly Hills after nine o'clock at night," that policeman explained, ending my confusion. "You broke the law."

Yeah, but you decide when you are going to enforce and use this law against a private citizen, I thought as I listened quietly. Then the policeman—restraining what I would have bet was an impulse to strike me—pulled out a pair of handcuffs from his pants pocket, along with a long chain. At that point, I knew this was serious. It was not a joke of any sort. "This will teach you," the policeman said, handcuffing my hands together as my arms stretched around the tree.

A second car pulled up, and another cop got out. He suggested that the three of them head into his car to discuss the matter. He was quickly outvoted and told to go back to his car and "stay out of this." He offered me a look of embarrassment, got back in his car, and drove off.

In time, I came to understand that this was just the way it was. Like so many of the guards and the crew at the studio whom I was about to meet, these men were the second or third generations of those who had left the South to come to California during World War II to work in airplane factories and war machines. They had inherited their families' sense of the status quo, and that status quo found the idea of a black star a hard pill to swallow. Unlike the progressive East Coast that I had just left, this West Coast permitted little tolerance for an "uppity" black man.

At that moment, as the policeman tightened the cuffs around my wrists, I had little understanding about who these men were. "I'm under contract to Universal, for a television movie," I tried to explain as I winced in pain. "It's called *Companions* . . ."

At that moment, I did not think of myself as naive or a weakling. I'd grown up in Brooklyn during the race riots that had threatened my hometown of Coney Island. I'd seen *Blackboard Jungle* kids tearing up the streets and one another. And I'd nearly been killed myself when I'd put on a cousin's gang jacket and wandered unwittingly into enemy territory. That day, if it hadn't been for my cousin's vigilant protection, I might have been killed by the leader of an opposing gang. During all of my childhood, I'd felt as if I'd been the chosen one in my extended family, the one who would be better than the best, the one to be kept safe at all costs. Since those days in Brooklyn, though, I had learned how to take care of myself. In 1968, while working on men-at-war training films for the Army's Signal Corps, I had mastered martial arts and could have easily taken down both of these policemen, along with a few of their buddies, but I understood that skill was of no help now.

Violence had always sickened me; the scene of the three white men surrounding my father and our car after a small fender bender many years earlier was imprinted in my mind. My father had walked away from the confrontation, tire iron in hand, the knuckles on his right hand bruised and bleeding, but I'd seen the three white men staring at him with eyes full of hate, screaming obscenities. Alone in the backseat, I'd felt my mother's fear as she kept her eyes locked on the scene outside our window. Even at age six, I'd understood as we drove away that this terrifying encounter was not over. My fears came to life that night when Georgie Terra, my father's best friend, came to our house and used words like *mafia*, *contract*, and *big trouble*. Minutes later, my mother was taking me to my grandmother's house "till the trouble passes." When my father came to get us two days later, I saw the looks on both my parents' faces and knew we were safe again. For most of my life, I'd always recoiled from violence and done everything possible to avoid it.

Now, here I was, a grown man of thirty-two, my arms chained around a tree, my hands trapped in handcuffs. At 6'4" and 200 pounds, I towered over the short, stubby policeman, but I knew that to resist would cause even more trouble. He could have shot me there, and no one would have doubted his motives. An unwelcome black man creating a disturbance on the quiet Hollywood street, I had been resisting arrest. There might have been a small blurb in the papers about this rising star's unfortunate end, but I would merely be one more statistic. One more black man punished for disobeying the rules. My parents' hearts would have been broken, but the planet would continue to revolve. And the policeman would never feel a moment's regret or see a day in jail. Yet the truth was, I was so petrified I could barely think as the police car disappeared into the night.

For the next three hours, I stood there, miserable and humiliated, as passersby stared, some whistling, some with looks of revulsion, others with amusement. People shouted obscenities and threw bottles of beer at me, while police cars, their sirens blazing and horns honking wildly, passed by. The drivers shouted, "You stay there, boy!" or "Don't you move a muscle, boy!" The hideous images of lynchings that had filled so many newspapers and magazines, pictures of bloated corpses and burned bodies hanging from branches, flashed before my eyes. What was going to happen to me? What had I done to earn such viciousness? What kind of place was this city? My questions unanswered, my pants soiled from the urine I could no longer hold, I was finally freed when the original police car returned.

The policeman who had chained me to the tree took one look at me and said, as he released my arms and hands, "You smell too bad to put into a car. Get out of here. And make sure you don't make the same mistake twice." Despite my anger and confusion, I heard his words clearly. They were spoken with no venom or distaste. These Beverly Hills policemen appeared better trained and more educated than the eight I'd met while driving in my rented car. Those guys had been the L.A. county sheriffs. Their Beverly Hills counterparts were responsible for protecting rich folks from people like me. Somehow it seemed all the worse that at the end of my ordeal, these policemen were now acting civil, as if they were simply doing their job, like I'd made a mistake and they'd punished me for it. "Have a good night," the officer told me as he walked calmly away.

I felt as if I had been beaten with dozens of blows in a ring where I'd never had a chance to put on gloves. I walked back to the hotel. When I arrived, the bellboy took one look at me and immediately asked, "Are you okay, sir?" I certainly was not, and I told him why. Within minutes, word had spread to the hotel manager. He tried to explain to me that conflicts were ongoing between blue-collar L.A. cops and flamboyant members of the Hollywood scene and how the two mentalities clashed. Perhaps what had happened to me was a result of this conflict. I thought the manager was just being nice, and, only partly believing him but totally exhausted, I thanked him for his concern and went to my room.

Nearly thirty years later, when I had been living in California for twenty-five years, I would be pulled over in my beautifully restored 1986 Rolls Royce Corniche II, the last year of this classic automobile. As I drove down the Pacific Coast Highway on a lovely late afternoon, with the soft top down and music playing on the radio, a police car came up behind me and put on its lights. I took a deep breath as I pulled to the side of the road, and the L.A. policeman approached my car. "You look like someone we're looking for," he told me. Then he smiled, recognizing me. Five minutes later, I was back on the road, the officer's apology still ringing in my ears. But I didn't feel good.

That night in 1968, however, back in my bungalow at the Beverly Hills Hotel, I felt almost numb. I showered and tossed my clothes into the trash can. Then I called my parents, waking them up, and told them everything that had just happened to me. "I'm coming home," I said. "I don't belong here."

"You get right home, Junior," my mother answered. My story confirmed all of her fears that my honeymoon with fame was over, that the man had finally figured out a way to harm me. She'd clapped at my Broadway performances, filled with a pride that I could see on her face. But, deep down, she'd always suspected that this pleasure would not last. That trouble was just around the corner. That my safety had never been properly ensured. And now she'd been proven right: my life was in danger. "You get yourself on the first train out of that place and come on home."

"Do you want me to drive out there and get you, Junior?" my father had asked, his voice filled with the same pain I'd heard in my mother's words. "I'll be there in a few days. You just stay right where you are till I get there for you."

Yet somehow I had resisted the urge to say yes to their suggestions. I wanted to come home, but I could not. Not yet, anyhow. "I'm going to sleep on it tonight," I told them. "I promise to call you tomorrow."

So I tried to sleep. But every sound in the hotel terrified me. There were noises in the corridor, shadows on the walls, knocks on nearby doors. The policemen were coming to find me, to finish off the job they had begun. No one could protect me here. Not my father. Not my uncles. Not my cousins. No one.

The next morning I was awakened by Ed Bondy. Ed was the mother hen for all of his clients: Julie Harris, James Farentino, Ann-Margret, Ellen Burstyn, Ed Asner, and so many others of our tight-knit New York family. "Why didn't you call me last night?" he greeted me.

"I didn't have your number," I told him. Obviously, the hotel manager had made some calls on my behalf, to Lew Wasserman, to the people at Universal, and someone had contacted my agent.

"Well, what do you want to do now?" he asked me.

"Go to work," I answered.

"That's what I'd expect you to do," he said. "The best revenge is for you to get out there and knock their socks off with your work. You're the best I have. You know that."

I called my parents back and told them I was feeling better, that everything would be fine, and that I was staying in California. I could sense that they were not happy with my decision, but they just told me to be careful. I looked out the window of my plush bungalow and saw that the day was bright and sunny, but I was taking no chances. In the car, I kept the roof up and the radio off and drove slowly toward Universal Studios, telling myself that this was a different day and that last night had been a terrible mistake. Once I arrived at the lot at Universal, however, one guard rudely ordered me to park on the side until he figured out who I was. It took more than an hour, but calls to Lew, Norman Lloyd, the William Morris Agency, and Ed convinced the guard that I was an actor worthy of a parking spot. I never saw that guard again.

Once inside the studio gate, I was not at all certain I could perform the role. The first day on the set, I took Norman aside and said, "I've never had the experience of shouting at Melvyn. I don't know how I am going to raise my voice to one of the greatest stars of our time."

Apparently, Melvyn Douglas heard about my worries and wasted no time in getting to me. Putting his finger on my chest, he said, "Lay it on me. Do your job. Don't be a 'mamby pamby.' This is your shot. Don't lose it." He, too, had courage and made my work easier by giving me an emotion or a line that I could respond to. As in a tennis match, he kept the momentum of our scenes going at just the perfect speed, while always raising the bar to challenge me as an actor.

When I delivered my speech to Melvyn, I was shivering inside, but I made sure you couldn't see my nervousness on the screen. "Don't you be so brash," I admonished the good doctor. "You're not out of the woods. You're still a suspect here."

Even the listing of the cast members, however, seemed to be an issue, because their names were posted in alphabetical order, and there I was, the only black man in the company, with my name preceding those of Patrick O'Neal and Gig Young. I was probably more sensitive to that fact than the others were. As it turned out, the actor whose name was last on that list, Gig Young, was nominated for an Emmy for best actor.

As the filming rolled on, however, and I continued to play my role with authority and conviction, I could see the frequent looks. Who the hell is this guy giving orders? they had to be thinking. But I kept on doing exactly what my character needed to do. I started to feel that the rougher I was in my role, the more I was included in their off-camera conversations, and I felt accepted. I was aware that one actor, who will remain anonymous, always kept his distance from me, yet I preferred to believe that he may simply have been staying in his role when the camera was off. Today, if that actor is reading this book, I hope he will recognize himself and will find me so that we will shake hands, something I am dying to do.

Lunch at the commissary was often the highlight of my day, as I chatted with Gig Young and William Redfield and Dana Wynter, a gorgeous South African actress, about theater and Europe. More and more, I felt as if the cast members were reaching out and pulling me into their circle. My favorite in the cast was easily Anne Baxter, who blew me away with her ability to follow the instructions to alter her performance and try something diametrically opposed to what she had been doing.

I had never seen an actor do this since I'd watched the great Kim Stanley during our rehearsal for *Taffy*, a play that never made it onto the Broadway stage. Kim had this extraordinary talent for transforming herself, with no lights, no makeup, no costumes, into a different person. She would walk no more than five steps, do something as simple as remove a sweater, and either lose or gain fifteen years of her life. Imagine what she could do with a full wardrobe and makeup and scenery. Never before or since have I seen an actress that confident. She laid tape on the floor, and, with no lights on, she carefully figured out exactly where and how she would do that walk. I've never forgotten the way she navigated that scene, walking down to the front of the stage to talk to the audience while she performed.

As for me, I was working doubly hard on my first major Hollywood role, not only to be perfect in that part, but to be perfect when the camera was off. I knew the rules well. I'd followed them before. I was the exception, the token black. I could not wear or say or do the wrong thing. I had to be twice as good as anyone else. I knew from experience how agonizing this role would be to play. It was a tightrope. I was acting in one role and being on my best behavior, yet somehow, in the other role, not honestly belonging to my people. It was going to be a lonely position. But it was mine, and I could not turn it down. Too much was riding on my success.

Yet even when I had convinced myself that it had been only the city of L.A., not the creative people at Universal, that had treated me with such disdain a piece of me had been irrevocably damaged. I understood clearly how the world viewed me. Never before had I felt my skin color as poignantly as I did that first day. Never before had I felt that I was less of a person than a white man was. Anything I'd wanted, I'd managed to attain. Now I had come face-to-face with racism, and it was an ugly sight. But it was not going to destroy me. As long as I understood the rules of the game, I would win. The ultimate prize the game had to offer would be mine.

2

Twice as Good

1936–1952

I've always thought of my early career as a reverse Cinderella story. I started out on top. Sure, there were lean times, but from the very beginning success followed me, delivering me to the right people, pushing me onward and upward. So long as I obeyed the rules. And until I hit the brick wall.

The rules came to me early. My parents, my uncles, my grandparents, my great-grandmother, they all told me the same thing: "You've got to be good. Not just good, but twice as good. No matter how many awards you win or points you score or votes you get, or high grades you earn, you cannot make a mistake. You have to be the very best there is." Mistakes were traumatizing. I couldn't make them.

But in my section of Brooklyn, in Coney Island, I never found it hard to follow those rules. My parents made sure, from the very beginning, that I was in the right place at the right time. When I was seven and things started to get rough in Sheepshead Bay, where I was born, we left our brick two-family house in the predominantly Italian section and moved into a four-apartment building at 2832 West 35th Street in Coney Island. My father was the building's janitor, and we lived in the basement, where I often helped him put wood in the furnace on freezing-cold mornings. My dad worked for the gas company and was also a chauffeur and a numbers guy. Our apartment sat across the street from P.S. 188, the elementary school between Neptune and Mermaid avenues. The apartment's backyard belonged to us. Nothing made my father happier than that small plot of land, where he grew vegetables and planted flowers. This garden was his passion. He spent hours out there, tending to his squash and zucchini. His crowning achievement as a farmer came with the fourteen-pound, award-winning beefsteak tomato he grew. My father's second passion was fishing. Each summer, he and his best buddy, Georgie Terra, caught enough mackerel in Sheepshead Bay to last us all winter long. He salted it in the European manner of preserving fish and then, when we were ready to use it, let it desalt in the sink.

When it came time for his summer vacation, my father headed to Athens, Georgia, to the 148-acre watermelon farm of my mother's Uncle Guvnor. There my father and my great-uncle laughed like children, flopping rinds to the pigs, with some White Lightning in their back pockets. On this farm that smelled and felt so bright and good, I can imagine my parents giggling in the bedroom, so happy, so different from the way they were at home.

From the time I was six or seven, I was lucky enough to spend whole summers on that watermelon farm, working in the vegetable gardens, slopping the hogs with all of that organic garbage, making sure the mules were fed and watered. I'd never tasted food like we had there: fresh eggs from the chickens, cream from the cows and the goats, fresh vegetables from the garden, lots of fresh pork and chicken. Today it is illegal to buy fertile eggs like the ones I ate then or to drink the milk and the cream right from the cow, but the nourishment I received from all of this fresh food sent me back to Brooklyn each September ten times stronger and healthier than my Brooklyn buddies or my basketball and baseball teammates.

Whenever illness might be poised to strike, all of the older women in my Brooklyn family had their weapons ready. They would send me off to my school, a handkerchief engulfed in the pungent smell of strange unidentifiable roots, wrapped tightly around my neck. These herbs, painstakingly stored by the elderly women in my family, were used to ward off the illnesses that filled my classroom. Once I got to school, I usually saw a group of black kids all looking as miserable as me, their necks hidden by handkerchiefs emitting the same overpowering smells from their homemade remedies. Our white friends might point at us in derision, but somehow our group never got polio and we were rarely hit by the coughs and the illnesses that struck so many of our white classmates.

When something did manage to make it through these homemade defenses, the older women were prepared. They kept my mucus-filled chest covered with pieces of flannel, freshly warmed in the oven and spread with a carefully combined mixture of ointments and herbs. In addition, they smeared my chest with Vicks and Musterole. Sometimes they put the Vicks in my mouth, and, after I managed to get it down my throat, I could breathe easier. When all else failed, there was Black Drought, a boiled herbal drink made of senna and magnesia, which I had no choice but to swallow. Seconds later, I would cough up all of the phlegm in my throat.

All of these home remedies, most of them vestiges of our African heritage, did their trick and kept me safe from the diseases that the elderly women feared. They all understood that hospitals were not friends of black people, especially during the years when I was very young. Since the treatment we would have received in hospitals was unequal to those of whites, we had to adopt our own methods of survival. Ironically, modern medicine ultimately copied our treatments, and modern pharmaceutical companies recreated our "primitive" remedies—the expensive way.

For the older women in my life, these pharmaceutical companies would have no impact. They had all heard the sad tale of Bessie Smith, the Empress of the Blues, who supposedly died in 1937 at age forty-three because a white hospital would not admit her after she was injured in a car accident in Mississippi. This may well have only been a rumor, but whether true or false, it was enough to put fear into the hearts of all of my relatives, who knew for certain that they were not welcome at most white hospitals. The fact that Edward Albee dramatized the account in his 1960 play *The Death of Bessie Smith* did not help dispel that fear.

For me, personally, a wasps' nest in Georgia nearly destroyed all of the good health that the elderly women and the Southern food and fresh air had worked so hard to create and maintain. That hot summer day in 1944, when I was eight, I hadn't known what the nest was when, curious, I reached into it and the wasps attacked me. Terrified as the wasps swarmed all over my body, I raced toward the water trough and plunged in.

Sinking into shock, I lay there, barely able to breathe. My great-uncle Ruben, the first one to get to me, pulled me out. Knowledgeable about the importance of alkali, he took the juice from the tobacco he was chewing and soaked it onto each sting. He unquestionably saved my life. The second the juice touched the stings, the pain disappeared, and my mother and grandmother gently pulled out each stinger with tweezers. That was the first of my near-death experiences when some higher power, deciding that my time had not yet come, pulled me to safety from impending death (this time with the aid of a "primitive" home remedy).

Luckily, that particular summer, I made it back to Brooklyn feeling and looking great, as did my father. But it didn't take long for him to appear diminished again, the smiles to disappear from his face, and the alcohol to do its job on the rest of his body and spirit. I loved my Georgia cousins and was excited every time one of them moved up North. But, sadly, most of them never made the adjustment and ended up getting into too much trouble when they left the farm. The transition to the North from the South was a tough reality check for my Southern relatives. The South was our natural habitat; there we could live a simpler life where money wasn't as important as fresh food and making sure the children had the love and support they needed. The farm itself disappeared from our family when my Uncle Guvnor died, and the sheriff showed up with a dog and a shotgun and told my aunt she had to leave. He claimed the taxes hadn't been paid on the land, and poor Aunt Sib, who couldn't read or write, had no way to dispute his claims. The sheriff found Aunt Sib a small apartment in Athens and told her never to go back to the farm. The state eventually reclaimed the land, turning it, I believe, into the Agricultural Department of the University of Georgia. I've often thought about filing a repatriation claim to get the land back into our family, but knowing that it would be a difficult undertaking and would take years of work, sadly, I've never done anything to right that wrong.

My father, Louis Gossett Sr., was a complicated man. When his parents divorced, somehow neither was available to take care of him or his two brothers and sister. Rocco Sylvester, my father's Italian boss at the large newsstand where he worked as a teenager, accepted responsibility for the family. Rocco made sure that the three boys and the girl were never sent to an orphanage. My father looked a lot like Humphrey Bogart and even dressed like and imitated him perfectly in his mannerisms. My father grew up close to the Mafia and, with his horse and buggy, was given the numbers route that encompassed all of Brighton Beach and Coney Island. I remember him coming home with that "Chicago bankroll," all of those bills balled up into one giant roll, the one-dollar bills on the outside. But there was nothing sloppy about that pile of dough. The one time I removed five dollars from it, my father knew immediately that money was missing.

I suspect there were many times that my father's connection to the Mafia saved his life. I also suspect that he'd had no intention of becoming a father so early in his relationship with my mother. It wasn't until I was a grown man that I discovered that my birth certificate had been altered; my real birth date was several months before the birthday I'd always celebrated. My mother admitted that when she worked at the hospital, she'd changed my birth date "to make things look good." My parents obviously "had" to get married. But regardless of how my dad became a father, he always made sure there was food on our plates and a roof over our heads. He was the perfect example of the African American father and husband I would like to salute today—the one who does not make headlines, the one whom our new president acknowledged in a speech after his election, asking that African

American men accept the responsibilities of taking care of their families. His speech echoed my thoughts about working with Congressman Charlie Rangel, to honor these men specifically at a Father's Day event, hopefully in the near future. My father was one of these men who, despite hardships, always provided for his family. He may not have known how to say I love you, but he showed it every day when he went to work and came home with that check. I can't remember one day of my childhood when I felt poor or unloved.

One important thing I did learn from my father, as well as from my grandfather and all of the elders in my life, was that it is not the job that matters but how you do it. If your job is to wash the car or sweep the floor with a broom, then you take pride in that job and do it to the best of your ability. Everything my father touched—his shorts, his suits, his pants, his car—was clean and neat, perfectly polished, as shiny as could be. I share that love of order, but today I never have quite enough time to keep things organized and perfectly tidy the way my father did.

My father remained close with his brothers, both of whom lived nearby and, along with my mother's two brothers, spent hours teaching me how to play ball, developing my athletic skills.

His brother Timothy, the father of my cousin the famous Robert Gossett from the TV series *The Closer*, was a policeman, while my father's youngest brother, Woodrow, was a motor-man. Their sister, Helen, a nurse, worked in Brooklyn and the Bronx. Although my father's flat feet kept him out of the army, both of his brothers fought in World War II: Timothy with General George Patton, and Woodrow with General Douglas MacArthur in building the Burma Road. They came home from the war to find far too many doors closed in their faces. Like my father, they found work, but the daily frustrations they felt as black men working in low-paying jobs left them vulnerable to the excesses of drink. All three men worked hard Monday through Friday, but come Friday night, they would party. Yet the partying inevitably turned violent, and these special men whom I loved so dearly turned into alcoholics.

As I grew older, I saw my father withdraw into this destructive world of alcohol. He became only a small part of my life outside our home, never attending any of my basketball or baseball games, although he did make it to many of my Broadway plays. Imagine my surprise when, as a grown man, I discovered three neatly and perfectly put-together scrapbooks detailing every moment of my basketball, baseball, and acting successes. He had not missed one newspaper story or picture about me. I cannot remember any time that he ever hugged or congratulated me or told me he loved me, but those scrapbooks surely meant that he did love me.

My mother, Hellen Wray Gossett, was a different story. A churchgoing woman who abhorred alcohol or wild parties, she remained close to her parents, Etta B. and Tenny Wray, who lived in Coney Island on 30th Street. Every morning for fifteen years, Tenny walked five to ten miles to his job in a place where they made corrugated boxes. On Friday night, he would enjoy his little pint and then, fueled with his liquor, head into long-winded monologues that seemed to last forever. Yet come Monday morning, he would pour lemon juice, two raw eggs, and boiling hot water into a mason jar and drink it all in one giant gulp. He continued this ritual for more than fifty years. Tenny's mother, my great-grandmother Bertha, lived well past one hundred, although no one was completely certain of her birth date. She lived in Sheepshead Bay, a half-hour drive from Coney Island, but I have many memories of staying at her house and listening to the BMT train rumble by all night long.

When I was a little boy, I loved to watch my maternal grandmother, Etta B., who was part Cherokee, part Seminole, and part black, sitting at the table and combing her thick black straight Indian hair as she wound it into a luscious mound on top of her head. Grandma told me wonderful stories of her parents running across the border from Georgia into the Everglades of free Florida and their battles during the Seminole Wars with Andrew Jackson in Florida. I would never forget one story that I made her tell me so many times. It was about a Seminole Indian who fell in love with a Georgia slave and managed to free her. But a short time later, she was recaptured, and he was so heartbroken that he convinced the owner of the plantation to make him a slave and let him live near the woman he loved. So many other stories of how no one could capture the Indians and how hard they fought are as clear as the memories of her caring for me, an only child. She cooked sweet potato pie and cakes and cornbread for me on a coal- and wood-burning cast-iron stove when my mom didn't make it home for dinner or was too tired to cook. The oven was always full of delicious foods, and I have no idea how that stuff did not burn.

Despite having a stiff leg, my mother worked as a domestic. She had broken her leg in an accident on the famous wooden slide at Coney Island, and even after surgery she could never straighten the leg. She was employed by several families, cleaning two or three houses every day. She took her work seriously and did an excellent job with every house. The Helfgotts, a Jewish family, adored her and treated her well, as did Helen Steers, who was a highly educated woman on the board of directors of the Brooklyn Borough Gas Company. My father worked for that company, and somehow I was introduced to Mrs. Steers. She wrote me a few letters, in the most beautiful handwriting I'd ever seen, and made it a point to reach out and talk to me. "Your father and mother are good people," she told me when I was in high school. "You have fine examples to follow." She followed all of my activities and accomplishments and told my father that if I didn't get a scholarship to college, she would pay my tuition. When I did get the scholarship to New York University, she told me to consider law or medicine.

I took her advice seriously and decided to become a doctor. When I was growing up, I'd been devastated to see so many family members die too soon, cousins older and younger than me. I was especially attached to my uncle Yunnie, Etta's brother, who was unable to stand up on his own. He'd contracted polio when he was six and had never walked again. Still, he managed to be one of my favorite babysitters, always amazing me with the strength he had in one hand. I'd think about all that Uncle Yunnie was missing, how he could never play sports, never travel, never go to any of the wonderful places I was able to walk to. I wanted to become a doctor and make him walk again, and to save all of the relatives our family kept losing to disease. I just knew I had to work hard, which I did in order to get great grades, play good ball, and win that basketball scholarship to NYU.

Lacey Gossett, my paternal grandfather, lived in Bedford-Stuyvesant, an hour's subway ride from our home. Lacey was a sight to behold. Six feet four inches tall, barrel-chested, gold teeth gleaming in his mouth, his shoes spit-polished on his feet, impeccably dressed, he resembled the heavyweight fighter Jack Johnson. King of the barber shop, where he took me once a month, the man was larger than life. He always had a good-looking woman taking care of him. The one I remember, Miss Les, cooked delicious foods and ran to his side whenever he called. Unlike my father, who rarely complimented me, Lacey let everyone know how proud he was of me, especially when I became an actor. He would order me to stand on a chair. "That's my grandson," he proudly announced to anyone in the barber shop or wherever he took me. "He's something else."

All of my large extended family lived within close proximity of one another in Brooklyn. Every holiday, we all got together in one house. While the women were in the kitchen, preparing the savory meal and serving and cleaning up, the men kept busy in the dining room. There, the table was also laden with bottles of liquor, every single one of which was emptied by the end of the night. This table, the food surrounded by the numerous bottles, told the black and white of our family's story. Sometimes my father and uncles collapsed on the couches, exhausted, but most often the sound of a shattered glass signaled the change from fun to anger, from a family joined by love to one disrupted by drunken spirits.

As the years went on, I could not help but notice the gradual change as the alcohol took its toll and the violence increased. As each man lost control of his feelings, fights over nothing escalated into drunken brawls. Somehow, it was safe to get drunk with the family, in their own homes, as long as all of the women and children were safe and, at that moment, taken care of and well-fed.

I watched, heartsick, as the men hit one another or their wives, and one by one they stumbled out the door, barely able to find their way home. These were the same men who had taught me how to play ball, who had tickled and kissed me and taught me so much about sports and life. They were larger-than-life heroes to me, yet I saw each one disintegrate into a drunk before my eyes, often in my bedroom, which was now filled with empty bottles. Because I normally slept in the living room on a bed my parents opened up for me every night, I was usually sent to sleep on the bed in my parents' bedroom until the party ended. But the empty bottles were a reminder the next morning of what had taken place the night before.

It was only later that I came to understand how difficult it had been for my uncles to return home from the war, unable to get the good jobs that their white counterparts in the military found so easily. These men had sacrificed their whole lives so that their children could have better lives than they'd had. And when they finished working at the unsatisfying jobs they'd eventually found, their reward, their one way to get rid of the devil inside, was with alcohol. Diminished by frustration, they had sought the bottle as a refuge for their shame. They always hurt the ones they loved the most, following the same patterns as many of their Southern relatives and leaving a legacy of broken bottles and crushed spirits that I would regretfully and helplessly continue.

At that time, however, we children weren't allowed to drink with them. Since I couldn't stand the taste of the liquor, that was no problem for me. For us kids, the way to get rid of the same devil was to join our parents in their spirited hearty dances, the Lindy Hop, the Boogie Woogie, dances that would lose their fun spirit and turn wilder. I watched as the men knocked over tables and threw the women around, over their heads and through their legs. I sensed the tinge of violence in these masterfully performed dances, the same violence that disrupted and ended our holiday meals. But don't get me wrong: though alcohol eventually took its toll, there was a great deal of love in my extended family.

My family was far from unique in its behavior, which I see as even more prevalent among many low-income families, with alcohol abuse remaining one of the curses of poverty. Today, after I have met and, for the moment anyhow, put my demons to rest, something still happens to me when I am around people who drink. My nostrils become large as I smell the sadness at the end of an evening that has deteriorated into drinking. I feel a surge of sickness as I wait for the change when the laughter grows louder and harsher, the voices shrill, and the violence inevitable. I can no longer be part of this ugly scene and leave before the revelers stagger out, looking for cabs or fights.

Yet this scene of alcohol-induced violence inside our families' homes never spilled outside the doors into our Coney Island neighborhood. My neighbors—Irish, Jewish, and Italian, and just a scattering of blacks—along with the love of my family, nurtured and sustained me, keeping me nutritionally sated in every possible way during my childhood. Together, certainly well before advent of cell phones, mothers kept their eyes out for all of us, for every kid who walked the streets beneath their windows. "Do you have your sweater on?" they asked whenever I appeared on their brownstone's stoop, ready to play our own version of stickball or hide-and-seek. "Where is your hat and mittens? Go home and get them this second."

From the first time I held a ball in my hand, my best friend Melvyn Dick was at my side. Somehow, Melvyn got Sugar Ray Robinson to sponsor our baseball team and even managed to get sort of adopted by the legendary boxer. And my other best friend, Norman Ostrin, was an incredible basketball player. As were Alan Buck, Shelley Seltzer, and the ever masterful Barry Storik, whom we called "Stick" because he was skinny as a stick. But nothing fun could happen until the homework was done. "Did you do your homework, Labele?" the mothers would yell. "You better have, or you're in big trouble!" And these mothers were too smart for us to try and fool.

Somehow, they managed to see my marks before my own mother did. "Mrs. Gossett," they would tell her the minute she got home from cleaning her last house, "look at your son's spelling test. He got a C. We'll help him, if you want, but he can't play stickball unless he studies that spelling list." The worst thing to happen to any of us was a note sent home from our teacher. If you got one of those, there would be hell to pay. I learned early to do whatever it took to make sure I didn't get one of those notes.

31

The athletic prowess of the kids I grew up with was legendary. Once when I was about fourteen and playing for the Sugar Rays, the team sponsored by Sugar Ray Robinson (who was happily sponsored by the Mafia), I was up against Sandy Koufax, who was pitching for the Parkviews Fuel Company. All I knew that day was that this pitcher threw 100 miles per hour, and the day before had sent a kid to the hospital with his fastball. "Dig in with a swing, Louie," my friends yelled at me as I stood there, the only black kid on my team, clutching my bat. I did the one thing I was capable of doing. I closed my eyes and gritted my teeth, and suddenly I heard a sound and the manager was screaming, "Run, Louie, run!" I had no idea how it had happened, but I'd had one of the very rare hits Sandy ever allowed. He was one year older than I was and a student at Lafayette High. The summer we were both chosen to go to the basketball clinic for the Knicks, I said little if anything to him. But I was well aware that no matter what kind of ball he held in his hands, this kid was the number-one athlete of our city.

In my particular neighborhood of Coney Island, there were few black kids. My parents' move there had assured me a safer neighborhood than some of the adjoining ones. Here, my white friends treated me as if my skin were the same color as theirs. "You play Superman today, Louie G," they would say as they handed me the requisite towel for my neck. "Up, up, and away!"

Yet there were times when they couldn't ignore the difference in our skin colors—like the hot summer afternoon when we all decided to leave the free swimming pool at Washington Baths and invade the exclusive Raven Hall pool. We raced past the flabbergasted man at the entrance and were heading into the water when a hand reached out and grabbed me by the seat of my bathing suit. "What are you doing here, kid?" the man screamed at me and unceremoniously dumped me outside the gate.

I hadn't even made it to my feet when the roar of my buddies' racing feet reached me. "Let's get the heck out of here!" they screamed and led the way back to "our" pool. It's likely that some of their parents could have been heard asking, "What the hell are you doing playing with that *shvartze*?" But I never heard those words. All I heard were nurturing, encouraging, loving words from their mothers. We were like the Gas House Bowery Boys, inseparable, totally loyal to one another.

In honor of my Jewish friends, I started to take off for the Jewish holidays. I'd spent too many Rosh Hashanahs looking out the window at my Jewish friends playing basketball while I sat in school with three Irish kids and a substitute teacher. One Rosh Hashanah, I joined my friends in the yard. When I went to school the next day, my teacher said, "Why were you absent? You aren't Jewish."

"I'm in sympathy with the movement," I answered her, and she seemed to understand. From then on, I celebrated every Jewish holiday by staying away from school. I did date a few Jewish girls, in particular, Sandi Turner, from the Everhard pencil family, who, at fifteen or sixteen, seemed very glamorous, as did her mother. I also dated Ruthie Fleisher, who, along with Sandi, was in all of the school plays. We hung out together in Greenwich Village and kept our friendships going through our freshmen year of college. One of my best friends during high school and college was another Jewish girl, Sue Yellin, who ended up producing jazz festivals in the Caribbean. When we were growing up, I was invited to their birthday parties in Coney Island, affairs where I was often the only black kid in attendance. During my junior year of high school, at Abraham Lincoln, I made a new black friend, Doyle Scott. Together with Doyle and some more black kids who also arrived at the high school, we joined a group called the Riveleers and sang in the bathroom and the subway stations, where our voices echoed off the tile walls.

Most of my dates in high school, however, were black girls like Loretta Lindsey and Mary Andrews, nice pretty girls from intact families in other Brooklyn neighborhoods. While Mary married a man in the army and lived in Japan with the military for many years, I have no idea what happened to Loretta. I had learned at a young age that if I wanted to date a white woman like Sue or Sandi or Ruthie, I'd better leave the neighborhood and head into Greenwich Village.

Not all of my moments with my Jewish friends were pleasant ones, though. One particular night when my parents were working at a Jewish neighbor's party, serving drinks and appetizers, they decided to bring me along. Early on, dressed in a waiter's outfit, I saw a tiny snicker on my buddy's face as I passed around a plate of potato pancakes. My father was especially uptight that night and seemed to have his eyes on me every second. As the evening wore on and my friends' snickers grew into giggles, I felt more demeaned by the whole scene. In the kitchen, my father slapped me for some imagined mistake on my part and sent me home before the party ended. "Never again will you work at one of those parties," he told me when he and my mom arrived home that night. In retrospect, I realize now how desperate my family was for money and how much we had needed the money that night. But my father never asked me to work with him again.

Still, it is not that one memory, but rather many others of sitting in the houses of my Jewish friends, eating dinner or a snack, that stay with me. In that neighborhood of kitchens and opened windows I was protected, nurtured, loved, and educated about how to take care of myself, how to dress, and how to act. Nevertheless, my parents, especially my mother, never stopped warning me to be careful, to be aware of the danger that was all around me. I did understand that there were areas of my own neighborhood where none of my cousins ever went, places where Mafia-related gangs hung out. Because of my father's connections with members of the Italian Mafia, we did not worry about those gangs, but they were often in the news. I was five years old on the night in November 1941 when well-known hitman-turned-informant Abe Reles was thrown out of a window in the Half Moon Hotel in Coney Island. He had been under twenty-four-hour police protection there, preparing for his testimony against Albert Anastasia, the boss of the Gambino crime family. Reles never got to testify, but the movie *Murder, Inc.* with Peter Falk told his story.

When I was twelve, my family moved to the lower-income housing projects at 3020 Surf Avenue, overlooking the Half Moon Hotel and the boardwalk. The friends with whom I played basketball two hundred feet from the infamous spot where Reles met his death missed some good shots by glancing up at that memorable window. My father later worked in the freight elevator in that hotel, where he was suspiciously popular. I was never quite sure why they all knew him by his first name, perhaps because he was one of the first black Italians any of them had ever met. I only knew that he ran that elevator so fast, it made me throw up every time I rode it with him.

I was in awe of my principal, Leon S. Kaiser, at the Mark Twain Junior High School. There, I became the first African American president of a class and later was also elected, by a landslide, president of my class of more than fifteen hundred students at Abraham Lincoln High School. I was aware that somehow I was popular, both in the classroom and on the athletic fields, but it didn't make much sense to me. I did know that from early on, music moved my soul, and I loved singing in a gospel group in the intermediate choir of the First Baptist Church in Coney Island. Ethel McRae and Dorothy Jones, the original Raylettes, the Ray Charles background singers, were part of that choir, along with the Chiffons.

God had given me something that I couldn't identify, although later it would be explained to me as "charisma," something that drew people toward, rather than away from, me. Our senior year election had been a blast. My opponent, Paul Steinberg, who ended up a state senator in Florida, had used the motto "Think right; vote white." My motto, "Strike back; vote black," seemed to have appealed to more of the students. Today, Paul's motto would have been considered offensive, but in 1954 it was anything but that. I cannot remember one outwardly racist scene during my high school years. I never understood why everyone seemed to like me. I wasn't much of a drinker, both because my father was strict about my doing as he said, not as he did, about alcohol and because, at least back then, I couldn't stand the taste. Yet I did hear my friends say over and over again, "Without Louie, there is no fun."

Despite the ease with which I moved in the classroom, on the baseball field and the basketball court, and through the homes and the streets of Brooklyn, I was perpetually aware of my need to excel, of those rules that had been imprinted on me early, not only to be the best, but to be better than the best. Not just good, but twice as good. It was repeatedly drilled into me, by my parents and my uncles, that I was the chosen one, the exceptional one. I thought this over many times, trying to understand why this was happening. Why had everybody decided that I was the one who was going to succeed, to rise above everybody else in our family? Maybe because I was good in school and in sports and had lots of friends. I could never figure out the answer to this question, but I did realize early on that this role did not come without responsibilities—and its own share of problems.

In order to be the best, I could make no mistakes. Not only my grades, but also my respect for elders, had to be exemplary. While some of my peers hung out on the streets of Brooklyn on Sundays, I went to church. My cousins were always my protectors, fighting my battles for me. They found out that there was a contract to beat me up, and they did whatever fighting had to be done to get the contract removed. I had no idea what I had done to make these other black kids so angry. Perhaps I was acting uppity, or maybe they were sick of hearing their parents say, "Why don't you act like Louie Gossett?" Most of the time, I had no idea I was being protected, but sometimes my cousins came into my neighborhood and said, "You just stay inside, Cuz Junior."

When word was out that there would be gang activity or any sort of trouble, I was sent out of town, to stay with relatives in Georgia or, equally wonderful, in the Bahamas. Those annual summer trips to Georgia were motivated, in part, by an attempt to help me avoid the race riots that erupted as the temperatures rose. It was a concerted effort on the part of my cousins to keep me far away from the gang fights. No one could touch me. My slate was to be clean. If someone was gunning for me on those streets, my cousins would deflect the bullets—literally.

I remember going to church or even school and on the way seeing my cousins in an alleyway fighting with a rival gang or one of my cousins holding someone down on the ground. When I got home, I would find out that my cousins had taken care of someone who was gunning for me. In some strange way, it was as if all of my cousins knew that I would have lots of hard times as I found my place in the world outside Coney Island. They all knew that when I was finally on my own, I would be conned and ripped off, and I was. That I would be hurt and disappointed, and I was. But they also knew I'd have to leave Brooklyn and that there would be many places where they could not protect me.

Somehow, as a result of that protection, I developed an innocence and a purity that made me yearn then, and today as well, for an end to violence. During those childhood years, I felt as if I could do no wrong, that there was a shield around me, a feeling that continued until I rented the Ford Galaxie in Hollywood. Thanks to this shield, I was untouchable, safe, doing things no other black person could do, things I didn't have to pay for in any way at all. At the same time, I wasn't consciously letting God be in charge, but I did believe that somehow God was giving me a taste of what it should be like for all of us, especially for the minorities in this country. That may sound naive and unrealistic, but I have a suspicion that if we don't think in those kinds of terms, we are lost. I know personally that when I make the choice of believing in and trusting a higher power, I reap rewards I never thought possible. My newfound closeness with my sons is one example of this, but those days were far away when I was still a boy in Brooklyn.

During that childhood, the closest I came to violence occurred on the day I was visiting my cousin Eugene Hallums. Eugene was part of a gang and always wore a silver jacket and a round white hat. I was about twelve at the time and decided to bring that neat jacket and hat home with me for a week. The next time I went to visit my cousins in Bedford Stuyvesant, I put on the jacket and the hat, took the BMT train to Prospect Park and then the shuttle three stops to Fulton Street, went downstairs, and began the eight-block walk to Nostrand Avenue. I had not walked more than half a block when I was suddenly surrounded by six older black kids, all wearing their various-colored jackets and hats. And not one of those jackets or hats was silver or white.

Before I knew what was happening, these kids had pushed me against a wall, and their leader was pointing a zip gun at me. The gun was a homemade wooden contraption, with a barrel that was a hollowed-out tube of metal. It might have looked homemade, but it came with a .22 slug released by a thick rubber band. My eyes locked with those of the guy holding the gun, and I knew I was looking into the face of death. He never blinked, just pulled the trigger and broke the rubber band. I should have been dead, but I wasn't. The gun had not gone off. Shocked, the kids released my arms, and I took off. Until I reached Nostrand Avenue, I broke the world's speed record. When I finally got to Nostrand, my pursuers stopped, as if facing a wall that barred their entrance onto the street. After I raced across the street, I allowed myself a look back, and there they were, the six of them, standing and staring at me.

When I finally made it to my cousin's house, he pulled the jacket and the hat off me and made sure I never wore them again. When it came time for me to leave, all of my cousins walked me to the train. After I was safely heading back to Coney Island, my cousins, ever my protectors, made their presence felt. They called a meeting of their gang and paid a visit to the neighborhood of the rival gang that had pursued me. I heard later about the rumble that took place between these two gangs and considered it a miracle that no one was seriously hurt before the incident was finally put to rest.

As for me, I never forgot the look in the eyes of the teenager who nearly killed me with one of the many bullets I would miraculously escape during my life. It was many years later when I learned that the person who'd held that zip gun had the last name of Patterson. I was never sure whether it was Floyd Patterson or his brother. Floyd spent two years at the Wiltwyck School for Boys, a reform school in upstate New York. I have no idea what happened there, but when Floyd left Wiltwyck, all of the anger and unrestrained violence was gone. He became a two-time world heavyweight boxing champion, and that violence remained in the ring, where he performed according to the rules. His brother, sadly, went to Sing Sing for manslaughter. Years later, when I met Floyd and related what had nearly happened to me, he broke into tears. "It could have ruined two lives forever," he said as he hugged me.

I wasn't terribly scared by the whole scene until I got home that evening, and the thought of what might have happened overwhelmed me. It made me despise violence even more, especially glamorized violence, so much of which I would see later in life.

During those days, I was living a Walter Mitty fantasy life, dreaming that I could be the Green Hornet or Captain Marvel or anyone I wanted. Safe in this fantasy world, I could easily ignore any subtle racist slurs that might have come my way. It didn't take much to make me happy. Every Saturday I'd go to the movies and sit in the balcony with my friends, watching Superman, Hopalong Cassidy, Gene Autry, and Roy Rogers and Dale Evans. At home, when I was little, maybe six or seven, I sometimes got confused with the characters in my fantasy world. Once I wrapped my mother's bath towel around my shoulders and with complete faith jumped from the first stoop down the flight of small stairs. All that I got from my efforts, however, was a spanking, a fat lip, and a gap in my teeth. I knew there was a lot going on outside my fantasy world, but, like Walter Mitty, I was comforted by the characters in my head.

I needed a lot more than imaginary characters to comfort me one July Fourth, though. I was thirteen that afternoon when I crashed headfirst into a pile of concrete while playing softball. My friends and I were in a school playground that had been built on a landfill. Uttering the Lord's Prayer the whole ride, two of my uncles drove me, barely conscious, to Coney Island Hospital. Miraculously, I had escaped with only a badly broken nose, a bunch of stitches, and a concussion. The doctor straightened my nose with his finger and without Novocaine. At the time, I heard a weird humming sound, similar to the noise when the TV gives off a test pattern. I could feel myself walking to the end of a long path. Yet something happened, and I turned around and walked in a different direction, heading back from where I'd come, rather than moving farther down the path. Once again, it wasn't my time yet.

My Brooklyn friends, however, certainly had a lot of living to do in those days. For some of them, but not for me, it involved drinking a little Sneaky Pete. By the time I was fourteen, my father and my uncles had actually become concerned that I was such a goody-two-shoes and wondered whether perhaps I was a homosexual. When I got my first love pregnant that year, after dancing the grind in one kid's basement, followed by sex under the boardwalk at Coney Island, there was a lot of giggling, along with pleased looks behind my back that said, "The boy had it in him all along." I was led to believe that the girl got rid of the baby, but I never found out for sure, an unanswered question that has never left my mind.

Yet even though I had proved I was a man, I never ignored the messages I received from the churches, as well as from people like Mrs. Steers. "You're lucky that you're a black man who has a chance to go places, to be larger than life." "If you make a mistake, it would be horrible." "You could be shiftless in private, but never in public." I had a heavy weight on my shoulders. I had a job to do, and I performed it to the best of my ability. It was a job made far easier by the quality of the teachers who led me through doors that I might never have known existed. Teachers who taught me Latin at age eight. Teachers who had been college professors and were accused of being communists by the Tennessee senator Estes Kefauver and forced out of those classrooms by their accusers. Black-listed teachers such as Gus Blum, originally Gustav Blumberg, the playwright-director who was pushed out of the theater by the ugliness of the McCarthy era.

It was my very good luck that Gus landed, along with many of his fellow left-wing activists, in the classroom, where he was able to influence a host of young minds. These teachers carried me on their shoulders, making me feel, as they did all of the other Jewish, Italian, and Irish kids in my classes, that I was special.

My parents had known what they were doing when they moved to this neighborhood in Coney Island. My schools were the best in the city, scholastically as well as athletically. Abraham Lincoln High School had a magic that other schools in the country could only envy. The list of our alumni is beyond exceptional. It includes a Nobel Prize winner, a federal judge, and a pitcher for the All American Girls Professional Baseball League, along with Neil Diamond, Mel Brooks, Harvey Keitel, Joseph Heller, Arthur Miller, Marv Albert, and the fictional graduates from *Friends*, Ross and Monica Geller and Rachel Green.

The success and fame of these graduates have to be credited to our teachers. These brilliant men and women not only taught us in their vibrant classrooms, they lived in our neighborhood, opening their homes to their students, showing us their globes and photographs of other countries, teaching us the difference between French and Turkish coffees, welcoming us at their dinner tables, offering us their mentorship, along with stories of other countries that opened our eyes to the world beyond Surf, Mermaid, and Neptune avenues. Many parents of my classmates were professionals, and they, too, shared their experiences and knowledge with us. So many had come to Brooklyn from abroad, giving our neighborhood a genuine European feel.

Even the stores had that European flavor. Nearly every day, I went to the corner grocery store for my mother or grandmother and brought home a chunk of freshly cut farmers' cheese or meat or salami. Or garlic or challah bread or a pickle from the barrel. And, of course, I would have to stop for a knish lathered with mustard from the knish man to hold me until supper. To this day, when I walk by Zabar's on 80th and Broadway, I stop and inhale deeply and let the smells wafting from the store carry me back to Coney Island.

The food my grandmother prepared for my lunch every day was a feast in itself. Every school day at lunchtime, Al Strojan, an all-city linebacker for our high school football team and a true bully, would walk over to a kid and punch his sandwich, squashing it into an inedible mess. One day right after Thanksgiving, he punched the turkey-and-tomato sandwich my grandmother had made for me. I have no idea how I got there, but before I knew what was happening, my friends were pulling me off Al. No one in his right mind would have attacked a kid of his size, but it was my grandmother's sandwich we were talking about here. Oddly, after that scene, Al and I became good buddies.

Even though our parents had little money, my friends and I never seemed to want for a thing. When I grew older, I also remember that thanks to the amusement park at Coney Island, my friends and I had a chance to earn spare change for our pockets. On that two-mile boardwalk, I worked at the Howard Johnson's booth, with its pledge of "26 flavors," located directly across the street from the subway station, which was the last stop for all of the trains that left the city and came to Coney Island. As all of the riders spilled out of their trains, the first person they saw would be my father at his newsstand. And next to the newsstand was Howard Johnson's. Here at Coney Island visitors could throw a dart and break a water balloon or roll a ball into a circle and win a prize or take a chance at Pokereno—which was similar to skee ball, only with numbers like poker, such as the ace of spades—at which I became an expert. I watched elderly people sitting in oversize straw carriages pulled by bicycles, looking at the beach and having a wonderful time, as the music played all day long.

Eventually, I moved a block away from the Howard Johnson's booth when I went to work at Nathan's. Now let me reveal a personal secret I gleaned from those years at Nathan's. The reason Nathan's hotdogs and shrimp and French fries all tasted so delicious was because the cooks adhered to the European method of cooking: leave one percent of the oils in the pans and the pots when you clean them out. It was the residue of cooked oil that created those distinctive tastes.

I was there selling hotdogs that day in 1949 when the race riot erupted. Before I could understand what was happening, my white boss had pulled me into the back of the booth, protecting me from danger. So often, the streets of Brooklyn were calm from Sunday through Thursday, but when the weekend arrived, the Brooklyn gangs with their various-colored satin jackets—the Diddybops, the El Quintos, and the El Diablos—were ready to charge, releasing the anger they felt all week long in their battles against one another.

My life in Coney Island took an unexpected turn that led me away from those streets when a foot injury kept me off the basketball court during my junior year. My English teacher, Mr. Blum, who was never seen without his black beret, was in charge of the drama club. He urged me to take the lead in the club's upcoming performance of *You Can't Take It with You*. Playing the role of the maid's boyfriend, I never took it seriously and just had fun at the rehearsals. When my performance brought the house down on opening night, I had no idea what I had done. Yet the magic of that moment, of hearing the applause and laughter of the audience, of being carried away to somewhere I had never reached before, not even during the height of a fiercely fought basketball game, touched me in a place I never knew I owned. I was hooked—and so was my audience.

God had given me this gift that I had never realized I possessed. I might have been a bit nervous before the show began, but the minute I hit the stage, something kicked in. I got a feeling from the bottoms of my toes to the top of my head that directed me around the stage. It was an ability that I learned later usually took other actors years to develop. I still wanted to be a doctor, but this acting experience had been something else. Mr. Blum told me I had a gift, one I should never take for granted. And I never have.

Still, when he insisted that my mother bring me into Manhattan for the tryouts of *Take a Giant Step*, telling us, "What could you lose? It wouldn't hoit," I went reluctantly. I was sixteen years old, and I would have rather stayed home with my friends to shoot hoops than be dragged into the city for some ridiculous tryout. There were three hundred aspiring black actors vying for the role of Spencer Scott. It would be a waste of time for me.

The tryout appeared to prove my point. My mother had made sure I was wearing the very best clothes I owned, including some new Thom McAn shoes that felt like wood on my growing feet. She kept telling me to prepare to be disappointed, that I was not going to get the role. But that I had to try anyhow because Mr. Blum wanted me to. When I got to the tryout, I felt an unexpected twist of desire. There was something happening on this stage that I wanted to be a part of, even more than I wanted to go home and play ball with my friends. I walked onstage, which was lit with one bright light, and read my lines. For those minutes I was unaware of anything except the words and thoughts of Spencer Scott. When I finished, at first I heard nothing. Then I heard giggles. The spotlight was in my eyes, and I couldn't see anything. People were laughing at me. I started to cry and ran off the stage, where my mother was waiting. "What happened, Junior?" she asked me nervously.

"Let's get out of here," I told her and started to pull her away.

As we walked out of the building, a skinny black man came after me. "My name is Louis Peterson, and I wrote the piece," he said. "And you sounded so much like me that I couldn't help myself. I'm sorry. We're not laughing at you. Please come back and read a little more for us."

So I did. They called me back four more times to read for other people. When they called me back for the fifth time, they told me the role was mine. "But we've got to change your Brooklyn-Jewish accent," they told me. "And work on a few other things." So they began an intense ten-week regimen of what they called "cleaning and learning."

After speaking with my parents for a long time, they came up with a plan for me to move into the Newtown, Connecticut, home of Jo Mielziner, a friend of Max Allentuck, the company manager. Jo was going to be out of the country for the summer and volunteered his beautiful home for my "summer drama camp." It would be here that a team of writers, acting teachers, actors, and directors would work on my accent and acting skills. My mother was delighted. It would get me out of the city for the summer, and I would be in a big house with good food and nice people. And they were going to pay me a great deal of money to be in this play.

What a team I had! I was now under the tutelage of the play's writer, Louis Peterson, and his wife, the actress Peggy Feury, from the famous Lee Strasburg Acting Studio, along with the play's director, John Stix; the producers Thomas Noyes and Lynn Austin; Max Allentuck and his wife, Maureen Stapleton; and Frederick O'Neal, who played my father.

Every day that summer, these skilled actors and voice and drama teachers took me from scene to scene, drilling me over and over on every word, presenting me with a concentrated course of acting with people whom I later learned were the top in the drama world. I repeated rhymes like "She sells sea shells down by the sea shore," "Ninety-nine nuns in an Indiana nunnery," and "Many mild-mannered monks in a Minnesota monastery" so many times, I was reciting them in my sleep. Slowly, my Brooklyn-Jewish accent disappeared, and a new voice came to life. I had no idea who all of these actors and producers and writers were, but each one was as kind as could be. They spent hours teaching me how to do a particular scene, blitzing me with words and instructions all day and night. I had no idea what blind providence I had fallen into, that I was working with such famous and gifted men and women, who were the soul of the acclaimed Actor's Studio in New York City. And each of them was concentrating his or her energy on this sixteen-year-old boy from Brooklyn who had no acting experience and was about to "take a giant step" on Broadway.

My parents came to visit to make sure everything was fine. They were pleased to see that I was on a big farm and that I was eating fresh vegetables and drinking lots of milk. I grew even taller that summer, and, at first, all I wanted was to shoot hoops in the big yard and swim in the pool. There were frequent barbecues, and I did have time to swim in the pool and play basketball with some of my teachers. Best of all, the house had the most incredible library I had ever seen. It was to this room, completely lined with books from top to bottom, that I headed every evening after my classes ended. Obviously, my teachers knew what they were doing and left dozens of books lying around, especially those by Chekhov, Ibsen, and Shakespeare. Although up to this time Shakespeare's plays had bored me, his sonnets blew me away. They were the best poetry I had ever read. I used to memorize them and let them carry me off to places I could never have even imagined. The words of "Shall I Compare Thee to a Summer's Day?" have never left my mind.

My imagination seemed especially vivid that summer, and often I sat in this book-filled room and mentally recreated the past lives I was sure I had lived. Perhaps because of an Errol Flynn movie I'd seen, I remembered a past life as a young pirate. In that life, my friends and I were strong pirates, sailing in a boat on the high seas when we were attacked by a European vessel. We fought off the sailors on that ship and kidnapped their women and carried them back to the harem on our own island. The women had allowed themselves to be captured so that they could stay with us and never have to return to Europe. I had so many fantasies about my life as a pirate that I was utterly convinced I had lived and loved that life. By the end of the summer, I was also more interested in Shakespeare's plays and was especially intrigued with Othello and Desdemona. Desdemona was a true lady of the court, while the moor was more like a pirate. Like me. It was more than possible that I had also been Othello.

John Stix made sure I saw lots of movies that summer, especially films by Orson Welles and those starring Laurence Olivier. John always pointed out which movies were good and which were not. But no matter which movie or book or play everyone in the house exposed me to, these theater people were relentless. I was there to learn—as much as they could teach me in ten weeks. During one of my parents' visits, I decided that I'd had enough and begged to come home, but my mother insisted I stay. By the end of that summer, I was glad I had. Something had shifted in my life. I was being allowed entry into another world. "You've got talent," they told me before I left, and although I had no real idea what talent was, I understood that it was a God-given gift and I should be grateful.

When my junior year in high school began, I was on a different schedule from the one my peers followed. Every afternoon, as soon as classes ended, I was driven across the Brooklyn

Bridge into the city, where I performed every evening. A tutor was there to help me with my homework and make sure I didn't fall behind in any of my subjects. Sometimes Frederick O'Neal helped me with my homework. On Wednesdays, I didn't go to school at all but spent the whole day at the theater, working with my tutor when I wasn't onstage for the matinee. Weekends found me back in the theater for three performances. Sometimes, when my parents allowed, I even joined the cast for dinner at Sardi's, where everybody knew me and watched out for me and made sure I met Vincent Sardi.

It was a rigorous schedule, especially for a kid who was on the basketball team and wanted good grades and a basketball scholarship to get to college to study to be a doctor. As always, I understood that onstage I could not simply be good; I had to be the best. And I was. Good enough, anyhow, to beat out Jimmy Dean in his performance as Bachir in *See the Jaguar* and John Kerr in *Tea and Sympathy* for the 1953 Donaldson Award for the Best Newcomer to Theatre. Yet the experience I received during that production was award enough. From the moment the summer ended and we went into full rehearsals with Frederick O'Neal and Estelle Helmsley, who played my grandmother, I felt as if I had joined a new family.

My greatest thrill was when my own family, my parents and aunts and uncles and cousins, drove into Philadelphia for opening night at the Forest Theatre, where we performed for three and a half weeks before moving to the Lyceum Theatre in New York. On opening night in Philly, the first person to get to my dressing room, even before my parents, was a West Indian black man named Frank Silvera. He'd screamed out "Bravo!" during one of my scenes, but backstage he was even more gracious. "You found your God-given talent," he told me. "It's been a long time since I found someone who's doing what he was put on the planet to do. You just keep doing it." Several years later, Frank became my main teacher at the Actor's Studio, and I've never stopped cherishing every word he spoke to me.

On our first performance on September 24 at the Lyceum Theatre on Broadway, I knew too little to be nervous. In retrospect, I should have been scared to death as I walked onto that stage, but I wasn't. I wasn't even bothered by the pain in my big toe when the backdrop of the revolving stage fell on it and cracked my bare toe while I was changing shoes. I didn't even realize my toe was bleeding and aching until I got home that night. Because we'd done previews in Philly and Boston, along with many rewrites, I had a good idea of how an audience would react and where the laughs should be. But that first night at the Lyceum, I will never forget the feeling I had when I walked onto the stage. Running away from home and looking for a date in the bar, I spotted the three prostitutes, Violet, Rose, and Poppy, three flowers, and uttered my first line: "Excuse me. Are you girls prostitutes or something?" It brought the house down and continued to do so every night, but I was too naive to realize why it was funny.

There were tears and laughter from the audience that night, and when the performance ended, my dressing room, number one, right by the stage, was filled with people I hardly knew. One I did recognize was Jack Palance, and when he came in to congratulate me on my performance, I couldn't speak. All I could think of was that this guy, who had played a killer in some TV show that gave me nightmares, was talking to me and offering me his hand to shake. In a soft, gentle voice, he said, "I liked your performance. Keep it up, Mr. Gossett."

My grandmother, however, was nowhere near as soft-spoken or complimentary. She walked right in and slapped me across the face. "Don't you ever curse like that again, Junior," she warned me. I realized right away that she was referring to Spencer's words: "Damn it, Grandma. I am not going to do it."

"It's just a line in the play," I tried to explain to her, my cheek smarting from the slap. "I'm not really talking like that. Especially not to you."

But she would not budge. "I don't care," she said. "I don't want to hear you cursing like that." From then on, I always looked over my shoulder and sneaked a peek into the audience before I said that line. If Grandma or someone from the neighborhood was in the audience, I said, "Doggone it, Grandma. I am not going to do it." Back at home, whenever she asked me whether I was saying that curse word onstage, I crossed my fingers behind my back and said no. You would have thought someone had put a contract on my life, the way I worried about her finding out that I was indeed swearing every night.

Four years later, when I was performing in Maxwell Anderson's *Lost in the Stars* at the City Center Theatre in New York, it was my grandfather Lacey Gossett who had the most to say about my acting. My character was dying, in a fetal position on the stage, with the most gorgeous music from *Cry the Beloved Country* filling the air, when, amid the sniffles and sobs from the audience, this deep-throated laugh, "Hee, hee, hee!" erupted in the back of the theater. Those near him could hear the rest of his sentence: "That's my grandson down there. That's my boy."

Of course, I heard it on the stage, and I also heard the stage manager utter, "Who is the fool laughing? Doesn't he get it?" I knew exactly who the fool was. My dear grandfather, whose distinctive laugh I would recognize anywhere. It was all I could do to hold it in and not break out laughing myself during my death scene.

During our seventy-six performances at the Lyceum for *Take a Giant Step*, so many famous people walked into my dressing room. Adam Clayton Powell, Hazel Scott, Duke Ellington, Paul Robeson, Ralph Bunche, Langston Hughes, Lena Horne, and

Walter White all came back to congratulate me. I had no idea who they were, but the men offered bear hugs, the women polite kisses. And every one of them told me that my performance had touched them, and they encouraged me to continue to do theater. "Yes, ma'am," "Yes, sir," I answered each one, grateful for their kind words but anxious to get home and get some sleep for my next busy day.

Back at school, I was even more popular than before. Everybody seemed to want to be my friend, but I was mainly interested in spending time with my old friends, playing ball and trying to have some fun in the midst of an exhausting but exciting schedule. My parents were beaming, over-the-top proud of my new fame. And I was making real money. Initially, I was paid $750 a week, a salary that was soon increased to $1,250. My parents got all of the money and put it in the bank. Whenever they needed money, they would borrow it from the account. I sensed, although she never admitted it, that my mother was tired, and I was so pleased when she was able to stop a couple of her cleaning jobs. I wanted her not to work hard, but she couldn't help it. It was her work ethic to work hard, but now she was doing what she loved: working with children. This was a love I inherited from her, because, like her, I have always adored the little people, the ones, I always say, who just got here.

My mother went back to school, working as a nurse's aide, then on to nursing school. She was happiest working in a child-care center, which eventually became the Hellen Wray Gossett Child Care Center. She even ran for councilwoman for the district of Coney Island, although she lost. She was some woman, my mother. But whatever money my parents borrowed from my account, they always paid it back, keeping my savings secure for college, in case I didn't get a scholarship.

I got a glimpse that summer and fall, when I was so young, of the fact that not many people in this world make a living doing something they love, the one thing that they were put on the planet to do. I know now that most people put their true chosen professions or dreams off into a corner or on a shelf, waiting for the right time to do what they have always wanted to do. Yet I had the good fortune to find this profession at the beginning of my life, to have the opportunity to make a living doing what I was born to do, to act and to create, and I am ever so grateful to have found that opportunity. It was certainly not in my frame of reference to act or go to Broadway, yet it happened, and suddenly I was making more money than I had ever imagined. I would love to encourage people to look for that one thing that brings them the most happiness—and we all have something—and go for it. Then their lives, as good as they might be anyhow, will be dramatically better. It is as if you put a plug into an electric socket; now you are in the right socket. Nothing is more exciting than to make that perfect connection, except to encourage someone else to find his or her own.

One of the best aspects of this profession has always been that I was able to pursue my profession for a society that loved and respected me and whom I loved and respected. It was this society that instilled in me a strong sense of racial security that made me feel good, even as a sixteen-year-old, as I traveled the streets of New York and dealt with people from all walks of life. As the years went on, more of these people saw me in one place or another, onscreen or in the theater, and allowed me to touch them in some way. These people, a list that later grew to include governors, senators, President Barack Obama, Bishop Tutu, Nelson Mandela, and so many everyday, ordinary, warm men and women, who have walked across a room to shake my hand and congratulate me on my work, allowed me to include them in my life. Everywhere I went, I felt as if God was in my life, helping me perform whatever role, on or off the stage, he had chosen for me. This incredible life began on that stage in

53

the Lyceum Theatre. And when I was handcuffed to a tree in Los Angeles, it was a total non sequitur. It made no sense. Nothing in my life, neither in Coney Island nor on the stage on Broadway, had prepared me for that event. Yet I did not remain chained to that tree and would never regret that I'd listened to Mr. Blum's words: "What can you lose? It wouldn't hoit." He was so right. It hadn't hurt.

And I was determined to make sure it never did. For that incredible year in 1953, I struggled to do the very best I could; in the play, in school, and in sports. Part of me was aware that I was missing out on many of the everyday pleasures my friends enjoyed, that I had grown up very fast that summer, and that part of my childhood had ended. But I had entered a world that entranced and intrigued me. I was hooked on theater. Whatever I had done in *Take a Giant Step* was winning me accolades and awards. I would continue acting, but only as long as I could be as close to perfect as possible. No mistakes. And I would be. That lucky sixteen-year-old kid, walking around that Broadway stage, was learning how to stand tall, and he knew, even then, that he had no choice but to climb to the top of the mountain.

3

The Beatnik Years

1954–1959

The years after *Take a Giant Step* were exhilarating, educational, and the beginning of my experience as a young adult.

There was so much happening in Manhattan, where I now lived. In the early fifties, bohemians like Jack Kerouac and Lenny Bruce were kings, as the years segued into the Beatnik Era, which kept Lenny in the lead, along with Mort Saul and Shelley Berman and Mike Nichols and Elaine May. Then, as the sixties approached and Vietnam came onto the stage, the hippies took their rightful place, until the flower children, offering free love and marches, found their apex in Woodstock in 1969. As the years wore on, I felt conflict in my positions as I stood with one foot in the beatnik world and another foot planted in the legitimate theater. As expected, it was hard to stand up straight when your legs are posed in opposite directions. I would finish my play, wash off my makeup, and head to the Village, where I always felt the safest and the most creative. All of these years were my salad years, my formative days of experimentation and adventure.

For the first part of those years, I was a college student, living in the Village, attending classes at New York University on a basketball-drama scholarship, studying medicine and theater. My short-lived desire to be a neurosurgeon died the day I was in a lab class dissecting a cat's brain. When I touched one part of the brain, a paw suddenly flew up into the air. I freaked out so badly, I just about fainted. Needless to say, this was my last pre-med class. Up to that point, I had loved the anatomy classes, but I now understood that dissection was not in my future. When I pulled myself together, I marched up to my adviser's office and officially changed my major to drama with a minor in psychology.

From then on, all of my classes were held on campus at Washington Square. I was reading plays and finally getting to know much more about William Shakespeare and Anton Chekhov than I'd already learned during my summer in Connecticut. Although I had an easier time with Chekhov, even though he gave me a headache, I found it nearly impossible to try to perform a Shakespearean scene. Shakespeare's sonnets had won me a lot of points on dates when I quoted lines from them, but it wasn't until I saw experts such as Sir Laurence Olivier perform in *Richard III* and *Hamlet* that I began to understand what was happening in these works. Shakespeare became permanently ingrained in my mind when I saw James Earl Jones do *Othello*. From then on, all of the moods of the play and the famous iambic pentameter became clear. Now I got it. Now I understood why this work was a classic—and I could never imagine anyone else playing this role.

At NYU, I easily made friends. Some were new friends, while most were buddies from home. We met in the cafeteria, which we'd nicknamed the Commons, where it seemed like all of the black students sat by themselves in one section, pretty much segregated from the rest of the student body. In my Coney Island neighborhood, I'd always been ambivalent about whom I should sit with. I was just as comfortable sitting with the white kids as with the black students. Once again I was unsteady, with my feet in opposite worlds, one foot in the white world and the other in the black world. Even then, I felt ill at ease with that awkward separation of the races. Just as had happened in Brooklyn, the black kids at NYU now called me "Turncoat" when I sat with the white kids. I could sympathize with what Jackie Robinson went through at the University of California–L.A. fifteen years earlier. Raised in Pasadena, he had been carefully selected to attend UCLA. His exceptional talent, his excellent grades, his ability to speak and express himself and to control his moods and temper all worked to make him the perfect candidate to move well in the white world, both in college and then in sports. Only he died way too young from a heart attack, but the ulcers that resulted after swallowing those "turncoat" feelings, along with outright expressions of racism, into his stomach ate away at his insides.

Ironically, I had met my hero Jackie Robinson through the Happy Felton Knothole Gang. This was the program in which the winners of the Little League sandlot baseball tournaments were invited to meet the Brooklyn Dodgers before every game. They could also bat or catch in little contests on the sidelines before the games. I was around twelve when I walked into that

Dodgers dressing room, which reeked of cigarettes, chewing tobacco, and beer, to meet my heroes: Pee Wee Reese; Duke Snider, who always hit the home run when it mattered; Roy Campanella; and, of course, the greatest of all ballplayers, Jackie Robinson. My grandfather had taken me to many games at Ebbetts Field, but the thrill of seeing these guys in their dressing room sent me flying.

Now a student at NYU, I couldn't act any different from the way I'd been raised. I'd been pretty much impervious to racism. I was sympathetic to the racial problems most black people encountered, but none of it hit me personally for several more years. At that time, I was just trying to do my thing, to be accepting of all people, regardless of the color of their faces. Of course, the real star during my years at NYU was Diahann Carroll, the winner of the TV show *Chance of a Lifetime*, the precursor to *American Idol*. She had a recording contract by then and was just gorgeous. I caught a glimpse of her once or twice at lunch, but I'd heard how heavy her schedule was, with managers and work. After all, her song "Why Was I Born?" was number one, and everyone was calling her the new Lena Horne.

My own living arrangements were easy and fun. My first roommate was my close friend Stanley Ralph Ross, God rest his soul. Stan was a smart Brooklyn boy whose mother was a love. Tall like a young Steve Allen, he was brilliant, writing songs and performing comic routines. He hung around with Joey Bishop and Buddy Hackett and opened for them in the Catskills. Like me, he'd grown up insulated in a protected Jewish world, but he was a Renaissance type of man and was comfortable in any type of environment. Years later, Stan—one of the many strong, successful, caring men to whom I've always gravitated—made a fortune producing the TV series *Batman* out of the comic books. But in those years, the two of us shared an apartment, one great big room on Broadway and 56th, around the corner from Carnegie Hall.

The minute I left our apartment, the smell of Horn and Hardart jelly doughnuts would draw me into the little store, where I used my spare change to buy a dozen jelly doughnuts and a carton of milk. Lunch and dinner those days was a hollowed-out hero sandwich filled with meatball gravy and green peppers, which I would cut into three sections for the rest of the day. You could smell the sandwich in the classroom all day long. Those days, I feasted on cheap, nutritious meals cooked by small places that prepared the same foods, such as knishes, pizzas, and heroes, made with love, for their families and their customers. No one could go hungry then. Not even a 6′4″ skinny kid who couldn't gain an ounce, no matter how much he ate.

I honored my basketball scholarship by playing freshman basketball for NYU, up in the Bronx. That basketball season, 1954 to 1955, I was the only black player on the freshman team. By the next year, when I made the NYU varsity team, the freshman team was nearly all black. I ended up taking many leaves, from classes as well as from the basketball team, in order to continue my acting. Some of my NYU teammates were Happy Hairston, who later played for the Lakers; Satch Sanders, who was a year behind me and became a Celtic; and Cal Ramsey, who went to the Knicks. I had a true passion for playing basketball, but I didn't have a chance to put in the time I needed in order to improve the way most of the players did. I had loved playing in the summer leagues before acting took up so much of my life. Still, I experienced a thrill on the basketball court when my competitive nature in sports kicked in, a feeling that would remain with me forever.

Soon, I began to find it difficult to fit in everything I wanted to do. Even though my advisers and my drama professors helped me pick classes that matched my work schedule, there were times during my freshman year when I was ready to quit school. The conflict between studying acting and making a living as an actor was a problem from my freshman year on. Because I was already making money as an actor, I wondered whether I should just quit school and concentrate on my career. As the first one in my extended family to go to college, however, I knew how important it was to my parents that I continue. After all they'd done to get me to college, there was no way I could disappoint them.

Despite the pressure I felt, I never missed the chance to fit in appearances on David Susskind's show or on Ed Sullivan's *Toast of the Town* and Red Buttons's show. During one of my live appearances on Red's show, we were doing a comedy skit about the army. We were all trying to ad lib about the sergeant who was about to arrive. When I said, "Jesus Christ, the sergeant is coming," everyone was shocked. Even Red, who was such a nice guy, went nuts. The calls came in fast and furious, but there was nothing that could be done. I'd sworn on live TV. Luckily, this mistake never cut down on the number of invitations I received to do these fabulous TV shows. All of the appearances paid a little money, which I sorely appreciated. And I even got to sing on some of them, such as Jack Parr's and Merv Griffin's shows. Merv was quite a singer himself and such a benevolent guy to the rest of us who were trying to break in. And it was great fun to sing on Steve Allen's show, accompanied by the piano player Charlie Smalls, who wrote *The Wiz*. I didn't make any money from these appearances, but they put me on the map in front of millions of viewers, so I could get other acting jobs. Financially, I never had to worry about tuition because my scholarship covered it all. I used whatever I could earn for my living expenses, while my number-one concern was to be sure my parents and my relatives were doing okay back in Coney Island.

I thought it was amazing that some of my acting professors at NYU who were professional actors themselves asked me to help them get acting jobs. I was delighted to recommend my talented teachers, such as Albert Quinton, a great Shakespearean actor, to the casting people or the directors whom I was now meeting and working with.

One of my first acting jobs while I was at NYU was reen-acting my role in the 1956 off-Broadway production of *Take a Giant Step*. During those years, the British were advancing on Broadway. It was a few years before productions such as *My Fair Lady*, *Equus*, *Becket*, *A Man for All Seasons*, *Separate Tables*, and Richard Burton's *Hamlet* would take over all of the lights of Broadway, but the trend was already beginning. American plays like *Gypsy*, *Pajama Game*, and *I Can Get It for You Whole-sale*, where Barbra Streisand was discovered, were still popular, as were Edward Albee's plays, both on and off Broadway, and the newly born Public Theater, founded as a Shakespearean workshop by one of my heroes, Joseph Papp.

At the time, many of the American productions were mov-ing off Broadway into different venues, attracting audiences wherever they ended up. *Take a Giant Step* was one of them. It played at the Jan Hus House, a theater underneath a church. Much of the original crew of the play remained, but not the three white actors who played my best friends in the play. These characters were easy for me to relate to, because all of them were replicas of my real-life best friends from Brooklyn, guys like Melvin Dick. During that time, I met a lady who would be one of my angels, Rosetta LeNoir, who played the maid. Rosetta kind of adopted me, becoming someone I could call anytime I had a problem or an issue to discuss. It would have been hard to design a play that more closely paralleled my exact life at the time than *Take a Giant Step* did. Because I knew my role completely by now, the off-Broadway run was more relaxing, plus more intimate, for me than Broadway had been a few years earlier.

Still, the schedule was a tough one, with eight performances each week. I made no more than $75 a week, but we performed to sold-out crowds, and the production received critical acclaim. One nice plus was that I was fed well, with dinners every night at wonderful neighborhood restaurants that opened their doors to all of the cast and crew.

A year later, I had to take a leave of absence from NYU to work on *The Desk Set* with Shirley Booth. I was thrilled with the chance to work with this brilliant actress, who had won national acclaim and a Tony in 1950 for her role as Lola Delaney in *Come Back, Little Sheba*, but a problem during the pre-Broadway tryout nearly derailed my role in the play and, quite possibly, could have ended my career. We were in Wilmington, Delaware, to begin the process of ironing out the kinks in the comedy before we moved on to New Haven and then to Boston and finally New York.

On our first night in Wilmington, I was dying for some seafood, so I left the hotel and walked down the street to the New England Café, figuring this was the best place to get what I wanted. I was standing in the entrance, waiting for a table for what seemed like a very long time. People who came in after me were being seated, but I simply continued to stand there while the hostess smiled at me, not saying a word after I asked for a table for one. I had just realized something must be wrong when another hostess came over to me and said, "We can't serve you here." She said it so softly and so nicely that it made the whole situation even worse for me.

Although I'd become more acquainted with racism than I had been while growing up in Coney Island, I'd assumed that a restaurant named the New England Café would be a safe place for a black man to eat. Still, after the woman spoke to me,

I didn't quite understand what was happening. "What did you say?" I asked her.

For the second time, she said, "You can't eat here."

I stood there, unable to move, when the manager came over and said, "We don't serve colored people."

"I get it," I said and turned around and walked away in a state of shock. Suddenly, I began to look at this town differently and wondered how on earth black people could live and work here. I had been so sure it was far enough north for this problem not to exist. I was very hungry, but I was in no condition to try another restaurant. When I got back to the hotel, I began to notice the small incidents I had been oblivious to before. The behavior of the black people who worked so quietly as if they didn't want the second shoe to fall. I imagined that they were secretly proud that a black man was in the play, but they all seemed so nervous, as if there was a foot on top of their bodies, holding them down. I saw the way the doorman didn't look at me, how the bell captain glanced away when I walked in, and the aura of fear in the entire lobby, as if these people needed their jobs and didn't want to make any waves. Whites would not deal with me; they didn't want to give me any time. In a fog as I walked into my room, the first thing I did was call my mother and tell her what had happened. "Now you just behave," she told me. "You can try to get something to eat somewhere else. Just stay away from the black section. I don't want you to get into any trouble there."

Once again, I promised her I would be good and stay away from trouble, but my mind kept returning to a scene I'd witnessed so many years earlier. I was no more than ten when I'd had my first encounter with Southern racism. I'd been traveling by train from New York to Georgia to visit Uncle Guvnor. Whenever we went by train, I understood that my family could ride in any car from New York to Washington, but from then on, we had to move to sit in the Jim Crow car for coloreds. During one trip, when we got out in Baltimore, I mistakenly wandered into a white bathroom. Someone pulled me out and hit me on the butt. One of the porters saw the scene and reminded me what section I needed to be in. I remember thinking that the Pledge of Allegiance was pretty stupid. After all, we were not all created equal. Someone had just hit me because I had acted as if we were. That incident never left my mind and obviously had more impact than I realized at the time.

My parents had always told me to be good on the train, to respect my elders, to be a perfect gentleman, but even at that young age, the burden of such a request was a hard one for me to bear. When I went to church, I felt as if the blacks were saying to me, "You're hanging around with whites. You think you're so much better than us. Get away from here and go hang around with them." Yet when I was in the black neighborhoods and churches, I saw the desperation and the hunger. Someone was always ready to rip me off, to take my jacket or my money. I had no idea where I belonged.

Now, at age nineteen, slapped with another racist act in Delaware, it hit me hard, showing me where I did belong and bringing back all of that frustration and anger at being treated like an inferior person. At the *Desk Set* rehearsals the next day, I couldn't concentrate, as my mind filled with scenes of lynchings and dogs attacking black people. I once again felt like the little boy who'd been hit because he'd dared to walk into a white bathroom. Only now I was a grown man, a college student, and an award-winning actor, yet nothing had changed. I'd done everything I was supposed to do, had been exemplary, but I was still being slapped. I had no way of knowing then that this pain would recur during my career at various levels of intensity, no matter how many awards and great reviews and friends of all races I would acquire. The bottom line was that the aura of being treated as someone inferior would always be there.

My performance at rehearsal was abysmal, and I knew I was in danger of being let go and sent back to New York. Finally, after the second day of my miserable performance, Shirley pulled me into her dressing room to tell me that she was very disappointed in me and that I was being fired. I told her I didn't care, that I wanted to quit. Then I started to cry, and, after more questioning, I finally told her what had happened to me at the New England Café. She listened and didn't say a word. "Stay in my dressing room," she told me. "I'll handle it."

I'd been in her dressing room for only a few minutes when the assistant director walked past and said, "You come out of Miss Booth's dressing room."

Before I could answer, Shirley reappeared and told him, "You leave him here," and then took off again. The assistant director shrugged and left. By then, I was totally embarrassed, certain I was now being marked as a troublemaker. From the dressing room, I could hear Shirley announce, "No rehearsal tonight." An hour or so later, she returned to the dressing room and told me to go back to the hotel and relax. She would see me at rehearsal in the morning.

I had no idea what she did, but the next morning a maid with a breakfast tray filled with food woke me up. While I ate breakfast, invitations kept sliding under my door. Many of them were for parties and gatherings at the Mansion Row and all of the fancy DuPont homes. There were not enough nights to accept all of the invitations I received. One particular hostess, a flaming redhead my age named Penny DuPont, was already seriously involved with theatrical productions and actually became a close friend.

I found out later exactly what Shirley had done. She had simply called the DuPonts, who were throwing a big party to honor her, and told them she would not attend unless I was invited. She also said, "If you don't treat this young man properly, we are packing up tomorrow and moving to New Haven, Connecticut. And I can assure you no future pre-Broadway shows will ever come to Wilmington."

From that moment on, not only was I well fed, but I enjoyed every moment of the show, especially the scenes I did as Kenny the Mailboy with Doris Roberts, who played a secretary in the comedy. There was no doubt that offstage, Shirley Booth was a gutsy lady, while onstage, she was the most generous actress imaginable. I learned so much from her during that run, lessons about acting and life that I will never forget. This wouldn't be the last act of racism I encountered during my long career, but it meant a great deal to me to know that someone of Shirley's stature was willing to go to bat for me.

On opening night in Wilmington, my mother, as always, was there. Shirley seemed to adore my mother, who had sent her flowers "for what you did for my son." My mother kept the thank-you note that Shirley sent to her in a scrapbook. My mother always seemed to have this charm, especially with white women, that made them all love her. It was, most likely, a charm she had acquired from all of her years as a beloved domestic for white families.

Every time I saw my mother at one of my plays, I was filled with love and gratitude for all that she had done for me. Not only did she never miss one of my opening nights, no matter where it was, but she roused all of the relatives, bought a bunch of tickets, and made sure they came, too. It was only later in life that I came to understand exactly how much both of my parents had sacrificed for me, how I had been their hope and their pride. Although my father was a quieter presence in my life, my mother was the visible one in my school and in my career, doing everything that needed to be done for me. Whether it was new shoes and new clothes, because I was always growing so fast, or keeping the refrigerator stocked with food for my never-ending appetite, they were there for me. As I grew older, I had seen my mother turn hard as my father became more dependent on alcohol. But she was never hard with me or with the children at the child-care center.

Today, I see remnants of the same problem between black women and the black men who have been raised by single mothers. This behavior started in slavery times, when the black women became highly revered nannies and were given respect and gifts because they were the ones who took care of the white children. Hattie McDaniel won an Oscar in *Gone with the Wind* for playing a character like that.

Unlike these women, however, the black men were considered shiftless and irresponsible, behavior typified by many movie characters played by Willie Best: men who were treated like dogs by the black women in their lives and were repeatedly ordered, "Get away from here." All too often, these men ended up feeling emasculated and resorted to abusing the women they loved, women who continued to make money as cooks and maids. They called the women "bitches" and "hos," terrorizing and beating them because they couldn't find their manhood anywhere else. Invariably, after each fight, they would end up in bed, making love. It reminds me of the song "You Always Hurt the One You Love." I could understand what these men were feeling. No woman could measure up to the mother who had raised them alone. These other women could never be as good as Mom. My fantasy wish is that some of those men would have the courage to go back and apologize to these women and their children, and that their apologies would be accepted so that healing can take place. How easy to say, but how difficult to do.

Yet today, I do see many beautiful examples of a different and healthier type of behavior. I rejoice as I see more and more successful African American relationships. Undoubtedly, this trend shows great promise when we have a president today who sets the bar so high for marital and family bliss.

I mistakenly believed that I could save the troubled women I came in contact with. On the surface, many of them seemed bitter and evil, but when you got underneath their skins, they turned out to be beautiful. These women told me heartbreaking stories about what had happened to them, but then, inevitably, they ended up running from me, losing respect for me, and returning to the men who had mistreated them in the first place. I never understood that dynamic with lost women from the dark side of life. To me, they were all like Billie Holiday, women who had been mistreated by men. I had been so protected by my family that I was sorely equipped to handle these situations. My mother warned me about drugs, but I didn't always follow her advice. She did so much for me that she made it difficult for me to find another woman who could measure up to her. In later years, I often found it hard to trust a woman.

Yet so much good stuff was happening during the time that I call my own beatnik years. I was so busy learning and falling in love—with just about everything. With the music scene, the people, the lifestyle, and even the drugs, which we all played around with socially. In whatever down time I had from my studies and my work, I savored the finest brandies and exotic marijuana hashish picked up from fellow actors and friends. Everyone did it, I told myself; I would have been square if I didn't. I tried cocaine, but it got in the way of my acting and made my nose run. Hard drugs, specifically freebase cocaine, didn't come into my life until the eighties in California. At that time, I was introduced to the glass pipe by the same kind of woman who had been mistreated by her man. These women, always beautiful, were sent by their hustlers or pimps to prey on celebrities, to use their wiles and their beauty to get well-known athletes or show business stars strung out on drugs. So much money could be made once the deed was accomplished. At that time, with my deflated ego, I was the perfect target for this type of seductive woman. It was the same story that could be applied to my brilliant good friend Richard Pryor. And I am sure we could all come up with more names of professional athletes and actors who fell and are still falling today into the same trap.

Before that painful time in California, I was part of this new society in New York. My drug of choice then was some marijuana and a decanter full of cheap Italian wine. When I tried the expensive hashish brought over from Afghanistan and Morocco, it coated my throat, and I couldn't speak or sing.

Something similar happened when I went to Jamaica on a vacation. Before I got there, I bought myself a costly silk shirt, not realizing how hot it was in Jamaica and that Rastafarians never wear silk there. As soon as I arrived in Jamaica, however, I was determined to wear my stylish shirt. It didn't take long for someone to tell me that I was going to get a chance to smoke ganja, the finest marijuana in the world, which only the Rastas smoke. Immediately, I was game. I approached a Rasta with red eyes and a machete stuck in the waistband of his pants. He looked like he wanted to kill me, but instead, he jumped into my rented car and drove me through rocky roads up to the top of a mountain where you could see all of Jamaica. By then, I had sweated through the ridiculous shirt, which clung to my chest like a limp rag in the 110-degree temperature. Out the windows, I could see where all of the coffee was grown, on the outskirts of the villages filled with naked children, goats, and dogs running around freely. Knowing how strong the coffee is in the Blue Mountains, one can easily imagine how potent the ganja from that area is. But once again, I was Errol Flynn, sophisticated, knowing exactly what I was doing as I hid all of my money in my sock, in a big lump that any idiot could recognize.

The next thing I knew, my Rasta escort, without a word, was leading me into a room in a Quonset hut with a metal ceiling. It reeked of pungent smoke, and a bunch of Rastas were sitting around the room. Every minute a fire was lit and I saw an illuminated face covered in smoke. Someone handed me a chillum pipe, which I knew you had to keep going or you would be deemed weak and worthless. I was a big man, so I took a big hit. Then, with my lungs on fire, I coughed so hard the tears ran down my sweaty face. It didn't take long until I was stoned like I'd never been before. From far away, I could hear the men laughing at me and asking me what I wanted. I managed to pull ten dollars out of my sock, which they grabbed and then handed me a shopping bag full of ganja.

By now, I was paranoid as well as stoned. Disoriented, I staggered out into the bright sunlight. The whole village seemed to stop to watch me. As I made my way to my car, I could see that the Rastas had machetes in their hands. With the ganja marijuana reeking out of my pores and my teeth chattering, despite the 120 degrees inside the car, I looked down and noticed that the Rastas had stolen the steering wheel. For the next twenty minutes, I sat there totally panicked, trying to plan my escape. Finally, the marijuana effect began to subside enough that I was able to notice that the steering wheel was right where it should be in an English car, on the right-hand side, rather than on the left as in an American car.

Feeling like a complete fool now, with what little pride I had left I made my way to the other side of the car, the silk shirt stuck tightly to my body. I tried to act, stoned as I was, as if this was what I had planned to do all along. All of their eyes were on me, and it was so quiet you could hear a pin drop.

It took me a while, but I got the gear shift moving and drove off. I looked in the rearview mirror and could see that the whole crowd, as well as the dogs, were laughing their butts off. As for me, I had never been so scared in my whole life. As soon as I got out of their sight, I dumped the shopping bag full of grass. By the time I got to the hotel, everyone, including the doorman, knew what had happened. I was, unquestionably, the laughingstock of Kingston. It took me a good two weeks to get the ganja marijuana out of my system. Repeatedly coughing, I took hot baths and smelled the tarlike resin of the ganja floating out of my pores. It's ironic that the place that produces the best coffee in the world is also home to the best marijuana.

In many ways, this behavior was typical of the way I tried to act—as if I knew what I was talking about, as if I knew how to handle myself, when I had no idea what was happening at all. With my protected upbringing, I had no street smarts whatsoever. Before that scene in Kingston I'd been bragging about my use of drugs, obviously making people jealous. I was also the worst possible candidate to indulge in alcohol and drugs. My system was too pure or something like that. Yet I now had some kind of strange connection to my father and uncles that made me want to be inebriated like the men I loved, to walk the way they did, to take a long sip and stagger and laugh at myself. Any connection I could make with these men, I would take. It was so strange that I wound up abusing drugs and alcohol when I had vowed to be the exception. Alcohol got my father and my uncles and almost got me.

During these years, however, the music part of my life led me in spectacular directions. Years earlier, back in Brooklyn at the Paramount Theatre, I'd been singing with the Gospel Brothers out of the First Baptist Church of Coney Island in competitions against the Dixie Hummingbirds and lead singer Sam Cooke, as well as against the Original Five Blind Boys led by

Ray Charles and another group led by Jackie Wilson. The Blind Boys had the manly art of looking like they were going to fall off the stage as they sank to their knees at the end of the song. But these guys knew exactly where the stage ended. They never fell off. And their performance always ended with the women screaming in admiration, as they later did with Elvis. Those same stages that held the gospels led by Ray Charles and Jackie Wilson turned into the place where R&B was born. It became quite a happening when Ray was bebopping the gospel. But it was also a problem when he asked whether they wanted him to stop and everyone said no, and he continued on. Some people left, thinking it was a sacrilege because these singers were insulting the music of the church, but they all came back. Today's church music has taken off by leaps and bounds, and it often includes some form of rap.

Now, living in the Village, I was meeting jazz musicians such as Max Roach and Miles Davis and folk singers like Joan Baez and Judy Collins, as well as Lenny Bruce and Mort Saul. There were so many great talents moving in and out of each coffeehouse, some, such as Mama Cass Elliot, were friends who were yet to be discovered.

Even there, I was aware of the undercurrent of racism around my sheltered world. Those of us who did not like it stuck together, finding places where we were safer from its effects. Music was one of those places, especially jazz music. This was our insulation. The people who came to listen to jazz thought of New York as a great melting pot, so full of life. While to many others blacks were second class, here, especially for actors and musicians, that way of thinking did not prevail. We all stayed together, rubbing elbows in subways and on streets. For so many of us, all that we had in common was our devotion to our art, to music, and to the theater, a shared love that led us to take care of one another in a nurturing, accepting society of artists, men and women, of every color and nationality.

The music connected us. Anytime I could find an empty microphone in a club or a coffeehouse, I was in front of it. When I went downstairs at these places and saw the straw basket being passed around, I said, "Hey, wait a minute. Count me in." On a poor day, I could make $50, while on a great day, I could bring home as much as $100, if not more. I knew plenty of songs, like "Wade in the Water," from my years of singing in church, along with some slave songs such as "Didn't My Lord Deliver Daniel," and "Hushaby, Don't You Cry," whose lyrics about the mother rocking the master's baby to sleep, while her own baby is screaming in the cotton fields, always tore at my heart.

When I got a guitar and learned three chords, I suddenly knew a thousand songs. After all, just about every blues and folk song has only three chords. By 1961, I had a partner, the late Felix Pappalardi, who later became a producer and discovered the group Mountain, as well as Eric Clapton's Cream. But during those years, I was singing at the same places as a nice kid named Bobby Zimmerman, who later changed his name to Bob Dylan. Some of my closest friends were Peter Yarrow, Noel "Paul" Stookey, and Mary Travers, before this group became Peter, Paul, and Mary. Paul and I shared the hootenanny, sometimes making ourselves a pretty decent salary. We sang in clubs such as the Bitter End, Folk City, the Gaslight Club, and Fat Black Pussy Cat—anywhere there was an audience and a microphone. It was a good way to add to the money I made from off-Broadway work, so that I had extra cash to bring home as often as possible.

At home, in Brooklyn, I was seeing more changes in my father. He had hardly reached sixty, yet he was getting old and drinking more. He was still making it to all of my opening nights, but it was getting harder to be with him at the opening night dinners at Sardi's. He got drunk way too quickly, and I had to drive him home. I saw a lump on his forehead getting larger and larger, which was somehow connected to alcohol, yet he wouldn't stop drinking. I was on the road some years later when the aneurism finally burst and ended his life. Black men were not famous for their external expressions of pride, but I came to understand how much he had loved me. There'd been a lot of pain in his life that pushed him to find solace in alcohol. I can understand his weakness; I even inherited some of it. Still, the web of protection he and my uncles and cousins spun around me allowed me to soar in places he never had the opportunity to travel. Ironically, as much as I loved the music scene, it was the drugs, especially the needle—which thankfully I never did—that made me step away from it. Yet so many years later, I still feel a regret that I was never able to continue with those fantastic concerts. I still remember all of the lyrics and often want nothing more than a microphone and a stool and a few people sitting there, listening. That feeling was the greatest high I ever experienced in my life.

Apparently, however, I was destined to travel in a different direction, and one of the most important tools I needed for that move came from the Actors Studio. You were required to try out for the Studio, but, somehow or other, I never did. I was not officially in, but I was definitely in. Around the time I made it into the Studio, it had experienced a natural transition in its racial composition when Sidney Poitier and Diana Sands became part of it. How reverential anyone felt to walk through those doors! The Studio's main location was on 44th Street and Ninth Avenue in the city. Here, Lee Strasberg would sit in a chair and reminisce about the good old days. The finest actors and actresses I have ever seen were part of the group. Peggy Feury, whom I'd worked with in Connecticut preparing for *Take a Giant Step*, taught the Stanislavski method better than Lee did. I also studied with Janine Manatis, a great actress and an equally wonderful teacher, who was married to the director Eli Rill.

This married couple taught in tandem, with one spouse's class on Tuesday and the other's on Thursday.

Yet my best teacher at the Studio was Frank Silvera, who was also my best friend for a very long time. He was my mentor. It was from him that I gained my deep love of theater. The man lived, ate, and drank theater. I was part of his roving acting class. There were times when I thought he was nuts, but to all of us, including Steve McQueen, Tony Franciosa, Ben Carruthers, Harry Guardino, and Ben Gazzara, he was our Pied Piper, and we would follow him anywhere. If he wasn't working in a theater, he would teach us wherever there was an empty space—in a field, a vacant store, a garage.

During the run of *A Hatful of Rain* in 1955 to 1956, where he played the father of Ben Gazzara and Tony Franciosa, we would gather backstage in the Lyceum Theatre. We all had our notebooks with us, and after the matinees or before the shows, Frank would be there studying with us, giving us scenes to play. He urged us to go deep inside ourselves, drawing on our own emotions from our memory banks, stopping at nothing to get inside our characters, deepening our personalities. Years later, Frank started the Theatre of Being with Beah Richards in L.A. to train aspiring black actors. "Being" was always his key word. When you play a character, you have to *be* that character

Our bodies and our emotions were our instruments, not unlike a guitar player who carried his guitar around or a piano player and his piano. Our instruments were our own selves. We were repeatedly told to pull emotions out of our life experiences, to use these experiences as part of our acting skills. Here, I was often at a loss. My protected world in Coney Island had given me little chance to grow emotionally. When I arrived in Manhattan, I felt at a loss for emotional experiences. I'd acted in a Broadway play, yet even then I'd been sequestered for the summer in Connecticut and later been driven every day from my home in Brooklyn to the stage. If I was going to be an actor, I couldn't merely fantasize about characters. I had a lot of catching up to do. I did the best I could, venturing out as much as possible to acquire these experiences and fill that void.

I did what I had to do to survive—driving a cab, carrying trays, working in bookstores, whatever I could to put cash in my pocket—along with attending classes and acting. In many instances, I was the sacrificial lamb, ripped off, lied to, too innocent for my own good. Too many times, I made a perfect target for those who were street smart, just as I had been made sport of in Kingston, but I was a quick learner, and I rarely made the same mistake twice.

At the Studio classes, I learned hands-on acting skills. It was tough work, and sometimes I seemed to have nothing to bring to the table, while at other times I felt blessed with a mysterious gift. When Frank taught us how to be aware of the camera, he would hold a hair dryer in his hands. While we were acting, he'd turn on the hair dryer a little bit to give us a sense of where the camera might be. As we felt the heat, we understood that this meant the camera was there. There was an actual dance that the actor did with the camera, and I came to realize how brilliantly Studio students such as Marlon Brando and Sidney Poitier performed that dance, moving in such a way that allowed the camera to reveal their thoughts and feelings to the audience without their speaking a word.

The person I considered the most talented actor in my class was Marilyn Monroe. She would walk into class with Arthur Miller's shirts tied at her waist, her feet in flip-flops, the sweet musky smell of Lifebuoy soap wafting after her. Her hair, pulled back with a rubber band, was always a little wet, as if she'd just stepped out of a shower. If she'd stayed with Arthur Miller, I believe she would have easily won five Academy Awards.

One afternoon I was sitting in my place on the Lower East Side when my phone rang. I picked it up, and a voice said, "Hi, Lou. It's Marilyn." "Marilyn who?" I asked, and when she answered, "Marilyn from class," I had a genuine fit. She was asking me to be in her love scene in Tennessee Williams's *The Rose Tattoo* at our next class. She was probably being nice to me because I wasn't one of the stellar students in the class, like Sidney Poitier, and no one else was asking me to do love scenes. But here she was, inviting me to play the sailor to her hot-blooded Serafina delle Rose.

I was a kid then, full of juice. I considered myself hot to trot, but I knew there was no way on earth I could play that scene. I was so star-struck, I wouldn't have gotten out one word onstage. I must have stammered something, because she got off the line pretty fast, and I think it was Marty Landau who ended up playing that scene. (I happen to think Mr. Landau is one of the most consummate actors I have ever seen on the stage or screen.) To this day, if I catch a whiff of Lifebuoy soap, my olfactory senses take over and I am undeniably aroused.

Somehow, no matter how many things I was doing, there was still time for pure fun. Some of these times were with one of my first acting friends, a brilliant kid named James Dean. We'd met in 1952 when he was preparing for the short-lived *See the Jaguar* and I was in rehearsals for *Take a Giant Step*. Jimmy and my understudy, Ben Carruthers, were good friends. A half-black, half-Mexican, completely talented guy, Ben was a rising star then, and, like Jimmy and me, he loved music. Ben became the leader of our little gang, taking us whenever possible to hear Miles Davis, where we sat in ecstasy listening to his jazz.

Jimmy, always charismatic, was five years older than I was. I was only seventeen when we met, but Jimmy was an imma-ture guy in his early twenties who, like me, hadn't had much of a childhood and was now acting like a kid. Although we never worked together at the Studio and he didn't stay there long, the two of us quickly became good friends, sharing that love of music. Sometimes, Jimmy, Ben, and I walked down the streets of New York City, noisily pretending that we were playing instruments. Jimmy would have an imaginary saxophone in his hands, while I banged on anything I could find with my drumsticks. Ben was our Miles Davis, using his hands to make muted trumpet sounds. Jimmy was great at pretending to play an instrument while making mouth sounds that sounded exactly like the instrument itself. It was almost as if our little trio were three rappers, making the sounds a rapper might create today with a microphone cupped in his hands. Although Jimmy, Ben, and I loved acting, it was music that made us explode.

Jimmy and I could recite every word that Anthony Quinn or Marlon Brando had ever said in a performance—in every play, every movie. Yet it was Brando's work that really got us going as we fed each other the lines, repeating scenes with perfect recall. We loved that scene in the schoolyard in *On the Waterfront* where Eva Marie Saint drops her glove and Brando picks it up and puts it on his hand to warm it up for her. We knew immediately that his action was improvisation, that Brando had improvised this to show his feelings for her. Jimmy and I loved to point out to each other all of the stuff between the lines that made Brando's work so brilliant. Brando, along with Anthony Quinn, Alan Ladd, and Jack Palance, were our idols, and we always repeated their words and their actions, like that scene between Jack and Alan in *Shane*.

"So you're Blackjack Wilson. I've heard a lot about you," Alan said.

Jack smiled and replied, "What have you heard, Shane?"

Then Alan said, "I've heard you are a low-down, stinking, Yankee liar."

Jack smiled at him and said, "Prove it," and the rest was a barrage of bullets and history. Over and over, we repeated those lines to each other until we had them down perfectly. Sometimes we just walked the streets aimlessly and giggled and talked about anything.

When Jimmy got killed in that car accident in September 1955, the entire industry experienced a deep loss. When I heard the news, I felt as if I had been hit in the stomach. I knew how much Jimmy loved cars. I did, too—especially a Porsche. Now, however, even all of these years after that accident, I still stay away from Porsches. I knew Jimmy would have been something; he was so far ahead of any of us. He'd sprung into fame so quickly, had been such a riveting actor. There's never been anyone quite like him.

When I think of Jimmy, I think of the two categories into which I have always placed actors, anyone in the entertainment industry, as well as athletes: meteors and comets. The meteor gets all the attention, lasts a good solid ten years, maybe less, and then like a meteor, in one big bump, he burns out, gone, leaving a flash in the sky that is almost too brilliant to view with the naked eye. People like Jim Morrison from the Doors are meteors. So was Jimi Hendrix, in his four-year reign as a superstar, and Lorraine Hansberry and Diana Sands and Janis Joplin.

But comets are around year in and year out. They are the Neil Sedakas, the Sir Laurence Oliviers, stars such as Robert Redford and Paul Newman, Ruby Dee and Ossie Davis, Sidney Poitier and Tony Bennett. Some people, like Oprah Winfrey, make a flash like a meteor, but then they stay around and become comets.

Jimmy was a meteor all the way through. Yet when you look carefully, the light he left can still be seen. All that you have to do is watch a few minutes of *East of Eden* or *Rebel without a Cause* or *Giant*.

As for me, I fervently hope I'll be thought of as a comet. But back in those days in New York, I was trying to do it all: acting, singing, acting classes, NYU, and even the basketball team. Yet the desire to be in the theater was too strong to overcome. Sadly, no matter how hard I tried, I couldn't help missing too many classes and had to leave NYU sixteen hours short of graduating. I promised my parents I would return for my diploma, a promise I have not yet fulfilled but still intend to make happen.

Although at my core I was still the kid from Coney Island, trying a little bit harder than the next guy, struggling against all odds to be the very best, I considered Greenwich Village my home now. It was easy enough wherever I went in the city in those days. I felt accepted, even though I still understood that racism loomed below the surface. I was too busy with my work and my friends to notice, too much in love with it all to worry. I found beautiful women, white and black, in the Village and added as many experiences as I could to my memory bank. I was growing as an actor and as a person. I would be extraordinary. I had no choice.

4

Hooked on Theater

1959–1963

This was a magical time for all of Broadway. It had been taken over by the British, which forced us to create off-Broadway. Jose Quintero had cofounded the Circle in the Square Theatre in Greenwich Village in 1951 with Theodore Mann, and the theater now blossomed with plays such as *Children of Darkness*, where Colleen Dewhurst and her husband, George C. Scott, lit up the stage. There were other off-Broadway plays—for example, *Once upon a Mattress*, with the indomitable Carol Burnett in 1959, and in 1960, The *Fantasticks* put off-Broadway on the map and kept it there. Ironically, during this Renaissance period, many of the stars who were soaring, Neil Diamond, Neil Sedaka, Barbra Streisand, Arthur Miller, Mel Brooks, and the world's greatest drummer, Buddy Rich, came out of those incredible high schools in Brooklyn.

The magic was all around. New York City had become a society of free expression. You could picket and scream about injustice, and no one would bother you, never mind send you to jail. This was the true melting pot, because everyone, from Europe as well as from Hollywood, visited Broadway. The entire city felt alive and joyous. Every day boasted "happenings" in parks and squares all over the country, especially in New York and San Francisco. In New York, on Saturday, from two to ten in Central Park or Washington Square Park, traffic was stopped, and we'd all show up to sing, play the guitar, dance, roller skate, or play chess. This was most likely where *Hair* of the sixties got its inspiration. The airwaves were filled with the beautiful voices of those years: Joan Baez, singing Pete Seeger's "Where Have All the Flowers Gone?"; Pete Seeger's "If I Had a Hammer," sung by Peter, Paul, and Mary; Linda Ronstadt's duets with R&B singers; Judy Collins's "Send in the Clowns"; Harry Belafonte's "Island in the Sun" and "There's a Hole in My Bucket," and his duet with Odetta, along with Miles Davis, sitting on top of the jazz hit list. These were just some of the magnificent voices crooning from the stages, the television screens, the concert halls, the radio stations.

My friends and I inhabited our own world in Greenwich Village. You could walk safely almost anywhere in the city, dance in the open nightclubs, and rejoice in this glorious pre-hippie time. In the summer, you could literally go around the world with folks selling food on Fifth Avenue from 59th to 8th Street. Each neighborhood had its own smells, the street vendors and the Jamaican, Indian, Italian, and Jewish restaurants sending their special aromas into the streets. Personally, I still liked the knishes and the kasha and the hot pretzels with mustard of my childhood in Coney Island, but I tried just about everything.

Sometimes the police wore flowers in their hair and off-duty police played drums and danced with us, enjoying our lifestyle. But slowly, and I can't put my finger on when, this open world began to deteriorate with the inclusion of hard drugs into our society.

But now I get ahead of myself and my own story. Here, in my world, there were joyous moments before the nightmares arrived. In my last year at NYU, I had been spotted by the Knicks at the Rucker Street tournament at 135th Street and Lennox in Harlem. They saw this big, skinny rail of a kid, a forward-guard, and sent me to their rookie camp in the Catskills. Mostly, what I saw there was a lot of violence and fist fights among the rookies, who were vying for a spot on the team. It was far more than I was willing or able to handle. Even though playing with the team was great, I stepped away. Because I would be getting more money playing George Murchison in *A Raisin in the Sun* than the Knicks could give me, it was an easy decision. I had more money in my pocket than most of those players had in their bank accounts. Some of them even asked to borrow money from me. Choosing acting over basketball was one decision, despite my never-ending love affair with the sport, I have never regretted.

When *A Raisin in the Sun* opened in 1959, the *Times* wrote that it "changed Broadway forever." It was the first play written by a black woman and directed by a black man to be produced on Broadway. I was twenty-three, and being a part of this play and working beside Sidney Poitier, Ruby Dee, and Diana Sands changed my life forever. I sucked up every morsel of the theater these generous actors gave me for the two years the play ran in the Ethel Barrymore Theatre on 48th Street. One line in the play, "Seem like God didn't see fit to give the Black man nothing but dreams," stayed in my head long after the play closed, as I found myself one of the blessed whose dreams were coming true. I saw how proud my father was when he came to see me in *A Raisin in the Sun*, as he sat beside my mother and my aunts, who always came to see me onstage, in nightclubs, and in films. I was grateful to be the main support for my family. I owed my family far more than the payment of some rental bills.

Every day that I went to the theater, from the first moment I became a part of the cast of *Raisin* to the final curtain call, I was transported to another world. To be working with Sidney Poitier, who played Walter Lee Younger, was everything I had dreamed it could be. I idolized the man so much that all I wanted was to be him. It took everything I had not to mimic him completely, but sometimes I could not help it. He was pigeon-toed, so I adopted his walk. He influenced me in countless other ways, becoming my role model for the type of actor, as well as the type of person, I wanted to be. I adored his style, his panache. He was a self-made man, the kind I have always respected. I knew that he and Harry Belafonte were good friends, and to me that was the way black men should be. They were stars, as well as clean, handsome, talented, responsible, and funny men. I knew that Sidney had suffered a great deal because of his race, but I had never seen him act like anything other than a perfect gentleman.

Once the play opened in New York, I found a way to be useful to this great man. Between matinees and evening performances, paparazzi hounded Sidney. He was, after all, the number-one man. But Ivan Dixon, who played Joseph Asagai, and I were determined to give Sidney a chance to have a relaxing, normal evening. Moments after the performance ended, Ivan and I would walk out the front door together.

My slightly receding hairline covered with a hat, I would turn left, while Ivan would turn right. Because I had the pigeon-toed walk down perfectly, most of the crowd would follow me, certain I was Sidney. While Ivan and I handled the crowd of paparazzi and female admirers, Sidney escaped out the back door. Soon he was sequestered, having a quiet meal in a restaurant.

I got to understand a lot about women fans during the matinees. During those shows, I heard the barrage of pocket-books open and knew the handkerchiefs were about to emerge and the muffled cries begin. Yet there was one woman in the show who tore at my own heart. Diana Sands had a fire that made her external beauty shine. It lifted her persona up, and she became the most exquisite object in the room. She was not unlike Bette Davis, who became any kind of woman you wanted to see in the movies, totally attractive, totally riveting. When these women were on the screen you could not look at anyone else. At the time of the show, Diana was twenty-five, and I was twenty-three. Famous, wealthy men were seeking her out, but somehow she was interested in me. We talked after the show or during rehearsals, although, for the most part, I was terrified even to be near her. She was so brilliant, and I knew everyone wanted her. Still, for some reason, it turned into magic between us. Like me, her first love was acting, and we understood that about each other. Although we tried to keep our relationship quiet, we were soon doing everything together. She was living in Harlem with her mother, but she cooked for me there or we went out together. Even when I was with her, she got calls from all of these men. "They are all womanizers and playboys," she told me. "I don't want any of them." Yet I knew these men were more sophisticated and more mature than me. I was like a puppy, following her around, adoring her.

We both moved on, me to Hollywood and her staying on Broadway in the theater, but I never stopped adoring her. When we were together in *The Landlord*, I watched from a distance as she began a special relationship with the first assistant on the film, grateful that I'd had my chance with this beautiful lady. We did a couple of television shows together before she went on to do James Baldwin's play *Blues for Mr. Charlie*, where she earned a Tony nomination and blew up the town eight times a week with her talent. I saw that magnificent performance as many times as I could. The four packs of unfiltered Camels that she smoked every day killed that talent, ending her life in 1973 at age thirty-nine. It's a heartbreak that she died so early. She was one talent no one was going to hold down and one of those wonderful people with whom you were so lucky to share even a moment.

Yet there were other incredible talents whom I could also touch, and some of them I did not meet onstage. Some I met underneath the stage. *Sweet Bird of Youth* opened at the Martin Beck Theatre on March 10, 1959, a day before *Raisin* opened at the nearby Barrymore. Paul Newman, who was starring in *Sweet Bird*, and Sidney were close friends, as well as poker buddies. I might not have been their equal on the stage, but beneath it, with cards in my hand, I was. Every Wednesday and Saturday, from five to eight, following the matinee and before the evening performances, a group of us, including writers and actors such as Lonne Elder III, Douglas Turner Ward, Ivan Dixon, and Lincoln Fitzpatrick, along with the stagehands, would meet downstairs at the Barrymore for our high-stakes poker game. There was nothing to do for those few hours between the two shows. You didn't want to eat a big meal or you could get sleepy during the evening show. I honestly think it was the stagehands who pulled us all into these games in a successful ruse to get our money. After the evening show, there was no poker. Instead, we all went out, usually to a downstairs place called Steve Paul's the Scene, in the Broadway area at 8th Avenue. There, the dancers, the musicians, the actors, the stagehands, and everyone connected to the production would pig out and dance and sing. I even sang nightclub music there with Charlie Smalls.

After those Wednesday and Saturday matinees, we were all ready for our fast-moving game of poker. Once I watched breathlessly as Sidney and Paul were making all of the money and throwing it around like water. In most games we all had to pull our cards, but in this one I held mine and waited and waited as the two of them stared at me with a "What the hell is he doing here?" expression in their eyes. I put every cent of my money onto that table. Finally, Paul tossed down his cards and said, "You can't beat this. I have four tens." And Sidney shook his head like I was nuts as he threw down his flush. When I put down my four jacks, the two of them looked at me like I was about to be fired.

I won a lot of money in that game, but for some reason, Paul was $175 short. "I'll get it to you," he said as he stood up to leave." He never did. But that was okay; I never asked him. I just wish that he'd written it down, and I could have put the IOU in my scrapbook, where it would have been worth a hell of a lot more than $175.

That was the last time Paul showed up. A week later the theater people closed us down, outlawing the games beneath the stage. They said we were getting too raucous. But that didn't mean we stopped playing poker, only that we had to find another place. By now, I understood the vital role of the stage manager, whose voice over the loudspeaker in every dressing room ruled your life. "You have ten minutes, Mr. Gossett." "You have five minutes, Mr. Gossett." Those cues were especially important when we played poker in our dressing rooms. Those rooms were one big hierarchy, with the bigger stars getting the larger rooms, the ones with the curtains and the fringe, nearer the stage. Mine was on stage left upstairs during *Raisin*.

After we were tossed from our spot underneath the stage, the games moved into these dressing rooms. There were times when an actor was holding a full house, and you'd hear him moaning, "Hurry up. My cue is coming up." Then, once his cue was called, frustrated and aggravated, he'd race up the wrought-iron stairs while everyone was yelling, "Who won?" The first thing he'd say once he walked offstage was, "Did I win?" Usually, the answer was no. But no matter who won or who lost, we were all winners, inhabiting the Great White Way, on 43rd to 56th streets from Eighth to Sixth avenues, with most of the theaters owned by the Shuberts, the great family of theater. During that time, Anne Bancroft and Patty Duke were playing in *The Miracle Worker*, and I had the privilege of rubbing elbows with these extraordinary actors.

When I was initially hired for *Raisin*, the producers weren't sure which role Ivan Dixon or I would play: either George Murchison or Beneatha's African suitor, Joseph Asagai. Before we started rehearsals, I wanted to play Asagai, but since Ivan was better looking, he got that role, and I played the slick George, a mercenary rich kid, who was famous for the line in the play that always brought the house down. I'd be sitting there with my size-thirteen feet wrapped up in those white buck shoes that were like two boats, taking up the whole stage whenever I walked across it. Sidney would take one look at me and my shoes and say, "How come you college boys have to wear those faggoty-looking white shoes?"

There was little humor, however, between Sidney and Claudia McNeil, who played his mother in the play. Both consummate actors, they managed to submerge the problems once the curtain came up. I did watch helplessly during one performance, however, as Claudia acted out her rage at Sidney on Diana, slapping her cheek much harder than was necessary. Not only did Diana's reddened face ache for hours, but she ended up needing serious dental work. There was no doubt that Claudia was the monster of the show. Sidney disagreed with the play's writer, Lorraine Hansberry, that the play should evolve from the mother's point of view. He preferred his character, Claudia's son, to be the center of the piece. I watched both Sidney and Ruby Dee fight with Claudia about their roles, but I stayed out of her way. I think Claudia felt that both Ivan and I were just kids, so she left the two of us alone. To me, it was Ruby Dee in her role as Sidney's wife, Ruth Younger, who was the centerpiece of the play, the way she looked at Sidney in that submissive way, and then, all of a sudden, her look would change, and he saw that she was proud of him.

When there were fights between Claudia's and Sidney's characters, they became vicious, and I could see my own parents fighting. I was playing a character of the upper class who had wealthy parents, and we were villains because we were rich. It was as if we were all characters in a tennis match, and you had to be prepared to throw back whatever they gave you. Sidney, with his Caribbean background, provided a certain vibration that moved all of us in a certain direction.

When Beah Richards took over Claudia's role a year later, things were noticeably calmer. And when Ossie Davis replaced Sidney, who headed to Hollywood for a major role, the play rose to an even higher standard. Lorraine Hansberry would be sitting downstairs, beneath the stage, during the rehearsals, continually doing her rewrites and racing them upstairs to hand them to one of the cast members. I met her then, but shortly after the play opened, she pretty much disappeared. I have no idea what was going on with this brilliant woman, but I knew she was an activist, and I wondered whether perhaps she was involved in some kind of subversive acts. She was only twenty-nine years old when the play opened, but she died of cancer six years later. What a tremendous loss that was.

The night the play opened on Broadway, when the curtain fell after the first act, it concluded the emotional scene in which the money is lost and everyone is crying. We all stood on the other side of the curtain, certain we had bombed. We heard nothing for the longest ten seconds imaginable. Then, suddenly, the silence was replaced by thunderous applause. At the end of the second act, this scenario was repeated—only for a longer period. As we stood there as silent as our audience, through the intercoms we could hear that no one was talking. Then, again, the thunderous applause, followed by fifteen curtain calls, after which we all returned to our dressing rooms as the applause continued.

I wish that every actor could share the experience we had that night. We were the talk of the town, as we performed every night, all of us emotionally exhausted from the concentrated energy we'd just exerted. It was as if we'd worked a long, hard, eight-hour day in one act. This electricity in the audience continued during the play's run and brought us out, holding hands, for never-ending curtain calls. It seemed as if everyone on the planet, politicians, actors, writers, and friends, came to that show and stopped backstage to congratulate us. The play also won the New York Drama Critics' Circle Award as the best play of the year. It lasted for 530 performances, some of which I had to miss to do a little TV work. When the last performance was over, it was as if a lifetime had ended. After that final curtain call, I missed everything about that show—the cast, the crew, the parties, the excitement of each and every performance, the poker games, and, without question, the salary.

But I had kept my options open with TV jobs even during the Broadway run. I'd learned early on that this was the only way to survive in this business. I'd been in three episodes of the TV series *The Big Story*, where I played a bad guy in a gang in the story about the life of Bob Thomas from the *Philadelphia Inquirer*. I was always grateful to David Susskind and Herb Brodkin for the opportunities to work in so many TV shows that they produced, such as *Judd for the Defense* and *East Side/West Side*. It seemed as if the whole industry was coming out of New York at that time, out of ABC, CBS, and NBC. Hollywood actors would have to travel to the East Coast to work in these shows. For me, it was no conflict. I spent six to eight days filming a TV spot, then headed to work in the theater at night. For the Saturday matinees, I had an understudy if they wanted me badly enough, but most of the time they scheduled my TV stuff around my theater schedule.

During those years, one great thrill of living in New York and working on Broadway was the chance to play softball in the Broadway Show Softball League. I was on the Negro Actors Guild team, and we played against teams from whatever play was on Broadway at the time, such as *My Fair Lady*, *Sweet Bird of Youth*, *A Hatful of Rain*, and *Bells Are Ringing*, along with teams from the Actors Studio and the Circle in the Square Playhouse. The Broadway musicals could have easily fielded their teams just with dancers, who, along with the stagehands, were incredible athletes.

Our commissioner was John Effrat, a stage manager who kept the order, arranged the schedules, judged any slight conflict that might arise during a game, and, most important, threw the party at the end of each season. Whoever was playing would show up at Central Park at eleven on Thursday mornings, so that there would be enough time to practice, play, wash up, and get back to work on time. Sometimes we even had practices on Mondays or Tuesdays. We always filled the bleachers that surrounded the four fields to overflow capacity, with a crowd of people who brought their lunches and came to watch us play. Most of us ended up with charley horses or stubbed toes or even worse injuries, but it did not matter. The game was worth it.

We Negro Actors Guild players looked macho with our red-and-black jerseys with red stripes, cut off at the shoulders like the old Cincinnati Reds shirts to show off our biceps. Other teams followed suit, as each show had its own uniform.

The quality of the ball games was almost professional, especially with our ringers—like George C. Scott, an MVP pitcher, who somehow ended up playing for the Negro Actors Guild team. Actors such as Ben Gazzara, who created the role of Brick in *Cat on a Hot Tin Roof*, and Tony Franciosa in *A Hatful of Rain* were also exceptional players. The best athlete of all was James Caan, who played shortstop for the Actors Studio team. Bruce Dern was all-star material out there in center field, always in his stocking feet. He'd been a barefoot Olympic runner, so it was no surprise to see him out there with no shoes. Paul Newman was a terrific player, as was Sidney Poitier, whose dresser, Stan Campbell, the man who helped him get in and out of costumes during his plays, was unbelievable on the field. Stan was a former professional athlete who had run track and played ball and was a true star out there playing for us.

I tried hard to take advantage of Peter Falk's glass left eye when he played left field for the Actors Studio team. I'd hit the ball past the shortstop into left field, where he'd have a hell of a time scrambling to get it. But Falk was a magnificent athlete and always got the ball. He knew I was going to try to cheat and get to second base, where he'd throw me out every time. I finally got smart and stopped trying to fool that guy. We even had some women on the teams. Gwen Verdon from

Damn Yankees, along with the dancers from *Gypsy*, played right alongside us. Serious players, they were often better than the guys. Most of the time, the championship game was between *Raisin* and *My Fair Lady*, and it was a hard-fought battle. We all had such a wonderful time out there. You would have thought I was playing for the Brooklyn Dodgers during those five or six summers I played in Central Park.

The highlight of the season was the big end-of-the-season banquet. We gave out awards, little statues the size of the Golden Globe. The last year I played, I finally won the Most Valuable Player award. I cherish that statue every bit as much as I treasure my Academy Award. When you look at those teams and that Broadway Show Softball League, which is still going on today, it's quite wonderful how we could all play together, regardless of race or gender or position in the plays, the way true sports teams should play. Playing for the sheer joy of it, on that field, every one of us was a true star.

I was having fun, but money was tight for me, so I found another way to make a few extra bucks during those years. I worked as a physical therapist. I'd had my first year of pre-med and made it through anatomy, so I had some understanding of the human body. I knew how to give an excellent massage and would be waiting backstage with my little kit, filled with liniment, bandages, and oils. I got right to work on the dancers' legs, on their ankles and toes, often between scenes, trying to work out their cramps and charley horses.

I'd personally seen how deeply those dancers suffered after their performances in the musicals. They'd been out there doing the near impossible, with their ankles and feet and especially their toes in terrific pain. Their legs and feet were black and blue, but you wouldn't have the slightest idea they were suffering until they staggered, nearly lame, off the stage after their performances. I'd seen some of them actually collapse during *My Fair Lady*. Yet no matter how much pain they were in, they would stand up and go right back out there and perform every routine to perfection, never missing a step. All of those dancers were in top athletic shape, and the women were all beautiful. But there was no romance in my work. I saw the pain, the black-and-blue marks, the strained muscles, the cuts and bruises, and I did what I could to relieve, albeit temporarily, some of this discomfort. I had appointments all day long whenever I could fit them in, along with emergency visits when someone needed my services immediately.

I was by no means a trained physical therapist or osteopath, although I seriously considered changing my profession to become one, but I saw and knew enough to figure out how to make these stalwart dancers feel better. And that was all that counted. Besides, in New York, it was all about survival, and whatever you could do to pay the rent, you did.

During this same time, I had one more "profession," this one involving my true love, music. I'd carry my guitar across the street from the theater to Avital, a coffee shop owned by and named for an Israeli man. Avital had seen me playing one day and hired me to work for him on weekends for a year. After the play, I'd hurry across the street, grab something to eat, and do two shows a night, three on the weekend. I sang and played with Skeeter Betts, one of the finest jazz bass players around, who was about to retire. I paid him a nice salary, and together we made a good bit of money, I thought, sharing the entrance fees with Avital. Avital made out well with us and even got new clothes, thanks to Skeeter and me. We filled up his restaurant with music lovers who watched me play on my guitar, perform a one-man show, recite poetry, do monologues, and sing. Skeeter and I built up a little cult following that year, many of whom would wait in line to see us.

In New York, there were plenty of other places to hear music and far more accomplished musicians to create and present it. My friends and I strolled all over the place to hear top jazz musicians such as Herbie Hancock and Wayne Shorter, with whom I had gone to NYU, from clubs like the Village Vanguard, all over the Lower East Side and the Village and the north and south of Manhattan. When the nightclubs finally closed and the sun was about to come up, we headed down to Wilt Chamberlain's place, Wilt's Paradise, formerly Small's Paradise, for a breakfast of chicken and waffles.

It didn't matter where we were, those of us who worshipped music found one another. In our living rooms, on the floor, on the couch, on pillows, we sat there and passed the guitar. Some glorious night, I might see Joni Mitchell on the floor and could watch her tune her guitar in her unique open-tuning method. Joni was a master of her guitar, and when she began to sing with that exquisite voice, she could make me cry. She transfixed me from her first note. John Sebastian Jr. from the Lovin' Spoonful might be there, with his string of harmonicas, each one in a different key. I'd watch mesmerized as he played each harmonica and then dropped it into a glass of water when he was through with it, presumably, I figured, to keep it moist until he needed it again. More regulars might be Spanky McFarlane from Spanky and Our Gang, a smaller version of Mama Cass with a voice just as strong, a personality equally charismatic, and a face as beautiful; Richie Havens; David Crosby; and Stephen Stills, along with Fred Neil, my best friend and running buddy in the Village. At twelve, Fred had won a country music award for a song he wrote, "You Don't Have to Be a Baby to Cry." Much later, he wrote the theme song for *Midnight Cowboy*, "Everybody's Talkin'," which was recorded by the singer Nilsson. Fred was a country boy, but whenever he was in the city, he would be in the middle of the circle, passing the guitar around.

Later, when I headed to L.A., our group met on 7708 Woodrow Wilson Drive at Cass Elliot's place out there and saw John Phillips after he had just married Michelle; Cass Elliot herself, the queen with the golden voice; and sometimes even the fabulous Linda Ronstadt. Every now and then, even Joan Baez or Judy Collins would pop in, but they were incredibly successful by then and usually on tour. Yet it didn't matter exactly who was there each night. It was a concert every time, practically a religious or spiritual experience, as we all sat around that circle doing what we loved most. Whether we were in my house or someone else's, in a restaurant in L.A. or in Central Park in New York, in the dressing room in the middle of a concert or in Washington Square Park, anywhere a bunch of musicians were together, the guitars were passed around. Sometimes, we even drew a crowd, providing priceless entertainment for free. Those were, unquestionably, some of the best times in my life.

During those early years in New York, I got a chance to go onstage with the glorious production of Jean Genet's *The Blacks*. Along with Genet's genius, Gene Frankel's direction put it all together in an equally brilliant manner. The off-Broadway production, which won Obies (Off-Broadway Theatre Awards bestowed by the *Village Voice*) for Best Broadway Play in 1961 and a Distinguished Performance Award for Godfrey Cambridge, was deeply confrontational with its audience. The avant-garde play carried the audience into Negro minds and imaginations, creating a mysterious atmosphere as if the blacks had captured the whites. It brought out a paranoid attitude with white or mixed audiences. I remember one show in the middle of the summer when the air conditioners suddenly went off, and a white man got so frightened, he had a heart attack. During another show, a woman fainted.

Every show was a bit different, depending on the mood of the audience. If people came in happy and relaxed, it was our job to shock them to get them under the control of the play. If they came in nervous and worried about what was going to happen, they were easier to handle. The set-up of the stage, the way the actors were under a canopy and the audience beneath them, increased the feeling that the audience was about to be kidnapped, to be taken hostage by the actors in this theater. It was as if they were in a warehouse, and we could lock the door and not let them out. We needed and received their undivided attention during the entire show. When the lights went off, you could smell the fear in the audience. When we put the lights back on and let them go home, we had all been through a true theater experience.

So much happened to the audience itself during the play. For example, a lady in the front row would be given a flower, which she would then have to place onstage, on the white sheet supposedly covering a dead body. At the end of the show, we would have evoked the sense of a real person being under there, so that when we pulled off the sheet to reveal two chairs, we would laugh at the audience. It was a play within a play, with an ambiance of mystery before the first character appeared. We actually started dancing a minuet, chiding and teasing the audience with our words. As soon as Roscoe Lee Browne called out, "Ladies and gentlemen," in his aristocratic voice, the cast would crack up. He would look at us with reproving eyes, and we would behave ourselves for a little while.

All of the actors and the actresses performed in black tie and evening gowns, playing white people, but my character, Edgar Alas Newport News, wore a black turtleneck and black jeans and ran around the most, heading to the outside world and reporting on the revolution that was succeeding outside the theater. I played several different characters during the run, including Archibald Wellington and Deodatus Village, because all of the actors switched roles and lines on different nights. The play ran for five years at the St. Marks Playhouse, which later became the home of the Negro Ensemble Company. No matter which role each member played, every night the cast was spectacular: James Earl Jones, Cicely Tyson, Godfrey Cambridge, our poet laureate Maya Angelou, Roscoe Lee Brown, Charles Gordone, and Raymond St. Jacques, just to mention a few on the list of distinguished actors.

I left the cast to do TV work and, most important, in 1961, to travel to Hollywood for the first time, for the filming of the movie *A Raisin in the Sun*. In it, I got to work again with Ruby Dee, Sidney Poitier, Claudia MacNeil, and Diana Sands. The love I'd felt in New York seemed sorely absent in this town, but I'd made a commitment to continue my career, and I understood that this meant Hollywood, with its increased pay and larger audiences, was part of that plan.

On the set, our director Daniel Petrie was smart enough to let all of us give him our performances as he watched behind the camera. Unlike during her stint in *Raisin* on Broadway, Claudia behaved and the filming went smoothly. After all, we knew our roles perfectly. Although I missed the intimacy of my theater audiences, I was fascinated with the intricacies of movie making. Every day in front of that camera, I learned how different the two mediums are. For the film, it was nonstop take after take, for hours at a time. If it didn't go well, they would cut, and you would do it all over again. This was so different from the theater, where you did your scene once and as perfectly as you could. Some years later, when Diana Sands and I did a kissing scene in *The Landlord*, Hal Ashby began to stutter. "I don't know how to tell you this," he said and then tried to explain how our lips were "poking out at the camera." The camera was making the image of our African lips even larger, so much so that they filled the screen. As a result, we had to regulate our kiss to fit the lens of the camera, something we never would have had to do in the theater.

Modulating my voice in the theater was so different from doing it for a film. In the theater, your entire body is your instrument. You have to extend that instrument every moment you are on the stage, so that your voice reaches the last seat in the balcony. In films, there were microphones in my shirt collar or above my head or anywhere they needed to be, to pick up and amplify my voice. There was always a sound director to modulate my voice so that it was balanced against the other voices.

In the theater, I always had to keep my eyes wide open and my face animated, but in a film, I now saw that the eyes were even more important. Through the camera, the eyes could tell the whole story. With the new film technique of Panavision, one eye could be magnified to five feet in width, so you had to be careful of your reactions on the screen and modulate them whenever necessary. The camera was a magnifying glass, capable of revealing your inner life. Prime examples were Marlon Brando and Steve McQueen, who didn't need to speak a word but could rivet the audience with their eyes and facial expressions. Much of what made McQueen such a magnetic film actor was what he didn't say. I believe that certain actors, such as Laurence Olivier and Brando, were simply born with this unique talent, as were Cate Blanchett and Meryl Streep, two of the most amazing actors I have ever seen.

I've always loved the Sir Laurence Olivier story about his conversation with Dustin Hoffman in *Marathon Man*. The two were about to film the scene where Olivier has Dustin in the dentist's chair and is about to start pulling his teeth to learn the answer to the question "Is it safe?". Dustin was a mess. He looked bedraggled and totally exhausted. He mumbled to Olivier that he spent the whole night running, didn't eat a thing, and got no sleep so that he would look the part for that day's scene. Olivier looked at him and leaned down and whispered in his ear, "My dear boy, why don't you try acting?" Olivier would have prepared for that scene by getting a good night's sleep and coming in ready to play his part.

Another of my favorite actors is Christopher Plummer. From his classic to his simple movies, I have never seen him with an empty moment. You could not find a false moment in any of his movies, no moment when you did not believe completely in his character.

Even when I was out in Hollywood, applying everything I had learned in the Actor's Studio and the theater to my budding film career, I managed to find time for physical exercise. I'd always seen a connection between sports and acting, something about the commitment to treat my body well, to keep myself in the best shape for my work. My respect for professional ballplayers, especially for my beloved Lakers, is as great as my admiration for superior actors. Ever since I was old enough to walk and my uncles put a ball in my hands, sports has occupied a huge part of my life. In Hollywood, when the day's filming was over, I usually found some guys for a pickup basketball game, just the way I had always done in New York. Years later, I often headed to Pepperdine University and used its gym or worked out in the one I ultimately created in my Malibu house.

For years, whenever I went to the Rucker tournament in Harlem, I used to say that I needed to make a new business card that read "A. S. Lou Gossett." I'd give the cards to those so-called crazy, bad-looking black kids holding basketballs, the ones who never missed a show on TV or a movie in the theater.

These basketball players would squint at me and then announce, "Aw, shit, Lou Gossett is in the house."

In Hollywood, during the filming of *Raisin*, I did find time for some pickup basketball, but mostly I went to the studio and then headed back to the motel. I spent whatever free time I had with my New York friends who had come out to Hollywood. I'd always felt more comfortable with my East Coast friends. They seemed more intellectual, more on the edge of politics, more vital than the folks I was meeting in California. I was aware of the racism present in Hollywood, but I preferred to look at it with tunnel vision and managed to avoid it as much as possible. Still, it was an eye opener for me. It appeared as if all of the races were separate, and no black person had a shot out here. Those of us in the cast were treated differently, as if we were special, which insulated us from the obvious racism. And we stuck together. If there was someone like Della Reese or Nat King Cole singing, we would all head over to Sunset Boulevard to hear them. Redd Foxx was hot, working at a club near our motel, so we went there, too. In many ways, I was just doing my job, passing the days until it was time to return to my home, New York City.

Three months later, when I did return to New York and *The Blacks*, the play was going stronger than ever, and I stepped back into the cast. Every night my dressing room was filled with celebrity visitors, from Jane and Peter Fonda to Vidal Sassoon and his wife, Beverly, with everyone anxious to come and comment on the production. Yet one visitor to my dressing room stood out above the others and changed my life off the stage dramatically.

She walked into my dressing room full of praise for my performance, on the arm of a man who will go nameless, except to say that he was the son of a famous man, and he abandoned her soon after that visit. The next night, the two of us had dinner together and quickly fell passionately in love, wanting nothing but to be in each other's arms. She was an exquisite combination of French and Italian, but when we met, she was very sad, recovering from the disappointing relationship she had had with this nameless man. We took long walks, went to movies, spent hours talking, and did everything together. I couldn't think of anything besides her and my acting. She was my first great love.

A talented photographer, she was also the daughter of an Italian ambassador or envoy of some sort. I had no idea exactly what her father did, but I understood that her family was like royalty in the United States. They maintained a lavish apartment for her on Fifth Avenue. We had been together for more than three months when I went to the apartment one afternoon to meet her. When I arrived, the apartment was empty. Even the furniture was gone. There was no sight of my darling. It was as if I had dreamed her. It took me several agonizing weeks, but I finally found out that her parents, whom I'd never met, virulently disapproved of her relationship with a black man. They had seized her and forced her into the back of the car and then into a private jet, which had taken her to a convent somewhere in the Alps. Here, her family was certain, the nuns would help her recover from this impossible romance.

Helpless and crushed, I could barely summon up the energy to continue my work, but somehow I did. I learned several years later that the young woman had fought tooth and nail about going to the convent, but she had been no match for her father's strength. When she came out of the convent, she was a different person. Unwilling to see any of her old friends, she'd insisted that she was now gay and wanted no part of any of them. For so long I had held hopes that my love would return to me and that we would continue the beautiful affair we had shared for such a short time. Despite the news I received, I clung to a small ray of hope that maybe, if we did meet, I could change her, that she would be able to love me again. I believed that it was still possible that we could marry and have beautiful children together. I understood the risk of such a relationship, but it would have been worth it for me. Yet it never happened for the two of us. Today the world is full of these beautiful mixed kids, but that was then.

It was more than five years later before our paths finally crossed. She had become a world-famous photographer and had come to take pictures of a play I was in. I barely recognized her. She in no way resembled the beautiful woman I had fallen in love with. There was nothing feminine about her now. She'd also grown heavy and bitter. When I tried to talk to her, she hissed at me, "Get away from me. I know what you did." Her tone and manner were so vitriolic that I backed off. I looked in her eyes, and there was nothing there. Yet when I saw her at work, I understood that she was living her life, quite brilliantly, through her camera, seeing and capturing the world around her through its lens. And I could understand why. She'd been disappointed by three men, including her father, who had sent her to a nunnery. It was over between us.

I had had affairs with other white women before her. In Manhattan and the Village, it did not seem to matter. I'd always been an adorer of women, of all colors—just a man and a woman, together, appreciating each other. It felt unnatural to me to have to adjust to the fact that black men could not love white women. Life should be homogeneous. To end a beautiful love affair, to destroy a woman's life because she might marry a black man, made no sense to my still-naive mind.

After I finally laid that relationship to rest, though, I saw life a bit more clearly. For the first time, I understood that I'd have to adjust my heart and my passions to the ways of the world around me. It was a tough, sad lesson but one I'm still reluctantly learning to follow. From then on, I would have to hold my breath whenever I felt myself falling for a white woman. I had been attracted all my life to women of all colors, but now with a white woman, red flags would appear as a danger sign from people both black and white, making sure I understood that this was taboo, Every now and then, I didn't care and followed my heart. But the older I grew and the more successful in my career I became, the more I understood that a black man and a white woman could not close their eyes to the world around them.

White producers and even black and white audiences in the sixties, seventies, and eighties did not want to see a black man walk into a room with a beautiful white woman on his arm. It was the kiss of death for an actor's career. A black woman seeing that black man with a beautiful white woman finds it equally offensive. And, of course, there was the danger from white society. It took a courageous couple to survive the onslaught such a relationship created. Julie and Harry Belafonte were married for more than forty years and created two beautiful children, while Joanna Shimkus and Sidney Poitier are still a gorgeous couple. Although Joanna has always been the loveliest and most loyal wife any man could desire, their marriage, like the Belafontes', was a risk for their husbands. Sidney's friendship with Stanley Kramer, whose *Guess Who's Coming to Dinner?* came along at the perfect time, reinforced audiences' appreciation of this magnificent black actor's talent.

After I lost my photographer love for good, I still felt a deep pain from losing the woman she had been before her parents ripped her away from me. I also understood that I would always have a fear about becoming emotionally involved with a white woman. Yet years later, I did fall in love with another white woman, who was German, Lillian Kyle. She had been the American soul music singer Edwin Starr's personal manager. I spent many an evening with Lillian and her flamboyant husband, Raymond. When she and Raymond divorced, Lillian and I began our beautiful affair, which seemed to raise little concern in our special Village society. Outside of the Village, however, we were both sensitive to the feelings our interracial affair created. There was no denying the fact that when a black actor starts to get a break, his personal life is affected. If he is seriously dating a white woman, he must make a choice. Although some white women understandably become bitter if the relationship ends, others come to terms with the difficult situation.

For Lillian and me, it was an excruciating decision that was brought to a head when it became time for me to move to Hollywood on a more permanent basis. I saw clearly that for a black man, it was a no-win situation. At the time, my number-one love was show business, which required my heading to Hollywood and making it as an actor there. I had so much energy riding on that success that anything that got in the way could be dangerous. Lillian and I understood how unpleasant the situation would be for the two of us in Hollywood, and I believe she made the unspoken choice of letting me go there alone. Perhaps, in a very sad way, it was for the best. To this day, Lillian, along with her son Golden, is a very special part of my life. Although she lives in England, rarely does a week goes by when we do not speak at least twice.

Yet at the time of our affair, I knew I had much work to do to continue climbing to the top of my chosen career. I certainly could not afford to do something that was not considered exemplary behavior for a black man. Doing what I had to do to succeed without her would make that climb to the top lonelier but easier.

That's my father, Lou Gossett Sr., and
his adopted father, Rocco Sylvester,
sometime in the forties working
at Rocco's newsstand.

Here is a photo my father
took of Uncle Govnor dur-
ing one of our wonderful
summers at Uncle Guvnor's
148-acre watermelon farm
in Athens, Georgia.

That's me, age ten, and my mom,
Hellen Wray Gossett, at home in
Coney Island, probably going to a
baptism or a graduation. Note my
mother's gorgeous Lena Horne
cheekbones.

Here's my family at Thanksgiving. Those liquor bottles would
be empty in a few hours. The man in the uniform (standing,
far right) is my Uncle Tim, who fought in World War II with
General George Patton, while my father's youngest brother,
Uncle Woody (seated, second from right), worked with
General Douglas MacArthur, building the Burma Road.

Look at my beautiful
maternal grandmother,
Etta Wray. We were
going to church. She
must have been close
to one hundred then,
but she'd been born a
slave and we never
knew her age.

This is a scene from *Take a Giant Step* in 1953, featuring Jane White and me. Jane is the daughter of Walter White, who was the head of the NAACP for twenty-five years.

This was the poster for the 1956 off-Broadway production of *Take a Giant Step*.

This is my special friend Lillian Kyle, in Paris, around 2008. I met Lillian in 1961 and still talk to her three times week.

Here are my good friends Cassius Clay and Richard Pryor at a benefit, I believe, for the United Way in 1962.

5

Finding My Place

1964–1967

In the mid-sixties, I was doing an off-Broadway show called
Blood Knot, with eight performances a week at the Cricket
Theatre. It was an early play by the South African playwright,
actor, and director Athol Fugard. It had been performed only
once in Johannesburg in 1961, then brought to New York in
1964. Set in South Africa, the play had two actors on stage, two
brothers who shared the same mother: one brother who could
pass for white and had done so for years, and the other one
black. The two roles were particularly exhausting. No actor

could do it for more than three months. I took over James Earl Jones's role for three months and was thrilled to be part of such an extraordinarily powerful piece.

At the same time, *Golden Boy* with Sammy Davis Jr. was floundering out in Detroit, where it was having its pre-Broadway run. Producer Hilly Elkins, who later went on to *Oh! Calcutta!* fame and became a cherished fixture in my life since *Golden Boy*, switched directors. He hired Arthur Penn and brought in Bill Gibson, who rewrote Clifford Odets's original script. Thank God for Hilly Elkins. He got that show going. Napoleon reincarnated, his fixation on the emperor evident in his own Napoleon hat and walking cane with a sword inside, he was the toast of Broadway for many years. He was an international raconteur, very flamboyant, and an exceptional producer. For a while, he was married to Claire Bloom, one of the great loves of his life. Today he is with another great love, ironically named Sandi Love.

Hilly was white, but we teased him that all of his clients were black, including Sammy and me and Ben Vereen, although Robert Culp, the English singer and Broadway actress Georgia Brown, Steve McQueen, and David Soul disputed that suggestion. Still, as my manager, Hilly broke down walls. A blood brother, regardless of his color, he was a mensch, brighter than any star he created. Although we didn't sign formally until two years after *Golden Boy*, when he flew down to Mexico while I was filming *Firewalker*, our relationship began during *Golden Boy*.

It was hard work producing Sammy Davis, but Hilly was up to it. The revised script created a new character for *Golden Boy*, Sammy's brother, the freedom fighter Frank, a worker for the Congress of Racial Equality. Hilly needed an actor who could sing for the part. He'd seen me in some nightclubs and knew I was at the top of my voice and dancing abilities, so, working with my agent, Ed Bondy, he brought me to the Fisher Theatre in Detroit. The cast was pretty tight-knit when I arrived, fresh and eager to play the role of this new character. The new director and writer shut down the play for a while and worked with it, revamping the entire show. They brought it up to date with new dances and put blood and guts into it.

Sammy was Joe Wellington, an angry prizefighter, embittered by constant prejudice, who used his fists to fight his frustrations. The originally subtle romance between Joe and the white Lorna, the mistress of Joey's manager, changed drastically in the rewrite. It developed into an explicit affair, capped by a kiss that shocked audiences who were used to musicals like *Hello, Dolly* and *Funny Girl*. An interracial romance with onstage kisses was pretty revolutionary for 1964, but Hilly was clear about it: "If you're gonna do it, you do it." And Arthur Penn was a genius at making all of that happen. I never knew of the death threats caused by that kiss, because Hilly kept us all insulated from what was going on beyond the stage. But I did know that there were people who came to the play just to see that scandalous kiss. I believe that this play, with all of its messages, would still work today.

After its revamping, *Golden Boy* opened to smash reviews in Detroit. When the Shuberts told Hilly, "Come to New York. We have the Majestic on Forty-fourth Street ready for you," Sammy announced, "Okay, this is how we are going to do it. We're going to New York by train. I'll have them add four sleeper cars, and anything you want to do or eat will be available to you there." And he meant it. We were one big family, all seventy-five of us, on that train. We played backgammon and poker and lots and lots of music and ate and drank champagne and had a ball.

By the time we got to Broadway, I understood what a special feeling it was to be part of this amazing musical entourage.

It created an indelible change in my identity. My parents, back in Brooklyn, couldn't have been prouder. They told everyone they knew, "You know what Lou is doing? He's in *Golden Boy* with Sammy." My father was there for opening night. He loved that play more than anything he'd ever seen before, identifying strongly with his contemporary, Billy Daniels. Although my dad got a little tipsy at times, he was never out of control and was relatively mellow and glowing with pride at that time. I loved to see him and Billy together when we all went out for dinner after the show, either at Sardi's or, if we wanted down-home cooking, to Jim Downey's restaurant on Eighth Avenue. The way Billy and my dad talked and laughed and giggled, sitting side by side, you would have thought they had known each other all of their lives. They always had so much to talk about, especially the good old days during the Harlem Renaissance in the twenties and thirties. They knew a lot of the same people from those days. Before my parents had married, my dad had been quite the playboy, and he and Billy had probably been regulars at Small's Paradise at the same time.

Although Billy was my father's favorite companion in my show business life, mother identified with and enjoyed the company of Estelle Evans, who had played my mother in *Take a Giant Step*. Just as my mother had done for that play, she came as often as possible to *Golden Boy*, organizing trips to the theater with her church friends and neighbors. She brought practically the entire community of Coney Island into the city to see my productions. She would buy a block of tickets, organize an auction to sell them, and make some money for the church. She even arranged for buses to bring the groups into the city. You can imagine the thrill it was for the women she led backstage to meet Sammy Davis, Lola Folano, and Billy Daniels. Especially on the matinee performances, I saw the people I'd grown up with in Brooklyn, my friends and their parents. I was as thrilled to see them as I was to meet the never-ending cast of celebrities who walked down that long alleyway to see Sammy every night. All of Camelot came: Sargent Shriver, little Maria Shriver, Robert and Ethel and Jackie Kennedy, and the entire Rat Pack, along with most of New York society, arrived to pay homage to Sammy.

One of the songs my character, Frank, sang, "No More," was openly admired by Martin Luther King. Its lyrics poured right out of me as my character sang his refusal to be second class.

I will never forget the night Dr. King came to the performance. He spent some time on the stage with Sammy and the whole cast, before he headed over to the New York hotel where he was having a fund-raiser with Sammy and Harry and Sidney and Eartha Kitt to raise money for a big march. Standing beside him, Coretta Scott King was a beautiful, quiet, graceful, regal woman, but her husband was clearly in charge. He was so popular then, totally charming, even a little loose. He loved the society of show business and was as charismatic and energetic as Sammy, both men loving the spotlight. As a minister of one of the largest churches, Dr. King had found his cause and was devoting himself full time to it. I was proud to be in the company of all of the young activists, men such as Andy Young and Dr. King's second in charge, Ralph Abernathy, who were with him that night. There was also a beautiful young lady there, Xerona Clayton, one of the young people in Dr. King's front line. Xerona was his secretary, his right hand, who later became literally the first lady of Atlanta and a strong Ted Turner confidante, as well as the founder of the Trumpet Awards. Now, many years later, Xerona is on the board of directors of my Eracism Foundation. It is a sign that she and I have always been going in the same direction.

I knew at the time that although a lot of white society accepted Dr. King, there was an undercurrent of blacks who supported Malcolm X instead of King. I have often thought that God had stepped in and changed Dr. King's life after he spent his seventeen days in the Birmingham jail a year earlier. It was as if, like Mandela, he had made a conscious decision that he would go all the way with whatever path God had chosen for him to follow.

Perhaps the jail time deepened King's resolve and changed him from being a charismatic man who was fighting for a cause into a man who made an internal decision to put his entire life on the line for a cause more important than life itself. Perhaps there is a lesson for all of us here: that there is a point in all of our lives when we have to make a decision to lead our lives differently. Personally, that would happen to me many years in the future, but we will get to that later.

With so much going on beyond the theater stage at that time, I found it harder to close my eyes to everything. Some years earlier, in 1956, full of piss and vinegar and the fresh awareness of black nationality and while living comfortably north of the confrontations, I had joined a group of friends who were ready to fix the racial problems in the South. We were certain that we could head down there, beat people up with bats, and settle everything. Our training in passive resistance changed that attitude somewhat, by attempting to teach us how to stifle our violent feelings.

I'd just completed *The Desk Set* when I went to Georgia for my first march. Although I was becoming a star, I was still smarting from the restaurant scene. On the day of the march, it seemed as if my friends had conspired to protect me—just the way I'd been protected while growing up in Brooklyn. I tried to turn away when a policeman came at me with a nightclub and a scuffle ensued. I'd gone through the training on how to march peacefully, but when the real thing happens and a police dog or a policeman comes after you, it is almost impossible to control your visceral response to protect yourself. My instincts were too strong to let the dog bite me or the man hit me. Just in time, I was pulled back by friends who had felt all along that I shouldn't be there, and I was kept sequestered until I was taken back to New York. Until I'd seen that first policeman, I had thought it was still possible for all of us to be peaceful together, just the way I remembered things during my childhood. But now, even with our passive-resistance training, that seemed an impossible task. Years before I met Dr. King, I thanked God for him, a man who wanted the same thing and was working to make it happen.

Nearly ten years later when I finally did meet Dr. King on the stage of *Golden Boy*, I didn't know how to feel about the civil rights movement. My life had changed; I was now a married man—even though for only a short time. I had been living, quite happily, with a beautiful woman, Hattie Glascoe, but our mothers, both church-going women, decided it was time for the two of us to stop living in sin and get married. I was twenty-seven and ran around too much for their liking. Our wedding was a reception at the Improvisation, a wonderful party with a long list of all of our friends, including Richie Havens and Richard Pryor.

Hattie was a strong-minded black nationalist. I didn't share her zeal or convictions, far preferring to live my life according to the laws of the land, rather than rip everything apart. I believed the words of the Declaration of Independence and the Emancipation Proclamation, as well those in the Pledge of Allegiance and the Lord's Prayer. I would not treat these words, some of them written with so much blood and sweat and tears, lightly.

As different as our beliefs were, Hattie was the first person to help me with my black identity, for which I will always be grateful to her. The two of us managed to have fun together and shared a love of jazz, especially for the jazz musician Sun Ra, a new sound in Harlem, along with Jackie McLean. For the first time in my life, here, I felt a little dangerous. But I remained on the fence, not sure whether I wanted to join the black nationalists, even though I respected so many of them, artists and politicians alike, who lived in our neighborhood. When I went with Hattie to the black nationalist meetings, I heard and even agreed about the need to return to our black roots. The music was enticing, as were the books and the words of James Baldwin and many in the tumultuous crowd of the Black Panthers. Malcolm X had become a matinee idol.

I listened and read and grew more uncertain about where I belonged. It was an ungainly existence to leave this world of racial politics and then head back into the lights of Broadway, where everything was joyous, although I knew that for me, this world had an Uncle Tom aura to it. I understood that if I changed my name and took on a black nationalist identification, this new identity would concern everyone who had supported me and would affect my employment. One thing I knew for sure was that when I returned to the Village, I could take off my suit and put on a T-shirt and find relief in the music and the art and all of the people who seemed to be able to get along with one another.

In my Broadway world, in the middle of a hit play, becoming popular myself in all of those worlds, I felt a strong affinity with Sammy. He had just become Jewish and was carefully studying the religion. It seemed as if he needed to belong to something powerful, to believe in something beyond himself. I understood his love for Judaism and had thought of doing the same thing myself. I sensed how that religion could pull you in. Before Broadway, I had gone to the Catskills with Al Evans and Stanley Ross, my best friend, to sing with the Sedacca

Brothers at Al's family's country club, the Nevele, where Al was the resident band leader. I especially loved spending time in the Catskills, where my Jewish friends' families took such good care of me, just the way all of our mothers had watched over us back in Brooklyn. No matter where we were, my Jewish mothers would say things like, "You're not eating enough, Lebele." "Put a sweater on." Their love was outstanding. And when I started on Broadway, they introduced me to everyone and said, "This is my friend Louie G. from Coney Island. He grew up with my Stanley. Look at him now. He's on Broadway." You can't turn that love around. When I did *The Zulu and the Zayda* after *Golden Boy*, I fell even more in love with my Jewish audiences, a love that I felt was requited. After all of these years, I'm beginning to feel that love again today.

While I was still in my role of Frank in *Golden Boy*, I began to salivate for the chance to play the character of Billy Daniels's Eddie Satin, Sammy's smooth, slick promoter. It was the part I understudied while playing Frank. Every day I rehearsed Eddie's role and sang his songs. Billy and I had become close, and he kept assuring me, "Don't worry. You'll get a chance. I have some gout, and I can't get up for the matinees." He was a true night man, heading over to the nightclubs after every evening performance. Getting up in the morning and performing in the matinees was too difficult for him.

Finally, a few months into the run, Billy told me, "The matinees are yours. You got it." How I loved that first smooth song of Eddie Satin's, the moment he hits the stage, standing in his penthouse with the world at his feet, and he sings about how the city sleeps. And the clothes! They were gorgeous. I looked at them and thought, There is a heaven. I couldn't wait to put them on and look like a king, just as Billy had. Those off-white, almost beige velvet shoes, the silk scarves, silk shirt and ties, the subdued brown-gray suits, the matching coat slung over his shoulders, as Eddie dressed just like his bodyguards, all of them hanging out. For the first time, I even got a dresser, who put me together for every matinee performance. It wasn't long until Billy's gout got so bad, he couldn't walk anymore, and the role was mine for every show. As Eddie Satin, Sammy's promoter, I'd have the incredible chance to scream at Sammy onstage. And when I did that part with him, I could see the respect in Sammy's eyes.

Although Billy was so generous about giving me that role, Sammy's attitude toward his understudy was different. His understudy was Lamont Washington, Sammy Davis Jr. reincarnated in every way, socially and professionally. When Lamont played a few matinees, he brought the house down. Sammy heard the reviews and never took another matinee off. There was no doubt Sammy was a better singer, but Lamont could sing almost as well and was a better actor. I watched Lamont perform dance steps that even Sammy couldn't do. After all, he was younger than Sammy. To watch Lamont perform, it was as if Sammy had given birth to his understudy. Although Lamont could not match the creativity of Sammy's tap dancing, he was the heir apparent, standing by in case he was needed. A triple threat, dancing, singing, and acting, he was unfortunately also a prodigal son who loved the girls and didn't take good care of himself. I pretty much adopted him as my younger brother, and the two of us were inseparable. It broke my heart when he died so tragically in a fire a few years later.

So there I was, working beside this spitball of energy who was taking Broadway by storm seven days a week. The best part of the show was the dramatic part, where Sammy raised the bar by demanding that everyone onstage rise up to his level. And we did. No matter how many nights I saw his dance routine, I was in awe of his tap dancing, which he changed for every performance. He brought his audiences to their feet, day in and day out, during the long run. Once the great man even gave me a compliment. "That's good," he told me when we finished a routine. "Do a little more."

I had no idea that when his door was closed before performances, no one was supposed to knock. One time when I did knock, he said, "Come on in." From then on, he always told me to come in. I would go into that dressing room and watch him sitting and drinking with his father and his uncle Will Marston. I soaked up some of that love that was right out there between the three of them, the former Will Marston Trio, where Sammy had gotten his start. I'd always known that Uncle Will was the brainstorm behind Sammy, that Sammy's wisdom and experience had come from him. During the play, I'd also seen how his musical director, George Rhodes, and his wife, Shirley Rhodes, the engineer of the entire operation, did all of the hard work. Shirley took care of all of the bookings, arranged for parties, for the cars in the train, for every little detail that was needed to make things flow smoothly, on and off the stage. And George made sure that the band was equally perfect. He had that band so well trained that at the drop of a hat they could do Sammy's song, give it all to him and make him look good. It would be very tough today to get such talented musicians as they had in that band, twenty or thirty virtuosos who took pride in everything they did.

It was then that I got my lesson on how intrusive the press could be. They were practically in bed with Sammy, following him everywhere—especially when his exquisite wife, the Swedish actress May Britt, then starring in *Murder, Inc.*, and their beautiful children came to visit him. I saw that Sammy did not have one quiet moment, that members of the press were on him all the time, just the way they had been with Sidney. As the run went on and Sammy began to run out of steam and needed his rest, the door to his dressing room was finally locked. Hilly and Shirley battled the press successfully and made sure no one came in when Sammy was supposed to sleep.

Show after show, I was dazzled by our star's talent. Since Sammy, nobody else has been able to do what he did. Some have come close, but no one is there yet. Doing a couple of duets with Sammy, along with a dramatic scene, was more than I could have hoped for. Luckily for me, Sammy had infinite patience, as well as infinite talent. He needed patience when we danced together, as I worked hard at keeping my big athletic feet off his small ones, shortening my steps so that I didn't step on his toes. He kept telling me, "This is dancing, not sports," and I made sure I followed his lead.

Sammy relished the acting and wanted to be a big Hollywood film star like Peter Lawford and Frank Sinatra. He was preparing to do a piece in a Western movie, and he spent hours in front of the mirror perfecting his draw. He wanted to be the fastest draw. I'd seen Sidney doing the same thing for an upcoming Western during *A Raisin in the Sun*. Many nights, I saw Sammy go off with Sidney and Harry Belafonte. I'd want to hang around with them so badly, I could not contain myself. "Where you guys going?" I asked pathetically whenever they left the theater together, but they barely noticed me.

Sammy and his Rat Pack were also having a hell of a time. As soon as the play ended for the night, that was when the night started for them. Sammy would finish up a show and then head over to the Copacabana, Radio City Music Hall, the Waldorf, or wherever one of his buddies, Frank Sinatra, Peter Lawford, Joey Bishop, or Dean Martin, was performing. He would join them onstage. Word always got out that he was coming, and they would close the restaurants at the nightclubs. Legally, the restaurant could not remain open after one in the morning, but if the door was locked and the restaurant officially closed, whoever was in there could remain and catch these guys performing together. Some nights, the group also included Angie Dickinson, Vic Damone, Marilyn Monroe, Debbie Reynolds, and Lucille Ball. Sammy was one of those meteors who shone so brightly but for a good long time. Years earlier, I went to some of these parties, the ones that had been held by the Rat Pack for John F. Kennedy's election. I had met Peter Lawford but never the president.

During *Golden Boy*, it never worked for me the few times I did go out with the Rat Pack. I couldn't stay up all night and go to work the next day the way they could. I tried as hard as I could to be as sophisticated and energetic as they were to handle that nonstop partying, but I always ended up in the corner, fast asleep, while they were still carousing. Sammy and his group sat in those nightclubs all night long with their cigarettes and booze and were still able to sing the next day. I couldn't drink anywhere near as much as they could. And, unlike them, I needed my sleep.

But that was a special world, and the world outside was getting more and more difficult for me to handle. There was anger, probably for good reason, in the hearts and minds of black people for their mistreatment and exclusion, but I was to find that resentment, even when justified, can destroy a person from the inside out. I still couldn't agree with Hattie's notion of black nationalism, which, in my mind, negated the racially united America that remains my dream today. At that time, Hattie's views made emotional sense to me, but they created a clash inside my head.

Then the killings started. Selfishly, I was having the best five years of my professional life, but outside of the theater, the world was falling apart. Suddenly, there were deaths and assassinations and all of our leaders were dying. Medgar Evers and President Kennedy died in 1963, then Malcolm X in 1965, Dr. King in April 1968, and Robert Kennedy two months later. Then there was the Chicago Seven trial after the riots at the 1968 Democratic Convention in Chicago. Too many holes had punctured my balloon, and I could no longer blow it up. In order to survive, I felt that I had to be calm and quiet, exemplary, but I wasn't sure how to do that anymore.

When Dr. King was assassinated on April 4, 1968, I was walking down Broadway, on my daily constitutional, when suddenly all traffic stopped. People were in tears. All I could hear was, "Martin Luther King was assassinated." Then I could hear nothing. It was like a movie. All of the noise in Manhattan either stopped, or maybe I couldn't hear it. I had no idea what had happened. I felt as if I'd been kicked in the solar plexus. But I hadn't fallen, and when I came to my senses, my face was covered with water as tears rolled down my cheeks.

I was also present at the Ambassador Hotel when Bobby was killed. I was in the dining room when Bobby left to go through the kitchen after his triumphant speech celebrating his primary victory in California. A few minutes later, I heard the shot. My emotions were set for heartbreak, and when I heard the gunshot, my systems immediately understood what had happened. I simply turned and walked away. I walked out without a word. I didn't want to hear any more. I got the point. We would never be a completely free country. The right-wingers and the white supremacists would never allow it.

I saw what was happening in my beloved New York. The word *dropout* became the mantra of my generation. I saw how the personalities of various neighborhoods were changing. There were a bunch of people fighting, and a lot of us, mostly artists, simply "dropped out." We dropped out of the responsibility of supporting the mainstream, no longer wanting to pay attention to the government. Personally, I went to work in a bookstore for a while, too shattered to know what to believe in or what to do with my life. When would we all be able to get along? All of the words of the beautiful Declaration of Independence now seemed like nothing but bullshit. Nobody was paying attention. The whole idea was full of holes.

As I watched the world around me turn ugly, I found solace in the people who said, "Make love, not war," and the three days of peace and love of Woodstock. In the Village, the Italians no longer welcomed the hippies. The Italians felt that they had lost their neighborhood. They came out with bats to beat up the blacks and interracial groups. I'd always had such a feeling of respect for these Italian residents. After all, I had grown up with Italians and loved them all. I knew that some of the guys I had grown up with were now in the Mafia, and they made me untouchable. "You got any trouble, Louie, you come to me," they all said.

I knew that Sammy had had his own problems. Although he had been golden in Vegas, he didn't seem to care about the racial limits that existed there. Because he was part of the Rat Pack, he acted invulnerable. Yet even though he was one of the first blacks to stay in a Vegas hotel where he appeared, that didn't mean he had free rein to do whatever he wanted there. On the streets, blacks could not do certain things, yet Sammy broke the rules. The most serious rule he broke was falling in love with Kim Novak, the number-one box office star at the time. It has been rumored that because of their romance, a studio head put a "contract" on him, and Sammy was taken to the desert, where he was beaten up and lost his eye. If it hadn't been for Frank Sinatra, the godfather, Sammy might have lost more than his eye, and we would have been deprived of one of the greatest entertainers of all time. Suffice it to say, God bless Frank Sinatra.

During the time we had worked together, I had felt an empathy with Sammy, as if I knew what he was feeling. He was a larger-than-life short man, but I could see that the two of us shared the desire to do anything that was necessary to be accepted in the mainstream. If you had something to offer mainstream society, you did it in the hopes that your talent would gain you entrance to that closed world. Now I could not reconcile the warring thoughts inside my head. I felt that it was important for all of us to try to work together. I might drop out, but it was difficult for me to forget what I had always been taught—not to cause waves, to be an exemplary black man. Not unlike my later role as Fiddler in *Roots*. Ironically, my role as Frank in *Golden Boy* had been inserted to keep up with the changing times. In his first scene, my character appears with a bandage over his head after being beaten up by a cop. The story on the stage had become reality. This was a very brave play. Kudos to Hilly Elkins for making it happen. As the times grew more turbulent, it was almost impossible to maintain that stance. The mood was so dark. It seemed as if people were hiding, and unreal thoughts of revolution were in the air. A point had been made with the killings of Medgar Evers, Malcolm X, and Dr. King. It was obvious that now we were not going to be equal. We were harking back to days when a white man could kill a black man and not go to jail. Even during my moments of success, my sensitivity to racial inequity bothered me. As with other successful black people, I was always looking over my shoulder, wondering where I would be safe. Although I never felt completely secure inside the world of the so-called flower children, it had been easier to live there than anywhere else.

I was well aware of the sad situation beyond the Broadway stage where I spent so much of my life. I watched my precious African-Judeo bond, the strong alliance that had been such a major part of my upbringing, being ripped apart. Riots were destroying stores in my neighborhoods. Leaders were being killed and put in jail. After the Lindsay administration, police got tougher. Again, I smelled a rat. Something was going on behind the scenes. Assassinations put a bad taste in my mouth as the riots became more frequent. Slowly but surely, New York was filling up with a death smell. All of its beauty was gathering dust. Happenings in Central Park and all of the block parties stopped, replaced by often riotous rallies, and it was no longer safe to walk my beloved streets.

This is where I have to insert my own particular opinion, one that has been substantiated by others far more important and knowledgeable than me and rejected and pooh-poohed by others. I believe that the hippie movement got life right, with its mixing of the races, free love, preservation of the planet and health foods, its powerful music and open lifestyle. It flourished until hard drugs like cocaine and heroin were introduced to make this hippie society disintegrate and collapse. I was around as acid was also introduced. Like everyone around me, I dabbled in cocaine and marijuana and hashish, recreationally, but not in such a way as to interfere with my work. I watched painfully from the sidelines as good friends began to deteriorate or go to jail or die. Drugs had snuck up on people who had been bright and shiny. Suddenly, there were massive arrests as demonstrations were broken up. Things got ugly, and everyone blamed it on the drug-crazed hippies.

I began to suspect that some of the policemen who had enjoyed us, who wore the flowers in their hair that the hippies gave them, along with the off-duty policemen who danced with us in Central Park and the Village during our "happenings," might have been living two lives. One of these lives was as undercover policemen, trying to dismantle our open, liberated, free-love society, where everybody got along regardless of gender, race, or religion.

Although this is just my opinion, I have always wondered how these heavy drugs suddenly appeared in the midst of this society. How did something so beautiful turn so ugly? Then there were lynchings and ultimately the assassinations, and we were drowning in pain and hate. The administration automatically turned Republican, because now fear ruled society. Way too soon, all of the entertainment moved to California, and we actors had no choice but to follow.

Personally, I was not yet ready to completely abandon New York City. Although my marriage to Hattie ended in an annulment six months after we married, she had stirred my social conscience in a way that made it stronger than ever. At that time, I was living on the Lower East Side near a black neighborhood, in Tompkins Square Park, somewhere around 7th Street. It was a pretty little park and a quiet neighborhood, but as soon as school ended for the summer, it seemed like a riot was going on each day. Every time I turned around, my windows were getting broken. One day I was so pissed off, I went outside, screaming to the crowd of kids about my broken windows and saying that I was going to do something about the matter. "So, what are you going to do about it?" one of them asked after I finished shouting.

"I'm going to do something about it," I insisted. "Yeah, I am." And I did. I did some research and found out about the Harlem Youth Act, which had been passed during the last part of the Kennedy administration. This involved antipoverty funds that might still be available. Indeed, I found $18,500 for a ten-week program that would allow me to hire some help and get a program running that would keep these kids away from my windows and maybe point them in a new direction. Because all I knew was theater, I structured the program around that.

My partner was a coffeehouse poet and an aspiring young actor, David Langston Smyrl. David and I used some of the money to hire teachers and to rent one entire floor of a building at 11 East 17th Street. This loft became our school, which we proudly named the Gossett Academy of Dramatic Arts (GADA). We had a great deal with the landlord, who was socially conscious and couldn't have been more supportive. He gave us everything we needed to make that place work for us. We offered our lessons and put on our shows inside the loft, but sometimes, when the weather was good, we performed under the band shell in Tompkins Square Park or even in Central Park. We portioned off the entire loft, creating office space for the theater, dressing rooms for the actors, space for the dancers, and rooms for the classes. It was very professional, and the kids loved it.

But what a lot of work we had to do before we could make that happen. The floor of the loft was a mess, and we had to fix it to make it suitable for the dancers and the shows we intended to put on there. The first weekend, a bunch of us rolled up our sleeves, sanded the floor, cleaned it, mopped it, and waxed it. Even with masks on our faces, all of that sawdust just about killed me.

David not only helped put the whole thing together, he even taught the kids fencing. He taught both the modern foil technique for dueling swords, where valid hits were made with the point of the blade, as well as the épee version of dueling, where hits were registered by an electrical scoring apparatus. It was something to see these gang members take to this sport. One of the kids who got his start there actually went on to the Olympics.

We had fund-raisers every Friday and Saturday night where the kids put on shows. We even had a concert at which Richie Havens sang. The school itself turned into a place where kids came every day and night, just to hang out, to make sets and curtains and costumes, skills that later translated into successful occupations for some of them. We had hoped to someday take over the whole building and turn it into a commercial school for kids.

Every day that summer, we had a different class going on, in dance, set-making, costumes, sword fighting, or psychodrama. Although we had a steady core group of eighty-six kids, Latin kids, black kids, and even some Ukranians, including some aspiring actors, plenty of other kids simply walked in off the streets every day. Even Richard Pryor showed up, both as a teacher and as part of a company I had put together. Liz Torres, the Puerto Rican comedienne who later made it big on TV, was the girlfriend of a member of a gang called the Dragons and was also my personal secretary that summer.

Although I was doing *The Zulu and the Zayda* at the time, I managed to get over to the school every day. I couldn't stay away. It was something to see the way that whole neighborhood changed. Everyone in the neighborhood would come to the park to watch the kids rehearse and perform under the band shell or to the school to watch another production. The mothers were so thrilled that for the first time, their children were onstage acting, doing something important that made them feel good, learning how to make sets and design and create wardrobes. Rather than killing one another in gangs, they were learning to express themselves in ways other than violence.

Yet David and I weren't alone. James Earl Jones and Paul Sorvino lived near the school, and both agreed to teach acting, with James teaching Beginning Shakespeare. Some of these kids, who had never acted before, had the chance to rub elbows with top-of-the line actors. Although GADA lasted only two years, there were some key actors and actresses from the academy who went on from there to join the Negro Ensemble Company and become serious actors.

I was especially fortunate to discover an actor and jazz enthusiast named Ernie McClintock, who ran the school full time for a year when I was busy working in the theater or on a movie and couldn't do both. Ernie was helped by guest teachers, who were in and out every day, working their butts off with us, producing and performing plays with the kids. Ernie later started his own school in Harlem, the Jazz Actors Theatre. What fun we all had with our school, especially with the psychodramas we performed outdoors at the park or in the school, teaching the kids improvisation, how to play the people they hated or somebody they weren't. They were coached to play the enemy with conviction. It turned out to be the most peaceful summer they'd ever had in that neighborhood.

To conclude the summer, we took a trip to the Berkshires. My good friend Lucille Lortel had heard about my program and said, "You bring 'em up here for the weekend," and I didn't wait for a second invitation. I'd been up there two summers earlier, doing summer stock, *Waiting for Godot* and *The Merchant of Venice*, with Alvin Epstein. In *Merchant*, which was done as a play within a play, we were a group of actors who got caught in a Nazi takeover and ended up in a concentration camp. As part of our escape plan, we volunteered to give the Nazis a performance of *The Merchant of Venice*, in which I played the king of Morocco. In the play within the play, I was a gypsy, as well as one of the leaders of our revolution. I was giving a final triumphant speech as the Nazis began, too late, to realize what was happening. It was a fascinating play, brilliantly created, with extraordinary performances by Viveca Lindfors, who played all of the major female roles.

I'd soaked up every second of that experience, which had been the height of artistic expression for me. It had been a complete visceral artistic triumph to go to the Berkshires and play with people who were the rank and file of the theater, people who loved the arts so dearly. I was anxious for my Tompkins Park kids to have the same experience. So we stayed in a camp Lucille set up for all eighty-six of us, and the kids did their productions, adding to their improvisations until these became what we called "playlettes," for which we acquired a license so that the kids could perform on the lawns of the campground. They took to the theater experience the moment we arrived. Everyone who passed by stopped to watch, impressed by the professionalism and talent of these kids.

How a couple of these city kids acted in the country was something to behold. They were terrified by the silence. The kids could handle gunshots and police and ambulance sirens every day but not coyotes or owls or, worst of all, silence. One of my most prized students, the toughest kid in his gang, a warlord with scars on his face, ended up trying to sleep on my floor, while he looked out the window all night long. "What is that, Mr. Gossett?" he'd whisper to me, shaking underneath the blanket.

"Just an owl," I'd tell him, and he'd be okay until a coyote cried out and then he'd be under my blanket with me. He wasn't going anywhere until it was light outside our cabin. Then, during the day, he was so terrified of snakes that he attached himself to me wherever I walked.

But what an exciting weekend that was! Something magical happened both nights around nine o'clock. If you looked up into the sky, you could see shooting stars and comets. These kids had never seen anything like that, and neither had I. Except for the frightened gang members, who counted the seconds until the weekend was over, the rest of the kids did not want to go home.

Sadly, after that magical summer ended, not everyone from the group made it. One kid ended up at Sing Sing. But four of those kids became the nucleus of what is now the Last Poets, a pre-rap group, with its brilliant protest poetry and improvisation, performing on stages, in nightclubs, and on TV. This group, including Gylan Kain, gave birth to the new art form being introduced by the rappers, which laid the groundwork for hip-hop.

There was no greater feeling for me than seeing my teaching come to life. Every now and then, one of those kids will come out of the woodwork, with a receding hairline or lines on his face, and introduce himself as a member of that group, and I feel like a million. That program not only healed the neighborhood, but it was also the genesis of my future dream, Eracism.

Unfortunately, but not surprisingly, the funds were dropped after the Nixon administration took over. Why not? The program was working too well.

For me, it was time to move on. I could not ignore the fact that New York was no longer the same town I had loved—and that had loved me. Things were changing, and I needed to change, too. Hollywood was my future, where I belonged, where I would have the chance to be the very best I could be. I had to move west. And up.

6

More Like Home

1967–1970

Before I headed to Hollywood, I was off to Kenya for the filming of *Bushbaby*. It was my first experience with the adventure-seeking director John Trent, who had the reputation of being a wild man. He was so wild during this filming that he nearly cost me my life. Twice.

From the moment I got off the plane in Nairobi, I was overwhelmed by a feeling of having come home. Although I didn't understand a word of the language, all of the smells and sounds in the streets felt deliciously black to me, evoking memories of my summers in Georgia. The inflections of the voices, the sounds of the laughs, were instantly familiar. What was not familiar was my experience of standing on the corner talking to a group of three or four black men, laughing and enjoying ourselves. The first few times that happened, I kept looking over my shoulder, expecting a policeman to walk past at any second and disperse us, saying, "What are you standing there for? Move on now." It took me a little while to get used to the wonderful new fact that here, in Nairobi, all of the policemen were black, and no one cared about a group of black men standing on a corner. Of all the black men I met, the Masai and the Kikuyu seemed closest to my relatives, some of them strongly resembling my Georgia cousins. But why shouldn't I have felt so at home? I was in the land of my slave ancestors.

When I walked to the waiting car, however, I noticed that a lot of the Africans at the airport were staring and pointing at me as if they knew me. I smiled back at them all, confused as to whether this was the way they treated all black Americans, but my attempt to be friendly seemed to set them off into more fits of babbling and pointing. When I arrived at the Nairobi Hilton, a crowd formed around me in the lobby, with some people even backing away from me in fear.

Finally, a British technician for the movie filled me in on what was happening. Nairobians watched TV in record numbers in those days. One of their favorite shows was the series *The Nurses*, with Zena Bethune, in which I had played a juvenile delinquent who dies from his chest wounds. "They all recognize you from that show," the technician told me. "They can't believe you're alive. Open up your shirt so they can see your chest. Maybe when they see you have no wounds there, they'll calm down." I did as he asked. There was a collective gasp as I took off my shirt, and then some people in the crowd walked slowly over to touch my chest, shaking their heads and talking to me in Swahili. I kept nodding, and finally they all backed away, smiling and chattering. I was alive. Obviously, the TV program had been wrong. I had not died on the operating table.

Yet a lot was happening in Kenya and other newly liberated countries, such as Tanzania and Zambia, that was far from amusing—or so easily handled. Africa was in a state of flux when I arrived in 1967, and Kenya was transitioning from a British colony to an independent country, a transition that was painful to the whites who had had such a great life here. These men had become obstructionists, doing all they could to make this transition difficult for the emerging new country.

For a guy like John Trent, who loved to skirt danger, this was the perfect place for his latest movie. I would be playing Tembo, a native who was the houseboy and was also responsible for child care for the ten-year-old daughter of a British family living in Tanzania. When the father, a park ranger who must hand over his job to the new government, leads his family onto the boat that will return them to England, ten-year-old Margaret sneaks off to set free her precious bushbaby, and the boat takes off without her.

The obstructionists insist that Tembo has kidnapped Margaret, and a price is put on my head. It is when a pygmy tries to claim that price that I nearly lose my real head. In his attempt to make everything in the movie authentic, John found a real pygmy to play that role. The pygmy was bald, closer to a dwarf in size, his entire little body a mass of hard muscles. Bare-chested, he wore shorts and sandals, with earrings and a necklace made of amulets to ward off evil. When the two of us first locked eyes, I knew I was in for a challenge. It was obvious that this pygmy had never seen a movie, and John spent hours trying to explain to him exactly what a movie was, time that turned out to be wasted. For this pygmy belonged to a unique class of people in Africa, a very powerful group.

No matter what he did, his life depended on his pride. Nearly all of these pygmies were poachers and stopped at nothing to remove the ivory from elephants, descending like ants on the carcasses until nothing was left. They always did their jobs well. They were always winners in whatever battle they fought.

To me, the script was pretty simple to understand: "Mr. Gossett comes in, and there is a pygmy, and there's a fight, sort of a wrestling match. Mr. Gossett gets the bow and arrow from the pygmy." When the translator read the script for the pygmy for the final time, the pygmy broke into gales of laughter and declared in Swahili, "No one can take the arrow from me. Nobody on the planet can run faster than me."

"Mr. Gossett is a big athlete," the translator explained. "He can run very fast. He can do it." More gales of laughter erupted from the pygmy, but somehow it was decided that we would do the test for this scene before it was filmed for the real thing.

I looked over at the pygmy, staring into his unsmiling red eyes as he crouched and listened to the words in Swahili. "When the rock hits the ground, Mr. Gossett will run twenty feet to you before he is able to knock you down and get the bow and arrow from you." The translator took time to try to explain to the pygmy that this was like a ritual, where no one gets hurt. Like when the warriors dance and do things, they don't hurt one another in the mock war. Nobody gets hurt. Nobody gets killed.

Still, I was certain the pygmy knew nothing about how a movie was made, what was real and what was not. He looked like a 4'10" boulder, laughing hysterically at the thought that anyone could run faster than him. Yet I wasn't particularly worried about the whole thing. I knew that it was literally impossible for this pygmy to run over to the bow and arrow, pick up the bow, position the arrow inside the bow, and shoot it at me before I reached his side.

Finally, we were ready. I didn't look at the pygmy but rather at the ground, ready to run. I had not even taken two steps before the pygmy had the bow and arrow in his hand and the tip of the arrow was positioned between my eyes. It defied reality.

Now I understood that I might die, right there, between this vicious little pygmy and our insane director. This had to be the same arrow, with its poison tip, that the pygmy would use to put down an elephant, sticking the arrow's tip into that hard-to-find, sensitive area behind the elephant's ear. Even if the poison were ten days old, it would still be strong enough to kill me. The pygmy, ecstatic that he had won, broke into a sinister smile. He laughed loudly and wildly, saying, "No way could you be faster than me."

Within seconds, all of the Africans jumped on him, yelling, "Stop! Stop! Stop!" in three different languages and removed the arrow from my face. But he was on his feet, jumping fiercely. He had scored the winning touchdown in the Super Bowl. While I sat there stunned, touching my throat to see whether the tip of the arrow had horrifically pierced my skin, John was trying everything he could come up with to bribe the pygmy into redoing the scene, the "right way." He promised him ivory, much more money, anything to make him let me get to the bow and arrow before he did. It took a while, during which time I kept touching my nose and forehead nervously, before the pygmy assented. He cooperated and let me win, but the whole time I was certain I was fighting a bear or a warthog. The scene came off fine, and the pygmy left the set, certain he had beaten the tall black chief. His life had changed, in many ways for the worse, forever. From then on, whenever I saw him, he pointed to me, laughing, and said to anyone who would listen that he was the winner. That he had defeated me. Sometimes he even brought an entourage of Africans to wherever I happened to be, whether I was reading the script, eating, lying down in my dressing room, or coming out of my hotel, and he pointed at me. He was Mohammed Ali, the king of the natives, having defeated the chief of the movie.

Yet sadly, this chance of a lifetime that made him a hero had also paid him too well, and he spent the money on alcohol, destroying the proud body and mind that had made him the king. He would have been better off had he never met John.

For yet another scene, I shared that sentiment. In his desire to make this movie authentic, John took another chance with my life. This time I was running from a helicopter, manned by two real-life obstructionists, probably the last of those romantic safari men who detested the idea of handing their jobs over to black Africans. In the scene, they had been sent by the police to bring me in, dead or alive, and collect the reward. I was racing across a plain, and the helicopter was gaining on me. As I ran, the lens of the camera I was looking at usually made objects appear closer than they were, so I was not worried. But then the copter flew even lower, faster than I had seen in the lens. At 6'4", I saw that it was suddenly flying at the level of my chest, and I caught a glimpse of the pilot's face. He was smiling. It was not a nice smile. And he was not stopping. I knew John wanted to make the scene look good, but something seemed wrong. I felt the wind of the blades of the copter and the wheel touch my head as I frantically pitched myself into a ditch and began to pray. The cameraman ended up in the ditch, too, frightened but amazed at the incredible shot he'd just gotten.

Proud of what he had just done, the helicopter pilot jumped out and squatted beside me, ready to shake my hand. Everyone, especially John, was shouting, "Great shot!" Before I knew what I was doing, I pulled the pilot to his feet, and it took three or four men to get my hands off his neck. I had completely lost it. Never before had I been that angry. I'd seen the ice-cold look on that smiling face, and I wanted to kill him now. He wasn't happy about it, but John finally realized what had happened, and he let the pilot go. It was a while before I could trust John again.

There was no question that John Trent was one crazy director. The scene did come out terrific, but, as with the pygmy scene, it had nearly ended my life. John was a true soldier of fortune, an adventurous man who knew no boundaries. About fifteen years after that movie, he died in Toronto, killing himself by driving too fast in a brand-new car. What a loss that was to the industry!

I learned so much about camera crews and racism during that movie. I had seen the way that pilot had talked down to the natives when he was preparing for the scene and the way they kowtowed to him. I had also seen cameramen, true professionals, nearly all British, who did not bring their past with them. I had no idea what they thought of the country's political changes, nor could I sense whether they liked or disliked working with the new African crews who were trying to learn the business, yet they managed to function with the natives, who were not getting much money to do most of the physical labor, carrying heavy stuff from one location to the other, doing the impossible. These British crew members simply came to work every day to do their jobs and do them in the best way possible. John Box, the set designer who had worked on *Lawrence of Arabia*, was exceptional, disciplined, a true pro.

What I was most grateful for was the way these men took the time to teach me the business. It was so different from theater, and I was still learning this movie trade. "Learn your marks," they told me. "Pay attention to your blocking, so that you will be in the right spot with the right prop when we return to that scene. Make sure you match what action you do on the master, which is the first shot you shoot, with every action you are doing in each take. If an object is in your right hand during that take, make sure it is always there for the master. It will become the axis the editor can use to cut from one angle to the other. Always be on time. Time costs money. The set is like a cash register, checking off every second you're late. Do a perfect job in your first take. Then the producers will hire you again. Tone down your style from the theater. Learn to modulate your voice. There is no room for ego. Form a team relationship with your prop man, your cameraman, your sound man, your stuntman. When you have no ego and want to learn, each one of them will help you." I devoured every lesson, never forgetting these words, no matter what country I was working in.

I also learned so much about the continent of Africa itself and especially about the country that had instantly become my second home. One night we were driving from one set to the other when we suddenly heard an ear-splitting roar. It was as if every animal in the world was crying out at the same time. Our driver stopped the car and announced that we were in the midst of the wild African migration. While I sat there stunned, the entire plain rocked with the sounds and sights of elk, jaguars, deer, lions, tigers, camels, elephants, and wildebeests, all led by the incredible zebras. The pounding of their hoofs grew louder until the thunderous pack was upon us, as the animals ignored the car or jumped over it if necessary. They had picked up the sounds of an approaching storm and were fleeing from it. It took fifteen to twenty minutes and then the plain was silent again, except for the sound of our car moving along the dusty road, trying to escape the storm. This was quite a sight for a kid from Brooklyn.

The lessons I learned about the Mau Mau and the Masai and the Kikuyu were equally important, but some of the sights I saw were far less awe-inspiring. There was an air of violence, something I could not define but which I understood meant that death was always just a step away. You were walking in a place so pristine and beautiful, but you could die at any minute. You could step on a snake or be attacked by a predator if you stepped out of the car or wandered off the set. You could be talking to a Masai or playing soccer with him and unwittingly insult his pride or show him disrespect, and he might take off your head in a split second. They all lived in tandem, these animals, these people, each one doing something to keep this chain of nature moving. I was the outsider, trying to learn the rules, all the while inhaling the inexplicably familiar scent of the land where snow-covered Kilimanjaro peeked out at me, entrancing me with its gorgeous majesty.

I was enthralled with all of these lessons and followed as many of them as I could. As I learned to walk the way Tembo would walk, I realized that his gait was, in many ways, my father's gait. But the custom of handholding was not at all as familiar. It took me a while to understand that when an African man took my hand and held it while we walked, it was not a sign of homosexuality. Rather, it meant, "We are at peace." Warriors who walked together had no need for a spear in the bush. As long as your hand was being held, it could not reach for that spear or a knife. If I pulled my hand away, it could be interpreted as a sign of impending violence.

One other Masai tradition took me no time to admire and emulate: their use of bush grass to increase their vision. I could see them squatting in a circle, shaping the bush grass into a mound that they would light, then inhale the smoke and remain in that position, talking. I could not understand one word they were saying, but their tones of voice and facial and hand motions made me think they could easily have been a group of my friends discussing the Dodgers latest game. For me, bush grass was an intoxicant. A few whiffs and I was in another world, acting like a fool, an indication that it didn't belong in my system.

The Masai cattle men, whose job was to keep the lions away from their herds of cattle, used bush grass to improve their ability to spot an approaching lion a mile or two away—not as an intoxicant. Once they spotted the lion, they were prepared to spear it before it reached the herd. These herders, most of them no more than eighteen years old, wearing sandals made of automobile tires so that their feet wouldn't get pricked with thorns, could run farther than anyone I'd ever seen, faster than the lions approaching the herd. Once the cattle herders had speared and killed the lion, they would string its teeth around their necks and put the mane on a spear or a hut as a symbol of their manhood.

I also learned that the Swahili word *bwana* did not mean "white man," as I originally thought, but rather "sir." I swelled with pride each time they called me *bwana*.

By the time I arrived in Hollywood after my stay in Kenya, I had reconciled myself to the fact that this was now my home. Although I still kept a small place in the Village on Sullivan Street near Broadway, which would always remain the true world of acting to me, I was pretty much living in a rented house at 8510 Ridpath Drive in Laurel Canyon. It was a small place on a 35-degree angle partway down a mountain. Some of my happiest times took place in that house. Here I emulated my father, planting beefsteak tomatoes and vegetables in the backyard, while inside I found room for all of my "things," all of the junk and the souvenirs, along with the books and the papers I always moved from place to place.

I was fast becoming the king of episodic TV, taping shows in Hollywood for series such as *Harry O*, *Bonanza*, *Little House on the Prairie*, *The Partridge Family*, *The Rookies*, *The Rockford Files*, *The Jeffersons*, *McCloud*, and *The Mod Squad*. The list goes on and on. It seemed as if whenever the script called for a tall, prematurely bald black man, I was in, and I worked as hard as I could to play that role to perfection.

Sometimes, as with one *Harry O* episode, my baptism-by-fire adjustment continued, as I learned that, above all else, money was the king in Hollywood, and losing time meant money pulled out of someone's pocket. I love working with David Janssen, but I wasn't thinking like an actor during one particular scene when I played a gangster, with a hint of black exploitation in the role. In this particular scene, I was eating beef ribs in a restaurant. Just before we did the scene, however, I had dumbly pigged out during our lunch break. The food was terrific on those Universal sets, and, as always, I denied myself nothing. Unfortunately, however, I had forgotten that after lunch, I had to sit at a table for two hours, redoing that scene multiple times and eating beef ribs the entire time. It was authentic, as was the miserable condition of my overloaded stomach during and after the filming.

My cowboy scenes were far more pleasurable, and I was getting to know every square inch of the Disney and Fox ranches where these scenes were filmed, as well as stars such as Dale Robertson and Dick Farnsworth, along with the wranglers and the cowboys and even the horses themselves. My stuntman, Tony Brubaker (we always called each other "Ooh-Aah" with the correct pronunciation on each syllable to indicate our respect for each other), taught me how to ride a horse, starting in *The Young Rebels*.

Most of my free time in L.A. was spent with the people I knew from New York, those who shared my love of music. It was with them, on August 9, 1969, that I dodged another of the many bullets in my life. That night I had been at a party at the Chateau Marmont, celebrating the success of a rock group with my friends John Phillips and his wife, Michelle, along with Mama Cass, and Denny Doherty, all of the members of the Mamas and the Papas, and Ben Carruthers and a few others. When the party ended, we were all invited to Sharon Tate's house for another party. I was excited about the possible opportunity to meet her husband, the legendary director Roman Polanski, but decided to head home to Laurel Canyon first to shower and change my clothes. It was this decision that kept me away from Charles Manson. As I was getting ready to leave the house, I heard a quick news flash on TV about Sharon Tate's murder. I stood there, unable to move, heartsick over what had happened but grateful beyond words that someone, some higher power, had saved me from certain death that night. There had to be a reason for my escaping this bullet.

When I got a chance to film a role as an African chief in Chuck Connors's television series *Cowboy in Africa*, I initially wondered whether this could be the reason I was spared. Perhaps this was a chance to make an impact on how the image of the black man filled the TV screen, as well as being an opportunity to continue my love affair with Africa—even if the stage this time was the Disney Ranch in Hollywood, rather than the plains and the mountains of Kenya. Yet what ended up taking place on that ranch disturbed me far more than what had happened a few years earlier when I'd arrived in Hollywood to film *Companions in Nightmare*. Both experiences were filled with ugly examples of racism, but what happened on the TV series felt more personal and more far-reaching than my being handcuffed to a tree.

I took my role as Fulah, the African chief, seriously and researched it carefully so that I would speak English with the correct African accent. In the show, Fulah is being asked to share his knowledge about the Kenyan Masai way to domesticate wild animals. After my four-month stay in Africa, I had a deep understanding of the country that I was certain would enhance my role in this episode. I had spent much time rehearsing my superb two-and-a-half-page speech and spoke every word with the correct dialect.

When we started to do the scene, it was a beautiful day at the ranch, with the temperature close to 70. Yet by the time we got to my speech scene, where I explain to the American cowboy how important it is for him to treat the horses properly, the sun had disappeared behind the mountains, the temperature had dropped into the thirties, and we were quickly running out of light. Chuck was on the horse and I was on the ground, wearing a loincloth, with some metal jewelry covering my chest and waist, holding a long piece of flimsy material around my shoulders. A type of Roman sandal covered my feet. By this time, the jewelry felt like ice, and my chest and arms were covered with goose pimples. Just before I was about to give my speech, Bob DoQui, who played the African Rendula and who was standing behind me, dressed in a similar manner, whispered, "What are we going to do about this? We're freezing."

"If Chuck can handle it, so can we," I answered, anxious to get the scene done before the temperature plummeted any more.

Suddenly, Chuck jumped off his horse and called out, "Wait a minute."

The director said, "Cut," as Chuck disappeared into his trailer. He emerged a few minutes later, wearing a shearling coat, a woolen scarf, some gloves, and a fur hat. "Okay," he announced. "Let's go."

By now, my near-naked body was shaking all over. My teeth were chattering, and my breath had turned to vapor. "I think the chief should put on some animal skins," I said to the director, who shall remain unnamed. "After all, this is his country, and he has been here longer than the cowboy. He is supposed to be a smart man who knows how to treat cows and practice animal husbandry. He'll look ridiculous out here shivering while the cowboy is dressed warmly."

The director took a long look at me and said, very carefully and emphatically, "Action."

Undaunted, I went on. "Wait a minute. Do you know how this is going to look to millions of viewers who will see a person who is not smart enough to dress properly? We'll lose all sense of authenticity. A chief would look ridiculous standing here, shaking . . ."

Before I finished my words, the director said, louder this time, not even looking at me, "Action."

I got it then. Time was important, more crucial than getting it right. I wasn't indispensible enough to merit special attention. They didn't care how ridiculous I looked. All they wanted was to get the scene shot and go home. Besides, it was only essential that Chuck be warm and look authentic. I glanced at him, but he looked away. I got that, too. He didn't want to cause any trouble. Money was important to him, and he wasn't about to take any risk that might lead to losing this series. There was nothing he could do to placate my silly need to be warm and authentic. What did any of them care? They had to get the shot in the can.

The Chuck Connors I saw nearly ten years later in *Roots* had changed a great deal from the man who thought only of himself, who was afraid to rock the boat. He'd become a fine actor and a pleasure to work with by then. But not during this scene.

We finished the scene in one take. I spoke every word of my speech carefully and with perfect modulation. I made sure there was not one slip in my delivery or actions. When I finished, one member of the crew came up and said, "Good job. We could have been there all night."

But the fury I felt as I walked away from the set grew with every passing second. The scene I had just taped for *Cowboy in*

Africa, a popular show that would be shown in millions of homes in the coming weeks, had been not merely inauthentic, it had been insensitive and disrespectful to an entire race of people. I had furthered a typecast I had seen far too much of, one depicting blacks as silly, happy to sing and eat watermelon. I had seen the same thing done for Mexicans, who were shown as slovenly, or Latinos, who were shiftless criminals, or Native Americans played by white men whose faces were painted red. The scene I had just been forced to do brought to the surface emotions that had been brewing in me longer than for just one afternoon. The show's producer had given me the gift of a beautifully written speech, yet it had ended up being delivered by a buffoon with quivering lips and a goose-pimpled body who, unlike his white cowboy counterpart, was too stupid to dress warmly.

In part, I was angry at myself for being part of this travesty. I knew all too well why I had not simply left the set and refused to do the scene. If I had done what I knew was the right thing to do, I would have been replaced within twenty-four hours, and I would never have worked another day in Hollywood. I would have ignored my parents' message: Don't cause a fuss. Be exemplary. Don't give anyone a reason to criticize your behavior. Had I not recently done *Bushbaby* and met real African chiefs and ordinary Africans under great pressure who were forming a new country, all highly intelligent men who took pride in whatever task they performed, I might not have reacted with such anger. I might have brushed off the whole scene and chalked it up to typical Hollywood respect for only the dollar. But I could not. Unlike in the real-life scene where I had been handcuffed to the tree and only my own pride had been injured, here I was injuring millions of young blacks whose ideas about themselves and their race came in large part from television. Television was more powerful to the younger generation than the atomic bomb was, and I had just misused this power. I knew all too well that if a young black man had no idea where he came from, he would not know where he was going.

From then on, from that one word, *cut*, which had jarred my black consciousness even more than a freedom march had years earlier, I pledged that I would work hard to improve the images of black men who walked across the TV or movie screens, that I would pay my dues, make every effort that I possibly could, and even take whatever insults were hurled at me, but it would all be worth it. If I did all of this, I could have a podium. I could be a role model for black youths, an instrument of change. But I needed to become the very best actor I could be and win more awards, important awards, perhaps the highest of all awards that could be given to an actor. And then, finally, I would find power to develop movies that showed respect for black men and women, stories that would illuminate the great African civilization, that gave young blacks images of black heroes that would make them feel proud, not ashamed, to be African Americans. This was one pledge I was determined to keep.

As it turned out, I ended up getting sick a few days after that scene, with a vicious chest cold that took weeks to go away. But inside I was growing stronger, more determined than ever to keep my promise: to safeguard and protect and inspire the youths, and no matter who tried to knock me down, to stand up tall.

7

A Rock and
a Hard Place

1970–1974

Never part of the Hollywood set, in the early seventies I felt as if I had one foot in the acting world and the other in the music world. At that time, I also felt growing admiration and respect for my athlete friends, most especially Kareem Abdul Jabbar, along with Magic Johnson and Byron Scott. Years later, in 1987 to 1988, these guys would thrill me to my core when they led my beloved Lakers to back-to-back championships.

When I was settling into Hollywood, some of my music friends, such as Peter, Paul, and Mary, were making it big-time and were no longer part of my world. I couldn't have been happier for them. One of my neighbors was the legendary folk musician and composer Tim Hardin, best known for the song "If I Were a Carpenter." Tim spent too much time under the influence of heroin, a habit he probably picked up during his Vietnam years but an addiction I still could not comprehend. I had tried LSD back in New York, but when I watched the cockroach in my bathroom sink turn into a dinosaur before my horrified eyes, I stored the drug in a closet. Hashish was too harsh for me and got in the way of my voice. It ended up in the closet, too. Most of my friends were more San Francisco drug–influenced: we were satisfied with some marijuana, which was the perfect accompaniment when I wanted to dance, play some sports, go to a concert, or make love.

It wasn't long before I could no longer ignore the obvious fact that my paycheck was considerably smaller than those of my white counterparts. I knew I was fortunate to be working continuously, so I did not dare complain. Still, it ate away at me when I allowed myself to consider that my time and talent were worth less than the skills of an actor whose skin happened to be white. And when I couldn't afford the same lodgings and lifestyle that my white acting counterparts could and had to search for much cheaper rents, it did gnaw at me.

At one point, when the intermittent episodic TV work temporarily dried up and there was no quality TV work for black people, I couldn't even pay that cheap rent and was faced with eviction. I was now, for the first time in my life, about to be homeless. Sadly, my friends helped pack up all of my beloved belongings into a truck, while I had no idea what I would do or where I was going to go. Holding on to the couch and the chair with the ball-bearing rollers my mother had proudly given me when I'd left New York, I miserably contemplated going home to Coney Island. If I let my furniture go, it would have ended up on Sunset Boulevard.

At that exact moment, the mailman arrived and handed me a few envelopes. With my hands still on the furniture, I contemplated throwing away the letters, certain that they were only more bills I could not pay. Somehow, I did manage to open the first one and nearly lost control of the furniture. It was, miracle of miracles, a royalty check for the song "Handsome Johnny" that I had written for and with Richie Havens years earlier and which he had recorded on his album called *Mixed Bag* and sung at Woodstock. Not only did the check evoke beautiful memories of that overwhelming high I had experienced at Woodstock, despite the sloppy mud and the endless lines for the bathroom, but it allowed me to put the couch and the chair back in the house and remain in Laurel Canyon. I call what happened at that moment a God shot, an unexpected event that occurs at the most opportune moments, seemingly coming out of the blue to save the day.

A few months later, my workload grew heavy again, and I was able to rent a place I loved at 754 Old Topanga Canyon Road. Laurel Canyon had been in Hollywood, while Topanga Canyon was in the Santa Monica Mountains between the San Fernando Valley and the Pacific Ocean. With this move, I was inching my way toward the water I so craved. In my backyard, I had a big compost pile that provided fertilizer for my garden, in which I grew amazing cantaloupes and tomatoes from seeds. The house itself was an antique jewel, with a stream flowing right across the street. Once the place where stagecoaches stopped to give their travelers a respite, the ramshackle all-wood house boasted three bedrooms and a much-appreciated room-warming fireplace with vents. Because the house was built on the secluded side of the mountain, the sun went down quickly here. For seven months of the year, I heated the house adequately with this fireplace. Simply walking up that hill kept me in shape, but cutting some of the wood for the fireplace was even better exercise.

The only complaint I had with the house itself was the gold bathtub, in which I could fit only about half of my body. It had been installed by the former tenant of the house, Linda Ronstadt. Because Linda was about 5′2″ tall, it made sense that my 6′4″ frame would not work in the tub. The tub, like Linda and her magnificent voice, was lovely to behold. But it had to go.

I adored this whole experience of living close to the earth. In Manhattan, I had lived near 56th Street and 9th Avenue, surrounded by three hospitals and the fire and police departments. Gunshots and sirens were music to my ears, so now, like the gang member kids I'd dragged up to the Berkshires, I had to grow used to the silence, as well as to raccoons running across my roof and the presence of snakes. I loved my makeshift Western kitchen, all wood and very rustic, more like what you might see in a Gene Autry movie than in *House Beautiful* magazine.

One of the best things about living there were the neighbors, Mimi and Henry Smith. He was a full-blooded Chippewa Indian, while she was a flaming redhead, albeit streaked with gray, a ravishing Irish Rhonda Fleming look-alike, more of a Native American than her husband. These two grounded me, exposing me to the restorative and plentiful powers of nature. The entire neighborhood was a true artists' colony, filled with dancers, sculptors, carvers, leather makers, and craftsmen of all kinds, along with some actors. I couldn't wait to get home every night, put on long johns or jeans and slippers, breathe in the fresh air, get my hands dirty in the garden, and settle down to a dinner of fresh bread and homemade soup at the country restaurant where we all hung out. At the nearby country store, I bought organic produce, much of it delivered from my neighbors' gardens. People came in from Malibu to buy fruits and vegetables here. I loved this country life and the warmth of the neighbors and friends who surrounded me.

On some of the studio sets, however, there were frequent moments when I did not feel as welcomed or comfortable. During my fifteen episodes as Isak Poole in the TV series *The Young Rebels*, an incident occurred when I suggested that it was finally Isak's turn to save the day. All of the other actors in the Revolutionary War series had had their chance to be heroes. By all rights, Isak, the brawny blacksmith who performed so much physical labor for the band of spies, deserved his chance. And he got it. When I was handed the script the next day, the message was clear: "In scene one, Isak receives a large blow to the head and remains in a coma for the rest of the episode." I took the news with humor. It was a minor retaliation, from people with whom I had worked well for the entire season. Yet the message was clear: "Your role is as a freed slave. Get used to it and consider yourself lucky. Remember what this all means, and leave us alone." Again, my paycheck was less than that of Rick Ely or Hilarie Thompson, but that was a given.

I did have one supporter who not only made my professional life easier, but also eased many of the difficulties of my personal life. Bobby Angelle was my stand-in and double for twenty-five years, and we shared a symbiotic relationship, much like two brothers. He stood in for me during the *Iron Eagle* movies, *Firewalker, Lawman without a Gun, Sadat, Satchel Paige,* and many others. Bobby was the man who walked down the alley, got hit on the mouth, and fell to the ground. Then the director called, "Cut," and Bobby took off and I lay there, my hand on my head, moaning, "What the hell did you just hit me for?"

When they needed to light the scene properly, Bobby would be the guy to stand in my spots so that when I got there to shoot the final scene, the lighting concerns were all worked out. He was also my photo double and was often used for shots when I didn't get that necessary twelve-hour turnaround, those long shots when you couldn't tell the difference between the two of us. Although Tony Brubaker was my stuntman in at least fifteen movies, it was often Bobby who was my double, running in my place during a scene.

Off the set, Bobby was a great help in providing security for me whenever the public or troublemakers harassed me. He also got my mail, picked up my dry cleaning, and did all of the things I couldn't do when I was working out of the country or putting in long hours.

Yet it was back on the set where I appreciated him the most. Whenever Bobby witnessed any mistreatment I received on the set or in my dressing room, he was my protector, the first one to speak up and tell the offender, "You can't do that to my boss." In many ways, it was easier for him to speak up than it was for me. Bobby had a lot less to lose than I did, but in many ways we protected each other. If it seemed as if he was about to be fired, I spoke up and said I was leaving, too. I just knew that on and off the set, he was protecting my back, and that felt good.

I first met Bobby in 1975 when I was doing *Cut Man Caper* with Raymond St. Jacques and Godfrey Cambridge. It was a ninety-minute episode of a weekly TV show, *Police Story*, and was a pilot for a spin-off of the show. He was an extra who dressed as if he had come out of one those black exploitation films, wearing a big black-rimmed hat, bell-bottomed pants, and shades over his eyes. He looked kind of like me, although he was five inches shorter, a height difference that disappeared thanks to a pair of platform shoes that he fashioned for himself. Bobby had a big broad smile that you just couldn't ignore, and it didn't take long until the two of us were working together.

The only negative side to my relationship with Bobby was that he looked and dressed so much like me that when he got into trouble, which happened more than once, I got blamed. But that was a small price to pay for his protective friendship. Although the two of us were out of touch for a good ten years while he lived in Ohio and I was fighting my own demons, today he is back in L.A., caring for his ten-year-old daughter after the death of his wife, and we are together again. No one could take care of me as well as this guy does, accompanying me on trips and ensuring that everything goes smoothly. Along with his watchful presence, he has also extended his friendship, a gift I have always welcomed.

We certainly shared some dangerous times on the set. In the late 1980s, I was working on *Gideon Oliver*, which was a particularly difficult series where I played an archaeologist and was in almost every scene that we shot each week. Truthfully, I often thought that Gideon Oliver was too verbose and spoke too many lines. We shot many of the scenes in Mexico, especially in Acapulco. In one episode, the producers wanted to shoot in the drunk tank of an actual Acapulco jail, rather than spend the money to build a jail on the set. Instead of a bathroom, a hole was sunk in the middle of the drunk tank's floor. The crew quickly disinfected the place and deemed it sufficiently clean for the scene. When I saw that cockroaches and other large insects remained everywhere, I refused and said it was nowhere clean enough. As soon as Bobby saw it, he said, "Don't do it, Lou." He had been in some of those Mexican jails himself and knew they were full of diseases, possibly even hepatitis. He might have gotten into some scrapes of his own in Acapulco, but he was firmly by my side on this issue. Some of the crew members told me quietly that they, too, agreed with my position. Most of them had to do whatever they could to hold on to their jobs, but a few volunteered to build me a new set for nothing. The ultimate decision, of course, was not in their hands.

It has never been easy for someone of my color to stand up for my rights and refuse to do a shot. Immediately, Bobby warned me that the scuttlebutt said that I was being difficult because I was on drugs and simply did not want to show up for the scene, which was not true. I was exhausted from often working overtime on the series, putting in fourteen or even eighteen hours a day, with little time off. There were times when I was so tired, I could not remember my lines. If there hadn't been an incident at my house with cocaine several years earlier, the producers might have ignored my inconsequential rebellion, but they had the ammunition and they fired it.

It was a tough situation for all of us but especially for the star of the series. The bottom line was that I was an African American trying to break down doors, and it wasn't easy. When had anyone seen a single African American male or female holding the starring role, with the entire show on his or her shoulders? Not since *Claudine*, Diahann Carroll's series fifteen years earlier. Before that, the only one who had done it was Hattie McDaniel in her 1950s sitcom *Beulah*, in which she played the maid. She was positively beautiful in that role. As for me, no matter how tired I was, I had to show up and do the work. I did the best I could, but for so much of the time, I felt as if I was between a rock and a hard place.

For an African American, earning a reputation as being difficult on a set could harm his or her career immeasurably. I already felt as if I were walking a tightrope, trying to do my work to the best of my ability as both my self-esteem and my health were beginning to suffer. I was a good ten years older than most of the actors with whom I was cast and for the roles I played, and I worked extra hard to keep up with these younger actors. I was also in uncharted waters as I struggled to sense exactly what kind of power I did or did not have, to flex whatever muscles I might have gained as the star of the show.

I often thought that my white counterparts had no idea how to handle an African American star. Those of us who hung in there to create a decent workplace for everyone are still my friends today. I would work with them again at the drop of a hat. My gratitude goes out to the conscientious and devoted Bill Sackheim for his unremitting efforts and dedication as the working producer of *Gideon Oliver*. I will never forget him. He was what they call a mensch during this difficult time.

Ultimately, however, with the cooperation of the crew, a new set was built. Despite the difficulties of this series, Dick Wolf's words on every script offered me a privilege not many actors receive. Television has since proved my opinion correct. Today, you can close your eyes and press your remote and chances are you will see a Dick Wolf show such as *Law & Order*, *Law & Order: Criminal Intent*, or *Law & Order: Special Victims Unit* at any time during a twenty-four-hour period, making him the most prolific writer-producer in the history of television.

As for me, I'd won the battle, but I feared I might have lost a war. Eighty-five percent of the jobs I got during those days were on TV, a place where I felt as if I had a chance to perform my best work. Embarrassed and frightened, I hated to think that my rebellion could harm that arrangement in any way. Ultimately, though, as time went on, my bad habits did invade my discipline, and I began a slow fall from grace.

Yet that jail scene was far from the only time when I was placed in dangerous situations, some of which I could not rectify. Another location in Mexico where we were filming was full of scorpions, so the crew spent hours spraying the field with DDT. As a result of the spraying, I couldn't breathe for days, but no one seemed bothered by that fact. I was certain that they never would have put the star of *Columbo* or *Hart to Hart* in such unhealthy situations; Peter Falk or Robert Wagner would have refused to work there. I can tell you that I hardly looked up once during the filming of that scene. I spoke my lines really fast, with my eyes glued on the ground, checking for any fast-moving black insects. But somehow I managed to survive the scorpions, the cockroaches, and the DDT.

For years before I met Bobby, I had no one to watch my back, and, for the most part, that was never a problem. In the black comedy *The Landlord*, with Beau Bridges, Diana Sands, Lee Grant, and Pearl Bailey and director Hal Ashby, Beau could have used someone like Bobby to protect him from Copee, Diana Sands's jealous and violent husband, a role I savored. When I find out that she is pregnant, I totally lose it, becoming insane and beating her into telling me the name of the father. Then I attack Beau with an ax. For this scene, I had a true out-of-body experience, one of those delicious acting moments when the passage between me and my character is open and he swallows me whole, pulling me out of myself and transforming me into the murderous Copee. Poor Beau thought I was going to kill him. It might not sound funny, but the roles of the mothers, played by Lee Grant and Pearl Bailey, are hilarious. The very best part of the whole movie was that it was filmed in Brooklyn, in my old neighborhood. When we filmed the scene where I am chasing Beau with an ax, all of my friends stood on the sidewalk, out of the camera's range, and screamed, "Go get him, Louie G!"

What is shocking in this film is the interracial romance, which ends in a pregnancy—pretty earth-shattering stuff for a 1970 movie. I do believe that it was this piece of the plot that prevented the movie, so ahead of its time, from doing even better than it did when it came out. I know of no other actress whose talent can equal that of Lee Grant. What a thrill it was to see her earn an Oscar nomination for the role as Beau's icy-cold, nasty mother, who ends up with a ham hock from Pearl Bailey in her designer pocketbook. Hal was such a subtly funny, brilliant man, and I do miss him.

During those early years in Hollywood, I played the role of Patrice Lumumba in the play *Murderous Angels*, which opened at the Mark Taper Forum in L.A. and then went on to New York, a performance that earned me a Drama Circle Award. It was an exhausting role, but I was in good physical shape and more than up to it. How I loved that role as a charismatic, flamboyant playboy whose real-life story had always fascinated me, including his assassination in 1961, when his murderers put him in a pit and kept shooting at him, terrified he would come back to get them. My assassination took place offstage, but the characters who walked across that stage were all real to me. It would seem that the next step for this play would be a masterful movie, but, sadly, this never happened.

Watching the actors who played Dag Hammarskjöld and the U.S. ambassador to the Congo and all of the UN personnel reenact real-life scenes brought back memories I had of meeting these remarkable people years earlier. How many times, at New York parties or in my dressing room or at the United Nations, had I shaken the hands of great men such as Hammarskjöld or Kwame Nkrumah, the first president of Ghana. For many years, I ached to portray Nkrumah's life story in a movie, as well as the roles of many other young African leaders. One of the first things I noticed about Nkrumah was the tribal robe he wore. I learned that each of these full-length robes was decorated in a special way, according to the tribe it represented. I later developed a special affinity for these robes and got to wear my first one when I went to Kenya for *Bushbaby*. They were incredibly comfortable, perfect for putting on after you swam or exercised, and they could even double as tuxedo wear. They were open on both sides, and you stuck your legs into the openings and folded the long sections back over your shoulders.

At the time, I was meeting these larger-than-life black men. Unaware of their magnitude, I also crossed paths with Andrew Young, Julian Bond, Ralph Bunche, and the young Nelson Mandela, as well as Thomas Mboya of Kenya and Bishop Tutu, Roy Campanella, and Harry Belafonte. I even had a second chance to meet my all-time hero Jackie Robinson. I encountered some of these legends at the frequent receptions sponsored by UNESCO, the NAACP, UNICEF, and CORE (Congress for Racial Equality). One particularly memorable reception was for Paul Robeson, with another for Lena Horne, who brought New York to its knees with her one-woman show. Yet it was the reception for cabaret performer Josephine Baker's show to raise money for her twenty-five adopted children in Paris that moved me the most, although I had no idea that twenty years later I would be a part of the award-winning HBO story of this remarkable woman's life. I will never forget the bear hug she gave me, almost picking me up off my feet. During that time, I also met a great woman whose legend has unfortunately not yet been portrayed, Katherine Dunham, a masterful dancer and choreographer. Way ahead of her time, with her roots equally set in Africa and America, Katherine possessed brilliance in choreography that brought the importance of African dance to the eyes of the world. It was her dance company that gave us Eartha Kitt.

To this day, I still smile whenever I remember how the charismatic minister of the Muslims Louis Farrakhan once confided in me that he had been a folk singer, Harry Belafonte's understudy, and the composer of the internationally famous calypso song "Back to Back, Belly to Belly." I must admit that despite all of the pros and cons about this man and all that he preaches, I had a fond affection for him.

Although years earlier I had been too young to realize the historical importance of all of those extraordinary people I was meeting, I played my heart out in the role of Lumumba, well aware at that moment of the cultural significance of the play.

It was a delight to move from the seriousness of the Lumumba role to that of Jason O'Rourke, a free man in New Jersey posing as James Garner's slave in *Skin Game*. This movie, by the award-winning director Paul Bogart, who had brought me in to play Jason, was a pure comedy romp. Jim and I travel through Missouri and Kansas in 1857, where he sells me along the way and splits the money with me, until we run into a bit of a problem trying to spring me loose on one occasion. Today, Jimbo, or Rockfish, as I lovingly call him, and I remain great friends and poker partners.

Although I had a blast in this movie, I still experienced the same problems with the cowboys I had encountered in much of my episodic TV work. I understood that many of these California cowboys were basically tobacco-chewing Southerners who had come West in search of better jobs. Excellent around horses, a lot of them worked on and eventually bought ranches and often landed jobs in the numerous Westerns that flooded the big and little screens. Living around people of other races did not initially please them, nor did they like seeing a black man such as me turn into a star. There were so many ways they could trip me up: put me on a poorly trained or wild horse; place feces in my dressing room; give me a particularly uncomfortable or broken saddle. The first time I found feces on the floor of my dressing room, I became physically sick, but I refused to let anyone see my reaction. Calmly, without any emotion, I called for some help from housekeeping, and together we removed the disgusting mess. This type of harassment continued, yet I never allowed myself to express my anger over such repulsive behavior.

Luckily, I was never hurt by any horse. If anything, the cowboys' antics at giving me difficult horses helped improve my riding skills. One particular horse, a blaze-face sorrel, became my all-time favorite riding companion. An American quarter horse champion that I owned jointly with Norman Danskin (of the Danskin clothing products), he was 17½ hands tall. I affectionately called him Blackberry, although his official name was "The blacker the berry, the sweeter the juice," a throwback to my great-grandma's saying. She used those special words whenever a child had been insulted for being black. I needed those words to salve my wounds when the horse racing officials found out that I was part-owner of Blackberry. Reacting to the fact that there were no other black owners, they had Blackberry gelded. Eventually, I brought Blackberry home for my kids and later donated that marvelous animal to the equine department at Pepperdine University.

As for the cowboys, with time and perseverance, I was able to win over these staunch adversaries, and I have always been proud of the deep and treasured friendships I ultimately earned with these multitalented men. I learned so much about relationships in those early days of my Hollywood career. Something as simple as saying hello and good-bye to the security men and genuinely appreciating their work brought me years of warm relationships with these valued personnel, habits I will never surrender. With a concentrated effort, I accepted the realization that these men were not reacting to me personally, but rather to long-held feelings of narrow-mindedness and intolerance that would take years to overcome. So I worked hard and often successfully to transform people from all departments, including those in wardrobe and props, from enemies to friends and teachers. It would be a lie to say that I erased racism from all of the minds and hearts of these industry workers or that I stopped being deeply hurt by their displays of bigotry, but

I knew that to work in this business, I would have to understand from whence the disease stemmed and to develop as thick a skin as possible.

Relationships with women were often far more difficult to "fix" than were those with the cowboys, but they certainly made my life a lot more pleasurable. Even today, I have never accepted the rule that I have to love women of a certain color, and I have always loved women of all colors. It had been natural for me since childhood to be comfortable with white women, which was what *Take a Giant Step* had been about. Yet all too often, in Hollywood and sometimes in New York and elsewhere, I was reminded that I could not come into many places with a white woman on my arm, especially to opening nights and restaurant parties. For other artists, such as jazz musicians and writers, whose faces were not as familiar as those of actors, the situation might have been easier. They were not pursued by paparazzi anxious to snap a photo of a black-and-white couple.

Today I feel there has been much growth and fulfillment for the African American woman. My hat goes off to my sisters, to exquisite women such as Angela Bassett and Halle Berry and Beyonce, who have evolved so brilliantly and become so secure in their blackness, their talent, and their beauty. Things are changing for African American men as well, but when I arrived in Hollywood many years ago, the worst thing I could have done, career-wise, would have been to marry Lillian Kyle or any white woman. Yet that did not mean it was the best thing for my heart—or for the rest of my life.

The most important woman in my life, however, did end up joining me in Hollywood. When my mother was diagnosed with ovarian cancer shortly after my sixty-one-year-old father died of an aneurism in the living room of our Brooklyn home, I returned home to check up on her. At the time, I was sporting a cast on my right leg from an injury sustained a few days before I had been due to start filming *Brian's Song*. I'd been preparing for the role by playing basketball and getting into top physical condition when I tore my Achilles tendon. The role went to Billie Dee Williams, but I used the injury as an opportunity to convince my mother to come to Topanga Canyon to take care of me while my leg was in the cast. It was easy to see how lonely she was for my father. She'd been such a vibrant woman, having gone back to school later in her life, founding her beloved Hellen Gossett Child Care Center, and even running for a seat on the city council. She was only in her fifties, and I desperately wanted to cheer her up and take care of her. She grabbed the bait, convinced that I was the one who needed help, and flew out immediately.

It was a splendid year for me, to have my mother living in my house while we took care of each other. It afforded me a once-in-a-lifetime chance to have a grown-up relationship with my mother. I made sure that she ate all of the organic fruits and vegetables that flourished in our neighborhood, that she slept like a baby and took long walks in the fresh air, just the way she had during her childhood in Georgia. I prepared her drinks from freshly squeezed oranges and grapefruits, took her to movies and opening nights, and watched her come back to life. Even the arthritic stiff leg she'd always suffered from no longer gave her any pain. She was deliciously happy in my Topanga Canyon home, loving the horses and the dogs in our neighborhood and feeling the love she received from all of the neighbors, who adored her warmth and vitality. She was, without question, the joy of our tightly knit group.

Personally, I was on my own mucus-free healing diet, with no dairy, eggs, meat, sugar, or anything that increases mucus. My mother and I ate lots of lentils, fresh fruits and nuts, corn on the cob, and avocados. Not only did my foot heal completely in six weeks, but my mother's cancer went into remission.

Still, by the end of our beautiful year together, I could see how lonely she was getting. She missed her house in Coney Island, especially the window from which she looked out at all of the neighborhood children she adored. She needed to be able to watch them, to yell at them, to be part of their lives. "I'm bored just watching birds and deer," she admitted one day. "I miss my kids." But she also made it clear that she still considered me her "kid." "I love you, Louis," she told me repeatedly, as if I didn't already know it. But she always added, "You be careful." I understood that, too, having always been aware of how much she worried about my safety. Over and over, I promised her I would be careful. Reluctantly, I brought her back to Coney Island and took off to London to begin filming *Travels with My Aunt* with Maggie Smith.

Ironically, a week after we both left Topanga Canyon Road, I was heeding her words about being careful without even realizing the extreme danger I had been in and what a bullet the two of us had escaped. One night, just when we both would have been sleeping, a severe rainstorm whipped through the canyon and dislodged a five-hundred-pound rock the size of a grizzly bear, which had been perched on a mountaintop above the house. Had I originally viewed the house in the winter when the trees were bare, the huge rock, not hidden by leaves then, would have been visible, and I never would have rented the house—but I would have understood why the rent was so low. During that storm, within seconds the rock had crushed the entire side of the house, demolishing the bedroom where I would have been sleeping.

If I needed a movie to distract me from concern about my mother, the Oscar-nominated *Travels* was the one, with my role providing comic relief as Maggie Smith's fortune-telling companion. There I was, a kid from Brooklyn, celebrating his thirty-sixth birthday in Paris in the springtime, with a per diem yet, intoxicated with the thrill of it all. For the first time, I was now part of this special international world, working with the world-renowned director George Cukor, who had directed Greta Garbo and Marlene Dietrich. Displaying complete trust in my acting abilities, he never spoke a word to me during the filming of *Travels*.

In London, where I met the Beatles and the Rolling Stones, there had been no concern about my playing the part of Maggie's black paramour. Surrounded by the same crew I had worked with during the filming of *Bushbaby*, respected as an artist who had come from the theater, I was seated at main tables at every restaurant or party we attended and treated like royalty in every instance.

I was living in London's tiniest house in Chelsea, where every room looked as if it had been squeezed in half. But I loved the milk and the breads and the eggs and the efficient subways and taxis. It was cold and damp that springtime, but everyone bundled up in those great sweaters and passed around the guitar and just had so much fun. One of my most pleasurable moments in the London music scene was when I did a set myself on the stage of the Roundhouse in Camden.

I even spent some time with Jimi Hendrix and his friends and was blessed with a good seat one night to watch that monster of talent, the consummate left-handed guitarist, sing all of his songs. In New York, at the Café au Go Go, the ceilings had been too low for his loud music, and no one had been able to understand his words, but here in London, he was revered. The man was a true genius. When I ended up sitting next to him at a coffee shop one night in London, we acknowledged each other, but neither of us spoke a word. I was too shy to talk to this true meteor. Like so many other meteors, such as Janis

Joplin and James Dean, he was gone way too soon, leaving us all a year later, at age twenty-seven.

Things were going so well for me that I seriously considered extending my stay in London. What luck it was for me to spend time watching and learning from disciplined British actors such as Maggie Smith and Alex McCowen, about whom I do not have enough words to express all of the good things I felt. Maggie was especially determined to get me into the Old Vic to do *Othello*, a possibility that thrilled me. Unfortunately, however, the black British actors blocked my entrance, insisting that there were already more than enough black actors in their equity group. I respected and understood their decision.

As it turned out, a call from Lillian Kyle in New York informing me that my mother had taken a turn for the worse made it clear that it was time for me to go home. I knew my mother had been in good hands while I was abroad, watched over carefully by our large extended family and close neighborhood friends, as well as by my dear friend Lillian, who came in from the city to see my mother at least two or three times a week and spoke to her twice a day. These two women, each of whom meant so much to me, shared a deep love, and I reveled in the affection they had for each other. Lillian's love for my mother was unselfish. Lillian never wanted so much as a thank-you for the attention she showered on my mother, bringing her healthy soups and delicious sandwiches and sitting with her, just the two of them enjoying each other's company.

My mother never stopped worrying about my safety and was deeply concerned that I might be in any danger. To her, danger included my dating white women. When she'd lived with me in Topanga Canyon, she'd had a chance to meet all of my friends of different colors and loved to spend time with them. For her, the magic word was *safe*, and in California, when we were all together, she had no worries about my safety. When I was with Lillian, she had also decided that I was safe.

Within two days of my return, my mother died. The occasion of her passing was a time to celebrate her wonderfully lived life with a two-day wake fashioned from the old school back in the South and in Africa. I have already put it into my will that when I die, I want a big party where everyone will have a good time and then throw my ashes into the ocean.

Strangely, when my mother died at age fifty-seven, I did not feel a sense of loss. Rather, it was as if she were still with me, the way it so often is with people who are close. All of the "stuff" of the person who dies simply moves into the heart and soul of the surviving loved one. After she made the transition into another dimension, my mother's spirit was way too strong to disappear. When people we are so close to, whom we think died too soon, pass on, we suffer a selfish loss. I have come to believe that those people were destined to have short lives. My philosophy about funerals is to take a photograph of the person when he or she was smiling and happy and, after the person dies, to look at it every day. If I don't have such a photograph, the loss will stop me cold, and I will miss that person too badly to move forward. For instance, with Michael Jackson, I prefer to look at a smiling photo of him and to remember all that he accomplished in a relatively short life. My mother's was the last funeral I attended. But my book of photos grows larger.

When I returned to Hollywood, things now seemed different. I resented facing the reality of this place, especially the message that I felt more strongly than ever: "Behave yourself, black man. Stay away from white women. Don't become too big for your britches." I obeyed, finding more solace and protection from "dropping out" into the hippie life, appreciating the momentary comfort of drugs. Still, no matter what drugs I used, I remained careful never to allow them to interfere with my work. Yet I grew more tired acting like the exemplary person I had so lovingly promised my mother I would always be. Often, I found myself saying, "F——k it." I didn't know it then, but these attitudes were the initial signs of an impending addiction.

8

Fatherhood

1974–1980

As I felt my initial romance with Hollywood turning sour, I was in a dilemma of trying to choose which direction my creative life would take. Did I want a career where I would sing or where I would act? The answer came in the form of Christina Mangosing, although I didn't have the faintest idea how drastically my life would change when we met. Yet when I heard her last name, my hippie persona said, "Far out." Now I had my answer. I had met a woman whose name was telling me, "Man go sing." That was it. Life would be easy and beautiful now. Yet it turned out to be a false euphoria.

I was living in Malibu at the time, in the most wonderful townhouse. I'd ached to be near the ocean and had found a way to do that relatively inexpensively. I'd saved up money from my episodic TV work, which was paying me about $5,000 a week, and with a couple of down payments, I was able to afford the monthly mortgage on a $46,500 townhouse. The front part of the house faced the highway, but the rear part was on pilings, sort of like stilts, that overlooked the beach. At high tide, there was almost no beach, but at low tide there was a bit of one. The best part of the house was the master bedroom with a porch overlooking the ocean. By being so close to the ocean, I'd come to understand how to live my life according to the rhythm of the tides. I could look outside and see no clouds but sense by the tides that a storm would be approaching in a couple of days. That exquisite view of an unlimited horizon had a glorious effect on my mind. I understood and reveled in the fact that this was all God's work.

My greatest joy was waking up in the morning and casting my fifteen-foot fishing pole thirty to forty feet over the breaking waves, then connecting the pole to the fence and going about my business. Within an hour or so, the little bell I'd attached to the pole would ring, and I'd reel in a halibut or an opal-eyed perch, clean it, and fry it right in the pan, along with some eggs, for my breakfast. There is something magical about fishing and eating what you catch. This brought back so many memories of my father and how he and my uncles were such good fishermen, not only for sport, but to bring in food for the family. I've never forgotten one cold winter in Coney Island when so many of us in the neighborhood were going hungry. People were eating inexpensive meals made of bread and soup to tide themselves over. My father took off for the weekend with a friend who was a commercial fisherman, and when they came home, they had more than a hundred pounds of mackerel and codfish in their car. Every neighbor had fresh fish for dinner that night. That was so typical of our neighborhood, with everyone adding his contribution so that no one went without food. I'd learned at an early age how people come to the rescue of one another in times of crisis.

As I settled into my life by the sea, I felt a newfound respect for my father, who had worked so hard, coming home bone-tired every night, sometimes even bleeding, to make sure his family was always taken care of. One time he'd even gone hunting in upstate New York with my uncles and a friend. As inexperienced as they were, they brought home pieces of a bear that they'd shot. They were so proud of their accomplishment that none of us dared to complain that the bear meat was filled with buckshot. I can imagine the fear they'd felt when they came face-to-face with that bear, which made them empty the guns of all of the buckshot they had with them.

Inside my Malibu house, I felt warmest and most secure in the kitchen, where I loved to cook. I was proud that I could survive so well by my own skills. Professionally, I was doing okay, working long hours in episodic TV. Yet I also found time to head off with my closest companion, my precious guitar, to sing in coffeehouses and even some clubs. I honestly wondered whether I could make a living with the music I so adored.

Then a lady friend of mine introduced me to a woman she was sure I would like, an exotic-looking waif, with long shiny black hair that fell gracefully to her knees. She was an exquisite combination of every race except Caucasian. And her name, irony of ironies, was Christina Mangosing. She seemed especially needy, and I, the great fixer of the century, was at her side. She moved in right away, and within two months she was pregnant. We had a small wedding ceremony in Malibu, and I prepared joyfully, albeit nervously, for fatherhood.

As the pregnancy advanced, however, Christina's personality began to change, which I attributed to the rush of hormones raging through her pregnant body. Her sweet shyness was replaced by outbursts of anger and wild behavior. One night, I came home from work to find the house empty. An hour later, a policeman delivered Christina to our front door, informing me that she'd been driving seventy-five miles an hour down the Pacific Coast Highway on the wrong side of the road. I couldn't seem to leave for work without her shrieking at me or couldn't come home without her continuing the same scene. Her eating habits had become bizarre, as she constantly filled herself up with foods decked in sauces so hot I could not taste them. One weekend when we were in New York for a press junket, we went shopping with a friend who was a celebrity hairdresser. The next thing I knew, Christina was following him into his salon for a haircut. When she reappeared at our hotel a few hours later, she had very short hair. It broke my heart to see her like that. I have often wondered whether that hairdresser sold her gorgeous hair for a small fortune.

As each difficult day wore on, I felt more helpless, unable to find a way to handle the mother of my unborn child. We tried some therapy but got nowhere. When I got the role in *White Dawn*, it seemed to provide a perfect plan. We would leave L.A. and spend a few months in stunning Frobisher Bay, 125 miles south of the Arctic Circle on Baffin Island, in Nunavut, Canada. For a while after getting there, I worried that Philip Kaufman would be another John Trent as in *Bushbaby*, but the filming, although we were three actors and seventy-five Eskimos, was not as traumatic. The experience itself was magical, with wonderful nights spent in igloos, wrapped in black sealskins, under which we slept naked. The Eskimos generously offered us women to keep us warm, and although Timothy Bottoms, who became an Eskimo the minute he walked off the plane, and Warren Oates, a Sam Peckinpah–type of actor who can adjust to anything, might have accepted the offer, I had my own large-bellied woman to keep me cozy. We moved through tunnels built twenty feet beneath the ground and learned to sleep despite the continuous daylight. In the movie, we are adopted and saved by the Eskimos and learn to live the way they do. In reality, we witnessed the killing of a polar bear, and I ate a raw piece of the heart, which flushed out my digestive system better than a dozen bottles of MonaVie would have. We ate raw Arctic char pulled out of the water with makeshift fishhooks, like safety pins covered with meat, as juicy and sweet as fresh watermelon.

Sadly, however, Christina continued to be unstable during the filming and terrified me by disappearing for two days on her own. She'd headed off to hunt with some of the Eskimos. I kept attributing everything to hormones and prayed that once the pregnancy was over, she would return to her normal lovely self.

Shortly after we returned to L.A., she delivered by cesarean section after a long, difficult labor. I took one look at my newborn son and was certain he'd been fathered by an Eskimo. He was positively beautiful, but he didn't look a thing like me. The more I looked at him, the more he resembled Harry Belafonte, with the same high cheekbones. But he was sweating profusely, deemed a "hot sauce baby" by the doctors who examined him. He was terribly agitated and cried all the time, and his temperature was sky high. No matter who held him, he screamed and screamed, unable to be comforted. I raced home, grabbed my tape recorder, and put in my Nina Simone and Miles Davis cassettes. Placing the earplugs next to the baby's ears, I watched as the music miraculously soothed his hot little body. The music that calmed him the most was the "Trois Gymnopedies" by the French composer and pianist Eric Satie, the serene piano composition that is played in hotels and elevators. The decision to name the baby Satie was an easy one. His middle name, Bertrand, was for the British philosopher and man of peace Bertrand Russell.

Once we got our beautiful little Satie home, I was the only one who was able to soothe him. We usually lay on the hammock on the porch off the bedroom, his little body against my chest, as I gently hummed to him. Within seconds, he'd be dead weight against me, but I loved to hold him there as long as possible. I could not get enough of the child, bounding out of bed the minute he cried so that I could change his diaper, singing and playing my guitar the minute he began to fuss. For four months, I was insanely wrapped up in my son and found it hard to leave him, even to go to work. I was especially worried about Christina, whose behavior was even more erratic and hysterical than before. I waited anxiously for the hormones to subside and for the woman I had fallen in love with to reappear. A lawyer friend of mine who spent time with her warned me that she was borderline insane and that I needed to keep a close eye on her and the baby, which made me all the more anxious.

Then the unthinkable happened. When Christina's mood seemed a bit improved and she encouraged me to go on location for a film, I followed her suggestion. But when I arrived home two weeks later, she and Satie were gone, along with his crib and toys and every piece of their clothing. I called everyone we knew, as well as Christina's sisters and brothers and parents, but no one seemed to know a thing. My lawyer, Wendy Herzog, did everything possible to get us help in locating the two of them, but not even the police were able to find them. It was as if my wife and infant son had disappeared off the face of the earth. I stumbled around in a fog, fearing the worst, waiting for the phone to ring, for someone to tell me they were all right.

Then one day, a year later, when Christina had gone through all of the money she had, I received a divorce petition, based on irreconcilable differences, from a lawyer, followed by a court order to provide child support and alimony. I was required to send two different checks, paternity money and alimony, to a lawyer. No one knew where it was being sent to, and not even the private detectives I hired could tell me anything more. Relieved that Christina and Satie were alive and well, I again put all of my efforts into locating them, but all that I learned was what the lawyer told me: the two of them were safe, and when Christina was ready to come home, she would.

Another year had passed when I got a phone call from a Hawaiian man who called himself Christina's boyfriend and cursed me out for treating my son badly. "How dare you not send money to take care of that boy?" he screamed at me. "When I found them, they were living in a commune, and Christina had one diaper left." I pleaded with him to take a money order that I would send for him to buy clothes and diapers for my son and let me come to get him. He took the check and, a week later, called to tell me that if I sent another check, he would put the boy on the plane and get him to L.A. I stood at L.A. Airport shaking with excitement and nerves until the plane landed and the stewardess carried my two-and-a-half-year-old son off the plane. He took one look at me and said, "Daddy."

Within a month, Christina came back into our lives, insisting that I return Satie to her. Luckily, I had in my favor the fact that she had been receiving welfare checks, as well as alimony and child support. It is considered illegal to accept welfare when you are receiving child support and alimony and are not broke. The judge did not look favorably on this crime. He was tough on Christina and basically told her either to give the child to his father or go to jail. It was unusual for a single man, especially a single black man, to win custody of his child, but that is what happened. We did work out court-ordered custody arrangements, so that she could have Satie every other weekend and once during the week, always with strict supervision, but from then on, until her dying day a few years ago, Christina hated me for taking her child away. She worked hard to poison our son against me and at one point almost succeeded in punishing me for what I had done.

For the moment, however, I was grateful to have my son back in my life and was determined never to lose him again. I hired a succession of excellent governesses to help care for Satie. Sadly, my professional life was very busy then, often too busy for me to be the kind of father Satie deserved, although I tried my best. One thing was certain, though. I was making a better living as an actor than I would have as a singer, another example of how wrong Christina Mangosing and I were for each other. With no woman in my life to help me with my son, I often felt tired and remembered how I'd been deprived of my own childhood once I started to work on Broadway.

All that I wanted now was a chance to relax and have some fun after a hard week's work. I tried going out and meeting women and attending parties but was never comfortable with that kind of social life. I was beginning to be able to decorate my house with the trappings of a successful actor. I filled it with all of the accoutrements that my love of music required, along with beautiful handmade wood furniture. I found it easier and more pleasurable to bring people to my well-appointed house, where I would cook for them and enjoy their company. I also played a lot of darts by myself and with friends. Yet no matter how hard I partied, I was still up and out of the house early Monday morning, heading to work.

If I did use any drugs, I did them inside my house, and I was no different from the others around me. One of the healthiest parts of my life during that time was walking on the beach with Satie and Lovey, our Malamute-Husky mix. Lovey was huge and

Satie adored him, sometimes even riding him like a horse and sleeping with him at night. Every morning, though, Lovey woke me up, standing beside my bed with a stick in his mouth. He always dropped the stick on my pillow, then ran outside and waited for me to throw the stick from my second-floor bedroom to the water, where he would swim to retrieve it, swim back to shore, shake off the water, and return the stick to me. We could play that game all day long if I had the time.

Satie and I had some other great animals then, including an oversized white cat named Blanco. Blanco's biggest thrill was trying to catch the seagulls that swooped down onto the second-floor balcony for pieces of bread I threw into the air. Blanco stationed himself in the doorway of my bedroom, then raced out onto the balcony, trying frantically to catch one of the gulls. The birds teased the poor cat mercilessly as he leaped off the balcony, desperate to grab the gull, which was always out of his reach. Like the cartoon character Tom from Tom and Jerry, Blanco never got so much as a feather in his mouth. Each session ended with Blanco falling one story down to the beach, shaking himself off, disgruntled, and roaring back up the stairs to try it again. Satie and I cracked up every day watching that cat knock himself out for nothing.

I tried hard to take good care of my son and give of myself to him as much as I could. I was continually amazed at how that boy could eat. I loved to cook for him and take him to all of the restaurants he loved, especially KFC and Sizzler, along with his favorite place, In and Out Burger. When he was a little older and I brought him on location, he remembered every place we went to by its restaurant: the great steak place in Austin, Texas; the Imperial Peking restaurant in Australia.

Something else he loved from the very beginning was the ocean, and it didn't take long for him to learn to swim like a fish. As often as possible, I took him to the Bahamas to spend time with my cousin Yvonne, whom I had always adored, and her son Tiger. Satie and Tiger had a ball together, and it was a joy to watch them swim and play until they wore themselves out. Yvonne took excellent care of Satie, and he was never bereft of love and attention when she was around.

Back home, however, all too often I left for work before Satie got up, and I came home after he went to sleep. I kept telling myself I was doing all of this to make sure he had everything he wanted and needed, even though I knew that what he needed the most was a mother and a father. I worked harder than ever, taking every possible opportunity to earn money and further my career. In 1975, I co-produced *The River Niger* with Ike Jones, a former all-American player at UCLA and Nat King Cole's manager. A great friend of mine, Ike was a black man married to a white woman, Inga Stevens, which, as I've already said, is never a good thing for an African American performer.

In 1977, I received a giant break, as did just about every African American actor, with the twelve-hour ABC mini-series *Roots*, which aired for eight consecutive nights in January. Based on Alex Haley's best-selling novel about his African ancestors, *Roots* followed several generations in the lives of a slave family. As we filmed for a week in Charleston and then back in California, we never expected that a show with black heroes and white villains would be a success. But it was, with 100 million viewers all over the world watching the final episode.

It was the commitment of the white actors to play the hell out of their roles, no matter how painful, that helped make the show a success. Before Vic Morrow did the whipping scene with LeVar Burton, he came up to me and said, "This is going to be rough as hell for me to do this."

Vic was a good friend, and I could see the pain on his face. "Go for it," I told him. "You have to." There was utter silence on the set when he finished, and he looked as if he was the one who had been whipped. Leslie Uggams was heartbreakingly magnificent in the back of the wagon as Kizzy is separated from her mother, just as Chuck Connors had been in the rape scene with Leslie, creating Chicken George, played by the brilliant Ben Vereen. Chuck was a much different actor and man from the one who had sat on his horse as I froze my ass off in *Cowboy in Africa*. I saw Lorne Greene, who played John Reynolds, Kunta Kinte's first master, go off into the corner and cry after he completed his scene. Robert Reed's personal feelings about slavery also made it tough for him to play his role, but he was excellent.

Although I did not realize it at the time, my role as Fiddler in *Roots*, at age forty-one, was a part I was already playing and would continue to play in my acting career and my real life. Reading the script for the first time, I was envious of the roles of the other actors, including O.J. Simpson, who appeared in the first hour of the week-long series. I mistakenly believed that the modern audience would see my character of Fiddler as an Uncle Tom. Yet Fiddler was old enough to know the difference, to understand what it took to stay alive in his world and how to teach the others, including Kunta Kinte, how to behave. In the first scene I tell him, "You in America now. You no more in Africa." And in so many ways, that is what I have been, an African American, acting properly respectful of his white employers and fellow actors. Too often, I was the only black in the white crowd, dressed in my tuxedo, clean and educated, teaching others to be properly respectful, to understand that this was the only way to survive in a white man's world.

When Kunta Kinte holds up his son, uttering, "Behold, the only thing greater than yourself," the words resonated through my whole being. Not only did I see my ancestors before me, but I understood that Satie was greater than myself—and more important. Every day, I was not just an exemplary black man,

I was also learning to be a good father. It was during the filming of this series that I legally changed my name by adding "Junior" to honor my own father.

Even though *Roots* earned thirty Emmy nominations, and I personally received an Emmy for my role as Fiddler, African American employment in TV subsequently sank lower than it had been for twenty years. I am not certain why that happened, but the scuttlebutt among African American actors was that the word in Hollywood was, "That's enough for the black actors. They've done more than enough. Now let's get back to normal." I do know that about a year later, things began to change, with Norman Lear adding black characters to many of his sitcoms. Thank God for producers like Norman Lear.

Luckily for me, after *Roots* I did find work and received a greater degree of notoriety and fame. For my role as the first black county sheriff in a small Southern town in *Lawman without a Gun*, I traveled to Kentucky. This movie was set in 1968, when race relations were especially turbulent in our country. It was a powerful movie, and my role was an exhausting one. I looked for ways to relax. One evening after I returned to the big house in Kentucky, which had been rented for some of the crew, I was dying to cook up some of the acres of collard greens filling the huge yard that I could see outside the kitchen window. I pulled a bunch of the plants myself, tossed them into a pot of boiling water, and waited excitedly for my delicious meal to cook. Within minutes, however, the kitchen was filled with a disgusting smell that sent everyone scrambling outdoors. A crew member walked in during the confusion and announced, "Those weren't collards, Lou. You just cooked up a pot of tobacco leaves." It took days until that awful smell was gone from the entire house. I felt terrible, but the truth was that the tobacco plants looked an awful lot like collard greens.

While working on the TV series *The Lazarus Syndrome*, I was even able to move my little family to a larger home in Hancock

Park, one block south of Wilshire Boulevard. I sold my $46,500 house on Pacific Coast Highway for $200,000 and bought a stately house, almost a mansion, with its own guest suite. The house, beautifully situated at the junction of two streets, was a mere fifteen minutes from Paramount Studios, where I was doing a lot of work in various TV series, in particular, *The Powers of Matthew Star*. The only problem with the house was that the master bedroom was on the street side, and people on the street could look right into my room. I always heard people yell, "Hi, Lou," when I got up in the morning or prepared to go to bed at night. Another drawback was that there was no more ocean outside my window, and I had lost my contact with God as I used to see the tides ebb and flow. I had no idea that this would have such a drastic effect on my spiritual side.

The neighborhood was filled with celebrities, including the mayor of L.A., Tom Bradley, and Mohammed Ali, who used to come over to do his workouts in my gym and play with Satie. Satie had his own little workout area in his bedroom, a miniature gym set with a ladder and a swing arranged over his bed. In this house, as well as in our house on the Pacific Coast Highway, his birthday celebrations were over-the-top events and included all of the kids in our neighborhoods. I hired clowns and magicians and staged huge events in his honor, making sure that the food was exactly what he wanted.

When we moved to Hancock Park, I hired a new nanny for Satie, the irreplaceable Willie Lea Coleman, a consummate chef who baked us cakes and cooked us incredible chicken dishes, sending us both into food heaven. She loved to prepare for cocktail parties that I held at the house and made me the envy of all of my friends. But mostly, she adored and spoiled Satie, feeding him breakfast in bed, picking him up at his private school. She was ready to do anything he wanted at any moment of the day. I knew she was spoiling him rotten, but I also knew she adored and protected him from any possible harm that might come his way. My fame was growing, and it was crucial that my son be protected from the press and anyone who might want to get to me through him. I was working longer hours than ever and regretted that I was not home to read to my son at night.

Yet even though I was making more money than before, I saw that despite my heavy work schedule, the money never increased the way I had expected it would. I noticed, as I had so many times before, that when I worked together with white actors, they received larger salaries than I did. I could not help resenting that I was being paid less than my white counterparts. As a result, it seemed that when I was through paying my manager and my agent their percentages of my earnings, there was much less left for me and my own bills than these white actors brought home. Even today, Hollywood scuttlebutt spreads stories of the millions I have squandered from the fortune I earned during my fifty-eight years in the entertainment industry, but those rich wages never filled my pockets—not in the later years of my career and certainly not in the early ones. Even though I was given multiple opportunities to hone my acting skills, I still felt the effects of forces that made it difficult to survive as a black actor. Just as sadly, drugs were playing a more important role in my life, although, miraculously, they still never in any way affected my working ability. I had earned a reputation as a solid, reliable actor, but for some unfathomable reason, despite my excellent reviews in the theater and a string of laudable movie and television roles with their share of nominations and awards, I felt like a second-class citizen in the entertainment industry. My fans always treated me as if I was number one, but to the powers that be of the industry, I was still considered singularly unbankable. They needed the combination of me and a white star who was bankable to finance any movie I was in.

9

An Officer and
a Gentleman

1981–1983

There were lots of women in and out of my life during those
years, as I discovered that little kids could be babe magnets.
I found out that a man caring for a small child without a woman
was somehow attractive to other women. "Where is the mother?"
they usually asked when they saw me walking into a restaurant
with Satie or buying groceries in the supermarket.

"She's gone," I told them, and their eyes lit up with a mixture of sadness and admiration. This led to some delightful experiences. As I got more involved in projects, however, and my fame grew, I had to be extra cautious. I was learning that I could easily become a target, especially to women who might take advantage of my situation. I was slowly becoming a quasi-playboy while being a full-time single father. My need for a little downtime from the constant work was too often time that I filled with women who dealt in drugs and alcohol. Still, despite my media-illuminated missteps, I always had work, and, far more important, I clung to the role of proud and primary parent of a beautiful, loving, albeit spoiled, little boy.

Working on the ABC movie *Don't Look Back: The Story of Leroy "Satchel" Paige*, which we filmed in Hattiesburg, Mississippi, was a special pleasure, particularly because I'd played baseball in high school. Satch was rail thin, so even though I was a little skinny, I had to resist some of the wonderful barbecues to stay that way during the filming. I also had to wear a hairpiece, which was a real pain, moving as it did all over my head in the oppressive heat. Having Satchel present on the set in his famous rocking chair a year before he died of emphysema added a special dimension to the filming. I have always felt that this movie, directed by George C. Scott, should have been a major film, rather than a TV movie. It was about the great Negro League pitcher who finally made his way into the American League at the age of forty-two, the first of the Negro League stars to be elected into the Hall of Fame.

In real life, I was in my mid-forties, often eight to ten years older than the roles I wanted to play. I was on the mature fringe of the artistic renaissance I saw taking place all around me. I saw so many interesting roles out there that gave actors chances to try new acting techniques, but the competitive edge for those roles seemed to be going to fellow actors who were younger than I was. I had to use up so much energy keeping my name out there, attending functions, being a celebrity, when all I wanted was to create my own family and be home with my son. I understood why so many of my fellow actors simply did not show up for these events, but I did not feel as if I had that luxury. My name had to be constantly in the paper.

So, the minute I saw the script for *An Officer and a Gentleman*, I knew that playing Sergeant Emil Foley was my shot. Originally, the script called for a white man to play the role of the hard-nosed gunnery sergeant, but somehow my incredible agent, Ed Bondy, got it for me. The second I'd officially landed the role of the drill instructor sergeant who whips his recruits into men by stripping them of their original identities and building them back up from scratch, ultimately turning them into marines, I knew I had to put myself through at least some degree of this all-encompassing transformation. If I was going to do this role, I would do it 100 percent right. The place to help me do this was the Marine Corps Recruitment Division (MCRD), an adjunct of Camp Pendleton, where they generously allowed me to enter military life for thirty days. Luckily, I was in pretty good physical shape then, running, swimming, and doing exercises of all sorts, which was a great asset for me. When I left the MCRD, I was in great shape. I had had the utmost respect for the marines before I got this role, proud that they were the first branch of the military to thoroughly integrate, from top to bottom, from commandant to beginners, and now the percentage of integration was even higher.

While at the MCRD, I got to hang out with the drill instructors (DIs) and saw how deeply they cared about each recruit, how important it was for them to turn these young men into real marines. To this day, every time I see a marine, I run over to shake his hand. Most of them simply shake their heads at this crazy tall black man, but some recognize me. "Ah, Lou Gossett," they say, smiling and warmly returning my handshake. Last year, I was invited to Camp Lejeune to commemorate an important anniversary for the oldest branch of the military. How I loved to watch those impeccable marine giants jump to attention at the slightest hand gesture from that black female commandant, Colonel Adele Hodges, the first woman ever to be in charge of the Marine Corps base, all 5'4" of her. Some marine units actually use *An Officer and a Gentleman* in their training programs.

There was so much to learn at the MCRD, especially how the gunnery sergeant, or "gunny," as they call him, teaches each of his men that in order to survive, he has to set aside his own self and all of his own personal motivations in order to defend his country. At Camp Pendleton, I watched the young boys arrive with their long hair, drugs, and cigarettes and go into shock as they were told, "Get rid of your former life. Throw everything into this big wooden box. As of today, I'm your mother, father, wife, girlfriend, and the Holy Ghost."

I was an athlete and in good shape, but not even my Broadway dancing skills could have prepared me for learning the cadence of marching. It was far more than simply placing one foot in front of the other. I had to learn the cadences of each marching drill, as I repeated over and over, "Company halt, two steps, company halt, one, two, to the rear, march, two steps, left." There were times during the practice for the movie when I led my platoon into walls as I struggled to figure out this fascinating but agonizingly difficult skill. Yet when I finally learned the precise moves, it was exquisite. It became a choreographed dance. What a wonderful feeling that was! "If you don't do this well, Mr. Gossett," the DIs told me, with only a tiny smile, "we're going to have to kill you."

During the movie, there is a shot when you can see how we had to turn corners. When Richard Gere's Zack Mayo, whom I call "Mayonnaise," comes to talk to me before the fight scene, I say, "Meet me in the blimp hanger." Then, seconds later, I order, "Company halt," and they all stop on a dime and head around the corner without touching the curb. It's far more difficult than it appears to have to act and march at the same time. Things were made easier for us by the fact that they had actual DIs, or gunnies, in the movie and that a real gunny was there to dress me properly for my role.

What was also difficult was that director Taylor Hackford decided to put me in separate living quarters, in a comfortable condo twenty miles away from the set. The purpose of the forced separation was so that I could intimidate my men more during my scenes. He had to put an end to what was happening during rehearsals, when I screamed at the recruits and they broke into giggles. The word in Hollywood was, "Have you heard? Lou lost his mind up there." Alone in my condo every night, I almost did.

The rest of the cast partied a lot, although Richard and the equally talented Debra Winger retreated to their own places. The onscreen chemistry between the two of them was terrific, but it was a different story once the camera was turned off. They couldn't have stayed farther apart from each other.

Taylor kept urging me to "lay it on him," meaning that I should scream at Richard, cornering him, transforming him into a marine who wouldn't want to leave. It was the first time I had worked with Taylor, one of the nicest and most brilliant directors out there. I like to be pushed, and he pushed me, with a vision of Foley that made me trust Taylor completely. During the shoot itself, I fell into the same trance-like condition as when I had played Fiddler. It is as if the spirits of these two men, Fiddler and then Foley, joined mine and carried me off to a place where I left myself behind and became those two unique and totally different men. It was utterly magical.

When Richard pulls those words "I got nowhere else to go!" out of the depths of his soul, I understand that he has to make it, that I have to turn him into a man. There I am, in 1982, a black father figure making a man out of a white playboy. This made quite a statement, reminding me of my role as the homicide chief I'd played in *Companions in Nightmare* some fifteen years earlier. Things had certainly changed, although in many ways they were very much still the same. My hat was off to Richard during the entire shoot. I have the utmost respect for that man, who made an internal decision not to act like a movie star but rather to do his part from the inside. It was his movie, but it was apparent that he never once thought of his character, "I can't let him do that. I'm a star." He got dirty and tired and acted his butt off. He should have won an Oscar. I believe he will win one soon.

Our fight scene was a well-orchestrated dance, in which we never intended to hurt each other. The martial arts expert coach Jason Randall, who was brought in to work with us, got the two of us worked up for the fight. "Richard says he's gonna beat your ass," he told me. "Lou says he's gonna beat you up good," he warned Richard. In one take, after five or six kicks, my leg got tired, and I struck Richard on the shoulder, and he went down. I felt terrible, but he got right up and said, "Let's get going." I ended up with a hairline fracture on my chest when Richard pulled me in and kicked me at the same time, and I got off balance. And then I ended up doing the same thing to him. We were both worried about hurting each other, but it was no big deal. After we completed that unforgettable scene in three days, we got a big applause from the crew. Richard and I shook hands and hugged each other and then hugged Taylor, aware that we had created some magic. Although we rehearsed that scene for weeks, it was the last one we filmed, just in case someone got hurt. The graduation scene, that memorable part when Richard says, "I will never forget you," and I say, "Get the hell out of here," was filmed just before the fight scene.

That whole time, despite the magic I felt when I became Emil Foley, I was struggling against an edginess that clawed away at me. I tried to use this role to get all of my devils out, because I'd been struggling to keep those demons at bay. Things were made worse when someone I thought I loved came up to Port Townsend, Washington, where we were filming, to cook for me and to bring me drugs so that I could be comfortable on the set. Although my actor's discipline began to slide away with each passing day, it was with reluctance that I sent her home. The rumor is that she might have been involved with other members of the company as well, but I never knew that for sure. All that I could think about was the work, but every night after the day's work ended, unable to hang around with the rest of the cast and the crew, I was very lonely.

After the movie came out, I had to remember that it took place in 1982, with the country still struggling over the issue of race. Unlike in *Roots*, when Kunta Kinte had been whipped, in *Officer* I had beaten a white man, a popular movie star, fair and square. Since that movie door was opened, even today I have had to be extra careful to stay away from bars. I'm aware that there can always be one hotshot anxious to take me on and prove that what happened in *Officer* was pure Hollywood. Although the acceptance for that role was overwhelmingly positive, there were still times when friends who were with me insisted I go out a back door rather than stick around certain crowds where they sensed a hostile person. It might be my imagination, but there are times when someone will come up to shake my hand and hold on to it for a few seconds too long, or the pat on my back is harder than it should be. At those times, I am grateful not only because I know martial arts, but because of my faithful friend and frequent bodyguard Otis Harper, who traveled with me often during those years. Sometimes the studio paid for my security, but whenever it didn't, I wouldn't hesitate to pay for it myself. One positive outcome, however, was that I made some wonderful martial arts friends who respected me for my performance in the fight scene.

One other wonderful reward for playing the role of Gunnery Sergeant Emil Foley came several years ago when I was in Baton Rouge accepting an honorary degree from Baton Rouge Community College. My security guard told me about a white policeman who had been shot in the chest during a raid on a suspected Arab terrorist's house. He was in a coma, but several of the policemen asked me to go visit him and talk to him. I did. I had been there only a few minutes, just holding his hand and talking to him softly, when he opened his eyes. The first words he spoke were, "I can't get down and give you forty right now, Sergeant. Maybe later." I couldn't believe it. I told him to take his time. He recovered completely, and I am sure that today he would be able to give me at least forty pushups. But what he gave me that day was a gift I will never forget.

One of the most fascinating projects I worked on right after *Officer* was *Sadat*, a role for which Anwar Sadat's widow, Jehan, personally chose me. Although this TV miniseries won me nominations for the Golden Globe and an Emmy, strangely, it was boycotted in the Middle East. Both the Egyptian and the Israeli governments found fault with certain details in the movie, but no one complained about my portrayal of Sadat. The boycott itself was odd, because the film appeared to be available in every private house in Egypt and in Israel. Personally, I felt revered in both countries and, remarkably, was able to travel from Egypt to Israel and back without having to show a passport.

Actually, we never went to Egypt for the filming but instead worked in five towns in Mexico for forty-two days. I brought Satie with me and enrolled him in the American Embassy school that the diplomats' children attended, but when my work became too challenging, I had to send Satie home. Playing a role that pays homage to such a well-known and well-respected person required every ounce of my energy and attention. I remember one particularly powerful scene in the movie. On the dark screen, a door opens and there I am, staring at the body of my brother, who has been killed. I have lost my brother and my best friend. I fell so completely into that role that I lost it, captured by the emotions that Sadat must have felt at that exact moment when he transforms from a "hawk" into a "dove." It is all in his face as he moves from there to his assembly and vows to stop the killing, telling the assembly, "If there is a way to make peace together, I will go to Jerusalem." This moment marks his transition from a fine president of Egypt to a great man of history. And we did it in one take.

Somehow, they found a schoolteacher in Mexico who was the spitting image of Golda Meir, and when I walk off the airplane at Ben Gurion Airport, she is standing there. I say, "I have been waiting a long time to meet you," and she answers with those memorable words: "What took you so long?"

Each day of this filming, I felt as if I was not acting. Instead, I was simply in the midst of a magic that consumed me, allowing me to glide effortlessly into my role and leave everything else behind. I returned to my own reality only after the cameras were turned off. Sometimes I believe that the reason I have been able to do such exemplary work on the screen is because this is the only place I can be free, neither censured nor judged.

Yet there was no screen to hide the ugly event that occurred in 1982, when Satie was eight, which caused irreparable damage to my personal and professional lives and, far more important, I believe to the life of my son. Christina, still anguished over my being Satie's primary parent and desperate to get him back, filed a lawsuit accusing me and the woman who, along with her two children, was living with me and Satie, of supplying drugs to the three children. It was an insanely ridiculous accusation that I was feeding Satie and this woman's two children a tablespoon of cocaine for breakfast every morning.

Despite the absurdity of the accusation, the police raided my house in the middle of the night. Although the detective told me, "This is pure Mickey Mouse. I don't know why we're here," the police removed Satie and my girlfriend's two children, sending them to foster homes for weeks. It took my lawyer, the late judge Edward Brand, a month to get through all of the necessary paperwork to return my son back home. I was allowed visits with Satie during that time, but he was miserable that month and returned home angry at not being able to see my girlfriend and her two children. It was obvious that he did not like me very much now. And, sadly, I was too busy to work out some of his anger with him.

Today, even though Christina is no longer alive, I am still trying to come to terms with her anger and the effect it has had on our son. I have always understood that Satie was her child, too, and that she loved him every bit as much as I did. Yet how could I have ever taken the risk of sharing custody with her, knowing that if I did, she might have taken off with him again, this time to a different country, and I might never have seen him again?

Ultimately, the court exonerated me, finding nothing, but it considered my girlfriend a negative influence on my son, who adored her and her two kids, and forbade her to come within ten miles of me and our house. All of the charges were dropped, but still the stigma remained. Other white actors were able to overcome worse predicaments with drugs and alcohol and self-destructive acts. For them, there was a hope of redemption and an even more successful career at the end of treatment, the drug problem only adding to the allure. But for a black man who was supposed to "mind his manners," the drugs were a permanent blemish. For me, the road was too narrow to have room to fool around.

I was beginning to become angry and resentful. I have since conquered those defects, understanding that the worst resentment one can have is the one he feels justified to keep. Although there are books and poetry and songs to help you feel justified about hanging on to those inequities, take it from me, they do you no good. It took time, but ultimately I began to use meditation and prayer to increase my conscious contact with God, eventually replacing my ego with humility and gratitude. This routine provides a daily inventory to help me discover what is darkening my soul and my spirit and allows me to eliminate those defects from my system, leaving a vacant space for God's light to shine through me to others, not unlike the diaphanous wings of a butterfly. After all, I quickly came to understand, God's light is brighter than any light I might have seen on Broadway and in Hollywood.

At that time, however, I had a long way to go before I created that vacant space inside my soul. Instead, my devils were enlarged, and I felt enormous guilt and resentment over the way things had turned out. Whenever that sad reality hit me, I called the dealer and got high and was ready to give it all up. But then I asked myself, "What am I doing?" and put away the stuff and got back into the fray.

Suddenly and unexpectedly, all of my sadness disappeared, and my world seemed filled with nothing but promise and redemption the moment Ed Bondy called to tell me of my Academy Award nomination for Best Actor in a Supporting Role for *An Officer and a Gentleman*. It felt like a huge vote of confidence from my peers for a performance they could not ignore. Actually winning the Oscar, although I'd already won the People's Choice Award and a Golden Globe for the role, was a shock. As I sat with nine-year-old Satie, looking handsome in his tuxedo, and Ed, who was showing signs of his age but was still vital and, as always, in my corner, I didn't have a speech ready. Stunned, I glanced at the two of them as I heard my name read by Susan Sarandon and Christopher Reeve. I'd been certain that James Mason (*The Verdict*) or Robert Preston (*Victor, Victoria*), both of whom were in poor health, would take the award for their stunning performances. It was a glorious effort to walk up to the stage and thank my parents, my grandmother, my cousin Yvonne Trenchard, and Ed from the depths of my heart and soul.

More than anything, it was a huge affirmation of my position as a black actor. After all, I was the first African American man to receive an Academy Award. Sidney Poitier had won earlier for Best Actor for *Lilies of the Field*, but although he'd been born in Florida while his mother was on a shopping trip, he was still considered a Bahamian, thus not an African American. Hattie McDaniel was the first African American woman to win an Academy Award in 1940, for her role as Mammy in *Gone with the Wind*. I was once told that Hattie had to come through the kitchen of the Waldorf Astoria to a small table in the corner of the ballroom where she could receive her award. We'd come a long way in forty-three years. We didn't have to come through the kitchen anymore.

10

The Eyes of a Lizard

1983–1985

All of the ugliness that had happened to me during the previous year was dwarfed by the momentous accomplishment of winning an Academy Award. Now I had the glorious chance to start over and fix the wrongs I had brought about myself and those that had been done to me. I believed that now that I had won the highest award of my industry, I would be able to reward African American children and, in fact, all children with the knowledge of our rich history through stories about heroes whose skin colors were not white. Yet I learned all too quickly that I was wrong. To make things worse, not only did I make the mistake of becoming resentful for not being able to do the projects I had always dreamed about, but I also complained to my agent and to some of the people in the industry. These projects' lack of success was a hard pill for me to swallow, and I could not contain all of my frustration. I had no idea how much that unresolved anger and resentment would continue to fester inside me, creating problems that would surface later in my life.

At the beginning, though, I had hope. Although I was starting to think about setting up my own movie production company someday in the future, I presented movie proposals about so many fascinating black heroes: Jomo Kenyatta, the first president of Kenya, who brought independence to his country; Dr. Martin Luther King; black cowboys (after all, one in seven cowboys in the Old West was an African American freed from slavery); Bill Pickett, who pioneered bulldogging on the rodeo circuit; James Beckworth, one of the chiefs of the Crow Nation, who led expeditions into the Northwest Passage in 1853; Benjamin Banneker, a mathematician and astronomer, who predicted the solar eclipse in 1789, built the first wooden clock, and laid out the plans for the streets of Washington, D.C.; and on and on, ad infinitum, each project exciting and eventually disappointing me. Over and over, the heads of studios and networks rejected each of my movie proposals.

Only the television industry gave these types of stories a chance, with *The Story of Satchel Paige*, which I worked on right after *An Officer and a Gentleman*, along with *Backstairs at the White House*, *The Josephine Baker Story*, *Roots Revisited*, *The Color of Love*, and the short-lived ABC medical drama *The Lazarus Syndrome*, in which I played Dr. MacArthur St. Clair. I saw then what became even more obvious as the years went on: if I relied on the motion picture industry for my livelihood, I would have been close to homeless, as well as completely unfulfilled. Yet even my successes in TV did not lessen my resentment of the fact that there was an endless supply of movies about the Vikings or the Roman Empire or the Greeks or Napoleon, but none of that magnitude being made about black heroes.

For me, personally, my success with the Oscar had changed nothing. My roles were all supporting ones, as with Jim Belushi in *The Principal*, where I played the security man and Jim the principal, and *Iron Eagle*, where again I was a father figure, this time to the young hotshot pilot searching for his father.

The lifestyle I had maintained—working hard, keeping in shape, caring for my son, while slowly becoming more reliant than ever on drugs—was taking its toll. Although I had won awards and had many successes, my inner life was not thriving. I had a son but not a successful marriage. I was up at two or three in the morning to get to the set, abusing myself on the weekends, and repeating the schedule every Monday morning. "Is that all there is?" I asked myself. Slowly but surely, I was duplicating the pattern of my father and my uncles and most probably the lifestyles of many other frustrated African American men. There were so many days and nights when I felt as if I was living a life similar to that of Dr. Jekyll and Mr. Hyde.

So often, when I came home after a twelve-hour day, Satie would ask to go to a movie. All that I wanted to do was take a shower and lie down, but then he'd say, rightfully, "You never take me anywhere." So I'd go to the movie and immediately fall asleep and still be exhausted the next day. I saw photographs of other actors, bike riding or walking on the beaches with their beautiful families, or just sitting at breakfast looking so happy and relaxed, and I tried to understand what I was doing wrong. I worked my butt off and didn't get the benefits of free time that other successful actors possessed. As I began to regret more and more that I had chosen this profession, I could feel how this disappointment took its toll in an expression of lower self-worth.

After my dear friend Ed Bondy died of an aneurism, I felt that I could trust no one else as I saw the evils of the business surround me. I was constantly being ripped off. I knew I wasn't being paid enough, and the resentment of giving people percentages of my pay simply for making phone calls grew stronger. "We know this is a struggle," one of my representatives said. "Take the low pay now. Next time we'll get them." Next time never came. Finally, there did come a time when I took a stand, saying no to a part unless the studio paid me properly. It took the studio all of five minutes to say, "Next," and hand the part to someone else. That scene broke it for me, sending me headlong into self-loathing. I felt older than my years, as my self-inflicted disease quickened its pace.

One of the few places that was a refuge for me during this painful time was my ringside seat at the Lakers games. Watching Magic Johnson, Kareem Abdul-Jabbar, Byron Scott, and Michael Cooper win back-to-back championships, I felt as if I was the invisible sixth player, that I was out there on that court playing with them. I sent them presents when they weren't doing well to keep up their spirits, such as a beautiful six-foot tree that Kareem and Magic ended up fighting over. I even sent mud from the Dead Sea to Michael Cooper when he injured his ankle while I was in Israel doing *Iron Eagle*. I loved every one of those players so much. Watching them play was my one and only healthy outlet.

Struggling to swallow the anger and sadness in my real life, I told myself repeatedly, "You will not become a bitter man. You will be a better man." Although it has been a struggle, I believe that now in the end I have become that better man. At the time, however, I made the most of the movies and TV work that came my way: *Iron Eagle*; *Enemy Mine*, one of my favorites; *Toy Soldiers*; and *Firewalker*. Still, I couldn't get the bad taste out of my mouth.

If it hadn't been for my cousin Yvonne, I am not sure how I would have made it through that dark period after the lawsuit and the Academy Awards. When she saw how I was floundering, she packed up her belongings and her son, Tiger, and moved from New York to California to take care of me. For the two years that she was there, she whipped me back into good shape. She answered phone calls, cooked for me and Satie, made sure I slept and ate well, and, most of all, for a while anyhow, protected me from the people who were trying to infiltrate my life, who used their wiles and beauty to get into my house and peddle their drugs. Before Yvonne arrived, I sometimes woke up to see men and women carting away some of my precious belongings, daring me to call the police. The women were especially conniving and were used to preying on the famous. "I'll come in and clean up the house for you," these gorgeous ladies would tell me, and I would stupidly say, "Sure," flattered by their attention. These predators indeed cleaned up, removing stereo equipment, cameras, diamonds, guitars, and computers from my home, certain I that would never risk going to the police and exposing myself to the curious public with these claims. They were parasites, no different from fleas on a horse.

Yet not every woman who came to my house was there to sell or use drugs. Desperately lonely and unwilling to go out in public under the relentless eyes of the paparazzi, I resorted to reading lonely hearts–types of columns and hiring young women to come for lap dances. For a two- or three-month period, in the privacy of my own guest house, I enjoyed the company of these women, most of whom were using the money they earned to pay their rent or college tuition or to buy food for their children.

More than anything, what I wanted from these women was their companionship. Their visits filled that lonely corner of my heart, and some of them are still my friends today, leading exemplary lives. I will always thank them for their friendship.

Alarmed at how everything around me was in shambles and how much damage had already been done, Yvonne stepped in and carefully scrutinized everyone who came into my house. My gift to Yvonne for coming to my rescue was a course in real estate, a present for which she repaid me with a terrific deal to sell my house at Dume Drive in Malibu, the home into which I had moved when I left Hancock Park. Yvonne found me another house in Malibu, and twenty-seven years later I am still living in it. This house, on a dead-end street, was better suited for me and Satie, with an indoor swimming pool for him and an exercise room and a nice guest house for me. Yvonne knew how I loved animals, and she set up goats and rabbits and even horses for Satie. She allowed me to rest and go on vacation without worrying about Satie, who was thrilled with Tiger's company.

Concerned over my increasing dependence on alcohol and cocaine, Yvonne made it okay for me to go to rehab in Arizona. Unfortunately, I was taken out of rehab too early, to work on *Iron Eagle*. At that time, it seemed that all of "my people" were relying on my money, while I was trying to seek my salvation. Eventually, the salvation won but not that time. It is never good when you leave rehab before your work there is finished. It simply means that you have not completed the work, and, eventually, you will have to return to do exactly that. By the time Yvonne left me, however, I felt healthy and strong, and we were both convinced I would continue to grow even healthier and stronger.

One of my first projects after *Officer*, the sci-fi feature film *Enemy Mine* with Dennis Quaid, brought me to Germany and

Iceland. As much as I loved this role, it did little to make me healthier or stronger. In addition, the scuttlebutt was out that I had been in rehab, and all eyes were on me. Despite the problems, this movie became one of my ultimate favorite films. Initially, I understood how no one else apparently wanted this role of the lizardlike Draconian Jeriba "Jerry" Shigan from a faraway planet, the first male to give birth in a feature film. Giving birth was a snap compared to the four hours of makeup that was necessary to transform my face into Jerry's, which required a complete body-and-face mask.

"Why take a role where no one can possibly know it is me?" most of the actors who were offered the part must have decided. Yet at that difficult point in my life, I viewed it as a form of resurrection, literally a complete makeover. The first day it took nearly eight hours for the makeup people to put the necessary prosthetics on my body while I lay prone on my back in a barber's chair. When the makeup crew finished, they were filled with pride over their creation as they airbrushed the final product.

The minute I stood up, however, I announced that after lying still for so many hours, I had to go to the bathroom. In addition, I was starved and needed something to eat. The makeup people stared at one another, and one of them finally said, "We have a big problem here." They certainly did. They had designed the outfit on a mannequin, never giving any thought to my bodily functions. Unfortunately, there was nothing they could do except destroy all of their beautiful work so that I could go to the bathroom and then eat some lunch.

It wasn't until many months later, when the new director Wolfgang Peterson's people came in, that the problem was completely fixed. (Wolfgang replaced the original director Richard Loncraine.) At Wolgang's suggestion, they cleverly designed the costume so that the prosthetics stopped at the waist, and inserted astronautlike pants that were in sync with the planet. They also reduced how long it took to apply my daily makeup, from seven hours to four. This time they carefully checked the complete outfit to make sure it worked before they put it on my body. They also contrived a way for me to remove my fake teeth simply by removing the mouthpiece so that I could eat.

For all of the hours that I was in costume, you could see the tubes that had been put into air pockets around the prosthetics in my face. Every time I got emotional, these tubes began to go in and out, and then I made the distinctive guttural sound that became Jerry's signature. I'd stolen that voice from the good old days when I was a child mimicking the way the Lone Ranger and Tonto communicated by imitating whip-poor-wills. To this day, the movie's legions of devoted fans all seem to remember those sounds. Even today, fans of all ages come up to me and duplicate that sound, and I find myself carrying on a Draconian conversation with them, sometimes even with a little Yiddish sprinkled in. For some reason, kids manage to do it easier than adults can. In fact, Satie was making that Lone Ranger–Tonto sound well before the movie, when he was maybe three or four.

No matter how I talked and looked in front of the camera, transforming me into a Drac was an enormous undertaking, and I welcomed the entire process. It was almost as if by turning my face into that of a Drac, covering it with piles of protective layers, I could change myself into a different person. The role itself was also a challenge I craved. With my face covered, this was a chance to prove my acting abilities, those that had won me an Academy Award. Instead of wearing a crisp marine uniform as a high-ranking officer of the most elite form of our armed forces, this time I wore a reptilian costume that represented an inhuman creature of reconciliation.

There were also some hilarious moments during the filming. The original director of the film, Richard Loncraine, who was filming the movie in Iceland, was eventually replaced by Wolfgang Peterson. After a two-month stretch, he moved the set to Munich. While we were in Iceland, however, I developed a rash on my face from all of the makeup. The producer put out a call that we needed a doctor to help clear the rash on the face of one of the actors in the movie, and a petite female country doctor arrived on the set, holding tubes of Vaseline and antibiotic cream. No one had told her any more than that, so when I walked out in my full lizard costume, the poor doctor nearly fainted. "Oh, my God!" she exclaimed. "I can't take care of that problem. You need to get that poor man to a hospital quick. I've been a skin doctor for thirty-five years, and I've never seen a man in that condition before."

I tried to explain to her that this was all makeup, and when I pulled off some of the facial mask, she looked at me even more wide-eyed and exclaimed, "Oh, my, there is a Negro in there!" I can just imagine what that woman must have told her friends when she got off the set.

The town of Heimi, where we were filming in Iceland, was actually surrounded by a snow-covered mountain and had been hollowed out of the volcano whose steam heated it. It was a popular port that merchant marines often visited, habitually enjoying a locally distilled alcoholic beverage that was strong enough to earn its name of Black Death. It was common to see these merchant marines walking through the town, drinking and falling down drunk in the middle of the streets. Local kids, figuring that was how you got to be a man, imitated their behavior and gulped down bottles of Black Death, which, no matter what your age, knocked you out.

I came up with something else, which never replaced Black Death but presented a much healthier alternative. Remembering what my father used to do with the codfish he caught in Sheepshead Bay, I removed the scales from the skin of the codfish, which were so easy to catch in Heimi, floured the scales, and fried them quickly in oil. After the scales curled up in the oil, I drained them and put them in a paper bag, and I ate them like potato chips. When the kids followed me, I handed them some of these crunchy chips, which they quickly devoured. They probably did not realize they were ingesting healthy cod liver oil, created from fresh fish that had been pulled out of their local waters. I was delighted to teach some of the parents exactly how to make the chips, by cooking the scales in a pan with some olive oil, salt and pepper, lemon juice, minced garlic, and onions for a minute or so, until the scales curled. When I left, I noticed that little stands had been set up around town, where enterprising kids were selling these chips. I can't say I got them weaned off Black Death, but I would bet that my father's recipe helped make their bodies stronger and healthier.

As I mentioned, when that production shut down and a new one began several months later, this time with Wolfgang as director, we headed to Munich for the filming. Things changed greatly for me when Wolfgang took over. Although I received decent money for this job, yet not as much as Dennis Quaid, I had felt that he was treated like the star of the movie. They shot his scenes first, and Richard Loncraine paid far more attention to his role. It could have all been in my mind, but I felt as if I had the harder job and he was getting all of the attention.

When Richard was fired, however, Wolfgang was determined to shoot it the way he wanted to, regardless of what Hollywood wanted. One of his first decisions was that there was too much Willis Davidge (Dennis's character) and not enough Jerry. Once Wolfgang settled the problem about my pants, he concentrated on my eyes, moving us from Iceland to Germany only after he spent several weeks in London trying to figure out what to do about my eyes. The contact lenses the makeup people had been using to make my eyes look reptilian caused me great pain. In London, Wolfgang brought me to see John deCarle, the inventor of the soft lens, who came up with a water-filled contact lens that covered the entire lens of my eye, over which he put the serpent's eye. Yet as creative as the new lenses were, the eye still needed to breathe, and it created nitrogen bubbles as it did.

Initially, I had not been prepared for the pain involved in the process of transforming my body into Jerry's. Nor was I ever warned about the possibility of developing temporary blindness, which I suffered from for ten agonizing days after these special contact lenses created nitrogen bubbles in my eyes. Despite all of Wolfgang's and deCarle's efforts and my trying out at least fifty pairs of the contact lenses, it still turned out to be a hit-or-miss affair. Blinking was agonizing, so my character became a creature that rarely blinked, which allowed me to keep my eyes open as much as possible. For the blizzard scene, Wolfgang used as little salt as possible, but when even that amount was injurious to my eyes, they switched to soap flakes, such as Ivory Snow Powder. When the Ivory Snow still caused pain, I knew I had no choice but to grin and bear it. One additional problem with my eyes was that when there was a lot of action, the serpent's eye would move, and they had to shoot the scene over again. There was nothing I could do about that.

One thing that was done to my eyes that I will never allow to be done again was applying prosthetics foam on the eyelid. It needed to be removed with acetone, which inevitably caused me additional pain as the granules and the vapors slipped into my sore eyes.

As a result of the lenses, my eyes became deeply sensitive to the sun bouncing off the snow in Iceland, which made them swell and bleed. When we filmed in Germany, a doctor gave me a certain jelly that helped to a small extent. Even when my sight came back after the ten-day period of blindness, bright lights hurt my eyes for a long time, and I could use only a candle to make my way around the room.

During the filming, my eyes felt as if they were full of sand. The sad thing was that the problem could have been avoided had I followed the doctor's suggestion to remove the lenses every twenty minutes to give my eyes some relief, but that was deemed financially prohibitive. Because of the change in directors and the move to Munich, there was legitimate concern about going over budget, so every minute and every penny had to count. When pain medication failed me, I finally found that the best way to handle it was to surrender to a Zen-like state. There were moments when I felt like ripping off the makeup, the reptilian costume, and the contact lenses and giving up the role. But I would not allow myself to do that and resigned myself to using both Zen and some drugs for the pain and spending many nights alone in my room with the curtains drawn to protect my swollen, hurting eyes.

Yet what bothered me even more than that pain were the rumors that I had lost my eyesight because of my use of cocaine, which everyone assumed had landed me in rehab. Toward the end of the filming, I did finally give in and use some drugs that an army sergeant brought me, but that was only after routine pain pills were of no use at all. When I took a few days off to rest my eyes, everyone erroneously decided that this was yet another example of my habitually not showing up. Even the insurance company became nervous that I would not fulfill my obligations. Working twice as hard as anyone else on the set to prove myself to the director, I was exhausted at the end of each day.

The redeeming factor of my time in Munich was that Satie and Willie Lea joined me there. For Satie, the highlight of the trip was our visits to the Munich restaurant Kafir's. He also became fast friends with Bumper Robinson, who played my son Zammis in the movie. The two ten-year-olds, who actually looked alike (after all, they were both my sons, sort of, and one I'd actually given birth to, sort of), were tutored together on the set, romped in the snow, and played with the dog I'd bought for Satie. They began a friendship that continued back in L.A. Willie Lea, who spoke not a word of German, argued over the price of pork chops at the market like a regular fräulein and kept us wonderfully fed with the high-quality meat that is so prevalent in that country.

When I returned to L.A., it was obvious that my cocaine problem kept me on the radar of insurance companies that took care of the movie companies. I suspected that I was now under surveillance by the Firemen's Fund, one of the new companies that insured movies and actors. The whole issue of insuring actors hadn't been a problem until more actors became dependent on drugs and alcohol and budgets grew bigger; with more money at stake, more diligence had to be taken. Many of us had the benefit of having a sympathetic doctor who understood and enabled us, a nice man who prescribed whatever we needed to make it to work. But the situation turned more serious when certain actors held up productions for days and weeks, which I never did. When productions were slowed down, the insurance companies were forced to pay for those down days. I am quite certain that the Firemen's Fund maintained zero tolerance for these problems, and, consequently, production companies hired very few actors who had a questionable drug or alcohol habit.

My guess is that early on, the production companies had doctors who would let actors go to work, knowing full well they were using drugs. But when insurance companies such as Chubb had to pay a great deal of money because of floods, fire, and tornados, things began to change. The insurance companies no longer wanted to risk insuring actors who might slow down productions and cost them money. Now companies such as the Firemen's Fund hired police to scout out actors they suspected were using. I have a feeling that happened to me and that there were gardeners and maids who worked for me and spied on my habits.

I find it ironic today that in my nearly sixty years in the business, I am responsible in my career for maybe three hours of not showing up because of my drug use, while others with much bigger problems than mine have shut productions down for days, weeks, or even months. Found asleep in dumpsters, drunk underneath tables, or simply home in bed, these actors have their misdemeanors plastered all over the media, but they have managed to be retrieved, propped up, and brought back into the studios' good graces. Yet there were a couple of years in the late nineties when I was deemed uninsurable and unreliable, when I could not get approved for a role and my parts went to excellent African American actors such as Samuel Jackson or Morgan Freeman. It sounds like a bad story, but God works in mysterious ways, and we needed to see the brilliant talent of those actors, anyway.

Despite the severe eye problems I suffered from in my role as Jerry Shigan, which included scar tissue in my eyes for more than five years, I have never, for one moment, regretted my part in *Enemy Mine*. In fact, the movie became a cult film, with its own special fraternity of those who know how to make Jerry's guttural sound. That year, however, and again two years later, my own private world was about to change drastically in ways that seemed positive and hopeful, offering me two new chances to live a more fulfilled and happier personal life.

Check out this outfit I brought back from Africa in 1972. I brought a bunch of these wonderfully comfortable robes home.

This is my exquisite infant son, Satie Russell Gossett, in 1974. His little chest rested on my shoulder while I sang and rocked him to sleep. A week or so later, Christina took him away from me for two years.

I thoroughly enjoyed training hard for the baseball pitching role in *Don't Look Back: The Story of Leroy "Satchel" Paige*, but the greatest joy was meeting Paige, who had been a star pitcher in the Negro League and later for the Cleveland Indians. He arrived on the set of this ABC-TV movie and sat down in his rocking chair. Sadly, he died of emphysema a year after the 1981 movie came out.

In the 1982 movie
*An Officer and a
Gentleman*, I played
hard-nosed gunnery
sergeant Emil Foley,
the role for which
I won an Academy
Award.

Here I am with my
Oscar in 1983. What
a night that was.

I will never forget the thrill of re-creating the life of Anwar el Sadat in the movie *Sadat* in 1983, from his days as a young officer fighting the British to his assassination in 1981, a role for which I was nominated both for an Emmy and a Golden Globe.

If I'm feeling unappreciated, all I need to do is look at these awards, stored mostly in one room in my home in Malibu Beach.

11

Losing Love

1985–1992

One morning in 1985, after a year of many unpaid public appearances but not much significant work, and lots of time devoted to making Satie happy, working with the housekeeper, and enjoying some time off with them, I was at home in Malibu watching *Good Morning, America*. I was very much in the mood to be of service and of a mind-set to try to unspoil my eleven-year-old son, who had become demanding as well as vocal about missing me terribly when I was gone. On the television screen, Pia Lindstrom, Ingrid Bergman's daughter, was reporting on a story about the homeless. She'd been going from city to city talking to the homeless, and that particular morning she was in St. Louis. She placed the microphone in front of a young boy, probably around seven or eight, and asked him, "If you had a wish, what would it be?" The little boy said, "Someplace to live and something to eat."

I could not take my eyes off the little guy or keep his words out of my ears. Immediately, I got in touch with my own special group of friends, who included Steve Allen, Casey Kasem and his wife, Jon Voight, and Valerie Harper and her husband. We always got together for causes that we felt were important or for some injustice we wanted to fix. The bottom line of our own push was that every child in America should have free health care, free education, free clothing, free shelter, and, most important, love. If every child started with that, then we believed his or her mind would be free to grow. We knew that every major city had at least a million of these homeless children between the ages of three and fifteen, and that the problem was increasing every day. We decided that I would fly to St. Louis to meet this little boy and try to make him a poster child to draw attention to the plight of the homeless and encourage lawmakers to do something about this heartbreaking problem. I would take photos with the young boy and get the ball rolling.

Because there were only two homeless shelters in St. Louis, it didn't take too long to find the boy, whose name was Sharron Anthony, and have him brought to the Chase Hotel, where I was staying. ABC, with help from David Hartman and Pia Lindstrom, helped make the arrangements, and cameras were set up for when I finally met Sharron. I intended to take the photos, write a check for Sharron's needy family, and get back to L.A., where I would make calls to lawmakers and do interviews about the homeless crisis, using Sharron as our example.

At the hotel, I was immediately blown away by the little boy's quiet, grown-up demeanor, by how neat and serious he was as he walked in, with a small paper bag firmly clenched in his hands, a bag that I later learned contained a sandwich. I recognized a loneliness in him that I still felt in myself. I spoke to him for a little while in front of the cameras and soon realized that he was smart enough to have learned that you could not go to the same shelter on two consecutive nights. He often went to the kitchens of fine restaurants with his sister, and the cooks gave him food. Sometimes he stayed up all night to protect this food from other homeless people, eating it on a fire escape so that the big guys wouldn't steal it from him.

I immediately thought of Satie, who had everything he needed but had been terribly lonely since my girlfriend's two children, followed by Yvonne's Tiger, had all left. How wonderful it would be to give Sharron the food and the home and the education every child was entitled to and also to give Satie a young boy who needed a big brother.

When I asked Sharron whether he knew who I was, he said, "No," and we chatted in front of the cameras for a while longer. When everyone had left the room, I turned to him and asked, "Do you want to live with me?" I hadn't meant to say it, but I had. He said solemnly, "Yeah." All I could think was, What have I done now?

Yet I had spoken the words, and I had no intention of taking them back. So I met his mom, who had many other children with different fathers, and asked her permission. Her eyes filled with tears, and she consented. The next day, I returned to California and asked Satie whether he'd like me to adopt Sharron, and he said, "Sure." I began the legal proceedings and returned to St. Louis a short time later to bring Sharron to L.A. When I saw him again, he was still neat as could be and had the same serious, stoic look on his grown-up little face, yet it wasn't hard to see through that look and understand that this young kid had seen a lot of stuff on the streets. We had just settled into our seats in the first-class section of our plane heading back to L.A. when we were served plates filled with shrimp salad. He took a mouthful and chewed seriously. "What kind of meat is this?" he asked me.

"It's not meat," I told him. "It's shrimp." He nodded and finished his plate. I have always found it ironic that this little guy, who once had to beg for food, eventually grew into a mini-Shaq, with a talent for cooking. But back then, he was just a young boy heading to an unknown place with a stranger.

Perhaps understandably, it was not a smooth transition into becoming a family for any of us. Neither Christina nor Willie Lea was pleased with my decision to add an eight-year-old boy to my family. Willie Lea didn't like a "dirty boy living with my Satie." I understood how much affection she had for Satie, how she protected him so diligently, even against me from time to time. She was as caring as his mother, God rest her soul. I couldn't have done anything without her.

It wasn't that easy for Satie and Sharron to become brothers either, nor for me to become a single father of two, but we did have lots of good times. Often, the door of one of their bedrooms would be closed, and I'd hear rumbling and giggles. I'd knock and stand at the door and ask, "Is everything all right in there?" and they'd say, "Yeah," and I'd know the two of them were having a ball wrestling on the floor.

About a year after Sharron came to live with us, the two of us marched with Jesse Jackson in the Washington March for the Homeless. You could barely see the little guy's head over the wide walking poster that about fifteen of us were holding up. I remember asking him whether he wanted to go to the march with me, and he'd said yes right away. But then again, he always agreed to anything he could do, just to hang out with me.

Even though I knew Satie was glad to have the company of a little brother, I also understood that it was hard for him to share his father. I wasn't around that much, and now he was getting only half of my limited attention. To make it more difficult, it was tough to be the child of a famous person, someone who is assumed to have a lot of money. I couldn't simply let him sleep over at any friend's house or take off for the day with another family. The fear of a celebrity's child being kidnapped, especially after Frank Sinatra Jr.'s kidnapping in 1963, was always in my mind. I knew that now there was desperation on the street, and I was too scared to let my sons go anywhere except with people I trusted. Having a photographer stick his camera in my children's faces, which happened often, didn't make it any easier for them. I had worked hard to keep the situation with Sharron out of the newspapers, anxious to avoid any publicity that might hurt him. The ever-present paparazzi made something as simple as taking the boys to a basketball game difficult, unless we sat in the owners' suites. Not that that was uncomfortable. Today I still hold onto that same fear of kidnappers and paparazzi, only now it is for my grandchildren, who carry my last name.

At that time, I was also dealing with guilt. I felt that it was not right to be raising my boys in a house so different from the loving one that I had grown up in, with parents, aunts, uncles, cousins, and neighbors around me all the time. Soon after Sharron arrived, however, he was wide-eyed with astonishment at our annual Thanksgiving dinner, as he viewed the piles of food Willie Lea had prepared. This was the one occasion when all of my family got together at our house. All of my cousins, about thirty of them, congregated at my house to enjoy one another's company and Willie Lea's incredible cooking. Some drove, but others flew in from New York, Washington, and Philadelphia, most of them staying in hotels so that we could be together for the entire holiday weekend. The one stipulation I had for that

Thanksgiving meal was that, unlike the Thanksgivings of my youth, which left all the adults drunk and staggering, not a drop of alcohol be served. I did not want anyone to leave my house drunk. Besides, alcohol just wasn't necessary. We had plenty of food and love to satisfy all of our hungers—never mind the pleasure of the leftovers.

The only thing our guest of honor, Sharron, said to me during that Thanksgiving meal was, "Where's the macaroni and cheese?" Although he was quiet that day, he was embraced by all of his new family members, especially the cousins, who all made a fuss over him. I was beaming with pride that day, convinced that I had done the right thing and that we were all headed in the right direction.

Yet there was no denying the fact that I now relied more often on some of my demons. Working harder than ever, feeling a huge sense of responsibility for my two sons, I saw things begin to untether. I found myself using more cocaine during my time off. I feared that the disease was seizing control of my life. The only place where I felt I had the freedom to tell the truth or express myself freely was in front of the camera, where I could lose myself inside the wonderfully stoic or high-spirited characters who did come my way. TV, which was more reliant on money from its sponsors, many of whom advertised when I was on the screen, was more than generous to me.

I was getting paid to play so many splendid people, yet in my personal life, there seemed to be no appreciation, only more guilt than I could handle for all of the things I was not doing right as a father. I had been told that this is one of the things that happens when you enter into the next level of alcoholism. To me, alcoholism is the name of the disease, not drug addiction or sex or power or cigarettes or gambling or food. I believe you can put them all under this one blanket. With each of these addictions, you have to repair yourself from the inside out. One trigger of all of these problems, whether it is deserved or not, is a feeling of guilt and low self-worth. Personally, I could not shake a sense of doom that there was no way out.

When I looked at the respect that excellent African American actors such as James Earl Jones, Charles Dutton, and Danny Glover were receiving, in roles more important than my supporting roles, I saw the effect of the blacklist that the scuttle-butt had put on my résumé. I tried to put as much effort as I could into whatever roles I did secure, and I gratefully accepted the nomination I garnered in 1987 for an Emmy for CBS's *A Gathering of Old Men*. In this movie, a story of deep-bred racial intolerance in the 1970s South, I played a sharecropper who is suspected of a killing a bigoted white Louisiana tenant farmer. Although I was disappointed that prestigious parts in major films did not follow my role in *Gathering*, this story of loyalty, friendship, community, and bravery in the face of racism was an extraordinary experience, one I would have performed in for nothing. It was such a treat to work with that fireball of an actress Holly Hunter in one of her first performances and another up-and-coming actor, Will Patton. During our off-time, the entire cast headed into my favorite American city, New Orleans, where I sang and played my guitar in Tipitinos, sometimes with the legendary Neville Brothers. Whenever I attend their concerts, even to this day, if they see me in the audience, they pull me onto the stage, hand me a tambourine, and call me Louis Neville. It's quite wonderful.

Back in Malibu, I was the single father of two, adoring both of these little boys, yet too rarely playing with them. Despite so many of the pleasures of my childhood, I had learned about responsibility at an early age, and now I needed to work even harder to provide for my sons. In hindsight, I wonder what would have happened if I had earned the salaries of the actors with whom I shared the stage and, like them, brought home millions of dollars for each project. I might have misused the money and harmed myself even more than I did. But I sure would have liked to see how I would have handled such an opportunity. Some of the young black actors today are amazed when I admit that I never got a million dollars for any of my movies. They look at me, speechless, certain that I must have squandered huge amounts of money on drugs and alcohol. The truth is that not much money ever came my way, and, sadly, at a later time whatever I did accumulate was stolen.

Everything in my life took on a different sheen in 1986 when one of the most beautiful woman I had ever known entered my life and gave me a perfect reason to work on improving certain aspects of myself. Sharron had been with us almost a year when I met Cyndi James Reece, who had just won *Star Search*, the precursor of *American Idol*. It wasn't long before the two of us were a couple and our life together full of promise and hope. She liked both of my boys but quickly became closer to Sharron, who was still smarting from the loss of his own mother in his daily life. I am positive that if I had been in a better place then, we would still be married today. I cannot imagine ever loving any other woman as much as I loved Cyndi.

We had been together for only a short time when Cyndi encouraged me to go to rehab. She would take care of my boys and my household, and I would return ready to live the beautiful life we believed we were destined to have together. When I did come home thirty days later, I was saddened to see that Cyndi had fired Willie Lea, who had been such a great comfort and support system for ten years, but I was pleased that Cyndi appeared closer than ever to Sharron. Feeling vulnerable and shaky, still in the midst of expensive ongoing therapy sessions for the four of us, I had been warned by my therapist not to make any major decisions in my life for a full year and to use that time to get back onto my still unsteady feet. But I did not listen. All that I knew was that I adored this woman and couldn't imagine life without her.

So, a few months after rehab, I proposed, with a gorgeous oversize emerald ring that I'd bought somewhere while on location. I gave it to Cyndi the minute I returned, and it blew her away. She loved it and never took it off. I just couldn't help myself. I don't know whether it was because I felt so vulnerable at the time or because my emotions were so raw; all that I knew for sure was that I hadn't realized I could ever love anyone as much as I loved that woman. I couldn't believe how lucky I was to have her in my life and in my boys' lives. I couldn't bear the thought of losing her.

I was certain that we were going to have the marriage of all marriages. And to make that happen, we had to have the perfect wedding: in the Holy Land on the holiest day of the year. Because I would be filming in Israel shortly, it would be easy to work out the details.

I knew that beautiful country well. Years earlier, during the filming of *Iron Eagle*, director Sidney Feuri had managed to shoot in a secret Israeli air force base, using the Russian Mig and the French Mirage, as well as the American F14, all part of the Israeli Air Force, the best air force in the world. The flying was spectacular and provided Sidney with exceptional footage, of planes barely missing one another in the air. I never went up with the Israeli camera pilot who followed the air action, but I heard that it was pretty hairy filming. I was told that the Israelis were using these same jets to bomb the enemy. Watching them do their maneuvers and fly like darts, I knew that if I were the enemy, I wouldn't want to have to fight with these guys.

For the six weeks that I'd been in Israel during that filming, I'd noticed how the handsome and beautiful sabra men and women, some of the most magnificent young people I had ever seen, would spend all night in the nightclubs, partying hard. Yet the next morning, men and women alike were in their uniforms, their guns in place, ready to defend their country. They earned my immediate and unbounded respect, and I made lifetime friends there. I was aware that there is something about the young people in any country where war is imminent that makes them want to party and stay up late and enjoy life. I'd noticed this heaven-be-damned outlook that young people adopted in other war-torn countries—not only in Israel, but in Africa and Egypt as well. It was sort of a "Let's dance tonight, because who knows if we'll be alive tomorrow?" attitude. The last thing these beautiful young people would do was hide in their houses and wait for the bombs to fall. After all, in prewar Paris, the most intense partying happened just before the Nazis arrived.

Not that my first trip to Israel had started off with much partying. When I'd arrived six years before *Iron Eagle* to film *It Rained All Night the Day I Left* with Tony Curtis, right after the Six-Day War, I'd never seen so much security. It had taken an hour and a half before they would finally let this big black man off the plane. But now, after I'd filmed *Sadat*, it seemed as if everybody in the Middle East, in Egypt and in Israel, knew me. This time, when I came to film *Iron Eagle*, a security officer approached my seat minutes after the plane landed, looking as if he were about to arrest me. Instead, he personally escorted me off the plane and made sure my luggage and I were out of the airport in record time. It was clear that I was now a friend of Israel.

While we filmed *Iron Eagle*, two years before my wedding, I had a chance to scuba dive in the Red Sea, with its glorious white sands and crystal-clear blue waters. I explored the columns and the monuments of an entire civilization thirty feet below the sea's surface. On Easter Sunday, I wanted to do some more scuba diving, so I went to the perfect spot in Eilat in the Gulf of Aqaba, where the Israel consulate walks or drives you the twenty-yard distance that separates Egypt and Israel. From there, the Egyptian counterpart drives you for about forty-five minutes, past Sharm-el-Sheik to the edge of the desert in the Sinai Peninsula. When I arrived at my appointed spot, I saw the area on my left where I planned to scuba dive. To the right, however, was a gate protected by soldiers stationed behind sandbags and machine guns. The sign read "UN Multinational Force and Observers Unit in the Sinai"—I realized that these soldiers were assigned to keep peace between Egypt and Israel. I had had no idea these forces were that close to where I had intended to dive. Because it was Easter, I decided to postpone my plans. I walked over to the gate, put my hands up in the air, and announced to the startled African American guard, "My name is Louis Gossett Jr., and I did *An Officer and a Gentleman* in the U.S. I'm here for another movie, and I'd like to have the chance to spend Easter with you guys." After all, I didn't want them to think I was a terrorist.

The officer studied me closely and said, "Damned if you ain't." Then he got on the phone and called the commanding officer, who welcomed me to the base. I spent Easter afternoon with the soldiers from the 101st and 86th Airborne Divisions of the U.S. Army out of Fort Campbell, Kentucky. I was invited to a holiday dinner with the men and some of their wives, who were also there. I enjoyed a terrific barbecue, consisting mostly of rabbit, with a little bit of chicken, and some corn on the cob. The men all seemed so blown away that I was there, but I was much more thrilled by the chance to enjoy their company.

After the barbecue, I finally found my diving instructor and went for a dive, but the highlight of the day was what I had found above the sea, with all of those fine men and women. I was heartbroken on December 12 to read about the plane that crashed, filled with men and women from that battalion who were heading home for Christmas from their peacekeeping mission. This tragic accident killed 248 Fort Campbell soldiers from the 3rd Battalion, 502nd Infantry Regiment. The DC-8 plane carrying the 502nd and eleven other units had stalled moments after takeoff from Gander, Newfoundland, where it had stopped to refuel, and plowed into a wooded slope about one-half mile from the runway. All on board, including eight crew members, had perished. I couldn't stop thinking of the smiling faces of the men with whom I had celebrated Easter just eight months earlier.

In Israel that Christmas, I had an experience that solidified my conviction that this land was magic for my soul. We had Christmas Eve and Christmas Day off from filming *Iron Eagle*, so I decided to head to Bethlehem and Jerusalem and Nazareth. After I put a note in the Wailing Wall, praying for peace, I walked around and saw a bunch of hawkers selling crucifixes and commercializing Christmas. This didn't feel much like Christmas to me, so I got back in my car and drove the other way, to the desert. I found a little motel outside of Jaffa, south of Tel Aviv, where I could spend the night, and after I registered, I took a walk. It was past midnight by then, and as I looked off into the distance over the sand dunes, I saw three Bedouins, the crescent moon illuminating their long robes flowing over the sides of their camels, as they headed toward a water hole. This was a scene from Christmas cards, complete with the solitary palm tree, that I'd received hundreds of times. Were they filming a commercial or something here? Dumbfounded, I looked around but saw no cameras. I stared at the three Bedouins, muttering, "Gimme a break," until they were long gone from my view.

These three "wise men" had no idea what I was thinking as they rode off, but I understood that this had been some sort of a message to me, making me feel more than ever that I had to play some part in making our world a better place. My body was covered with goose pimples, as I thought about all that I'd seen in Mexico, Africa, and Egypt; in Israel at the Dead Sea; in Masada and the city of salt, Sodom; and now in the desert. All of the stories I'd learned in Sunday school came alive, and in that one moment I saw so clearly how little sense war made and how necessary it was that we all live together peacefully. I needed to hold onto the word *peace*, not only for that memorable night, but forever.

During the filming of the movie, I found myself reliving memories of all of the Jewish people I had grown up with and especially of Gus Blum, who had picked a tall black kid out of a crowd at a Brooklyn high school and changed his life. Here in Israel, I was enjoying a perfect, drug-free lifestyle, experiencing that same feeling of having come home that I'd felt in Africa.

I loved playing the part of Chappy Sinclair in *Iron Eagle*, but I could hardly wait to play the role I was signing on for on December 25, 1987. Surrounded by Cyndi's mom and grandmother, my aunt Helen, Satie, and Sharron, Cyndi and I were married that day on a gorgeous spot in Herzilia, on the central coast of Israel, with a reception in a hotel that spared no cost. Yet nothing was more exquisite than my bride, which convinced me that Divine Intervention was at hand, assuring me that my marriage, like the Holy Land, would last forever.

For Cyndi's mom and grandmother and my aunt Helen, the day was equally memorable. Unbeknownst to the three women as they toured the Holy Land, a plainclothes military escort was shielding them from any possible rock-throwing skirmishes. It was the experience of a lifetime for these wonderful women.

Our honeymoon on the Greek island of Hydra was marred only by the billions of flies that the hot air had carried in from Africa, forcing us to sleep under tents of mosquito netting.

Shortly afterward, I had to take off for Australia to do *The Punisher* with Dolph Lundgren, about the comic book hero. Once I got settled, lonely for my new family, I sent for them to join me there. I found a special tutor to work with Sharron, who was still having an understandable adjustment problem. From the streets of St. Louis to the beaches of Australia was a lot for a ten-year-old kid to handle. Satie, on the other hand, needed nothing more than me and some mud crab from Imperial Peking Chinese restaurant in Sydney to be happy there.

Because Cyndi was doing episodic TV and singing on several different shows, she was unable to join us for more than five days. She was a great singer, and I understood that she wanted to work; however, I was still resentful that she would come that far and stay only five days. When Satie and Sharron also left, I felt utterly lost. I had just married the woman I adored, but I couldn't have been lonelier. Australia was filled with beautiful women, but I was going to dinner by myself every night. I kept telling myself that it was only fair that Cyndi, who had taken time off from singing to help with my boys, was now pursuing her career, but that didn't help the painful loneliness.

The night I returned home from Australia, I called the house the minute my plane landed in L.A. Disappointed that no one answered my call, I got into a limo and headed home, certain that someone would be awaiting my return. Yet when I arrived at the house, all of the lights were off, and no one answered the door. My heart beat like crazy, as memories of Christina taking off with our infant son or something even worse filled my mind. I dug my keys out of my luggage, opened the door, and stood there, paralyzed. A few seconds later, I found all three of them wrapped up together on the couch, completely engrossed in a movie and not the least bit interested in my return home. With barely a word from any of them, I unpacked and went to bed. Alone.

Unfortunately, problems in our marriage began to appear soon after I returned from Australia. I was working a great deal but never made enough money to take some serious time off. Cyndi complained to me and to the boys that I was never around for them or for her. She was right. Because I was working so hard to make money and be a good father and husband, while still feeling unsteady, the chinks in my armor began to show. It was not easy to remain sober, doing it "cold turkey" and without the support of an organized recovery program, but I was determined to do whatever I had to do to stay that way. Often tired, I was also brutally raw from our painful therapy sessions. The cost of our twice-a-week sessions for each of the four of us at $175 an hour was exorbitant, totaling more $40,000.

There was no doubt that I loved my wife and wanted this marriage to work, but from its beginning, once the blissful aura of the storybook wedding dissipated, the timing seemed wrong. Recovery, I knew, was a lifetime process, and I wasn't giving it the time and effort it required. Still, when it came time to finalize Sharron's adoption, because we were already a family, I figured that it was only natural to add Cyndi's name to the papers.

Work, as always, continued to be my escape from pain in my personal life. I spent a few months alone in Budapest in 1990, filming the HBO movie *The Josephine Baker Story*, about the fascinating African American woman who became a major performer in the Paris cabarets in the 1920s and 1930s. It was especially moving to me when I recalled being hugged by that vibrant performer herself in my dressing room on Broadway during *Take a Giant Step*. The scene in *The Josephine Baker Story* when she manages to have the black and the white soldiers shake hands, as part of the attempt to integrate the armed forces in Europe, is one of the most poignant scenes that I have ever appeared in.

I couldn't have been more shocked when I won a Golden Globe for what I considered a cameo role as Sidney Williams in that HBO movie. Sidney was the liaison for the army who made the arrangements for Josephine to sing for the armed forces in that powerful scene when she manages to integrate the troops. I sat beside Cyndi at the award ceremony, thinking how beautiful she looked that night and what a glorious couple we appeared to be. I have often thought of how different it is from reality when you look inside a marriage and see a house where the furnace is turned off and there is no warmth. To me, our marriage had quickly become that house.

When Rich Little asked me to open for him in Vegas, just me and my guitar and a bass player on the stage, as he'd seen me do in New York years earlier, I couldn't have been more excited. That was the opportunity I'd wanted for years, to be a Vegas headliner, to have the chance to be "in one," to have creative time, me and my guitar, in front of an audience. But the more I thought about it, the more I realized it was also the perfect opportunity for my wife to display the remarkable talent that had made her the winner of *Star Search*. Unfortunately, although Cyndi's performance was excellent that night in Vegas, the chemistry between her and Rich Little didn't work. I'd wanted Cyndi to have that chance, but I have to admit that it was a sacrifice for me to let her do it. To this day, I regret that I did not have that shot, that shot for the Golden Ring, which could have been the start of a different kind of professional life for me, one I would love to be practicing today. I had seen the reactions whenever I sang in coffeehouses, how my music, much of which I had written, worked like a charm on the audiences. Being an entertainer, as opposed to an actor, would have also given me an independence, removed me from my unhappy position of always being under someone else's thumb, that I would sorely have loved. Hindsight is 20–20, so I find it best to try not to think about it very much.

A trip to St. Lucia as part of a special Travel Channel program did provide the two of us with a much-needed vacation. Thanks to the work of Hilly Elkins, both Cyndi and I were hired for the show. We stayed at the Windjammer, snuggled on the side of a mountain, where we did a lot of walking and fishing and remembered why we had loved each other in the first place. If things had worked out better for Cyndi and me, we could have done a second program, this one at Easter Island, but that was not to be.

Back home, sadly, the same problems arose. I was working too much. She was working too little. And money was always tight. When the role of Honey Roy Palmer in *Diggstown* came my way, it seemed like the perfect vehicle to get myself back in shape and to fix the problems in my marriage—especially when the director, Michael Ritchie, asked me which actress I would like to have play my wife. "What about my wife?" I asked, and he readily agreed.

Just the idea of having a wife in a film was a positive step for me. For so many years of my career, I'd been acutely aware of the fact that in 90 percent of my films, I had had no woman. In *Iron Eagle*, *Enemy Mine*, and *Officer*, there was no female in the script for me, making me wonder, Where is *my* woman?

I well remember the time a famous white actress came over to hug me at an Academy Awards reception several years after I'd won my Oscar, saying, "I've been dying to meet you." Before she had the chance to touch me, she'd been whisked away. Not that this was anything new for me. As Ed Bondy had told me so many times, and as I well understood, "They don't like it." Ironically, Ed, who once had a family and children, had become openly gay at a time when there was zero tolerance for gays. Yet he worried about my going against the norm. Things have changed dramatically today, and I can't help wishing I were twenty years younger and could be a part of that wonderful change. Still, it is a plus for mankind and something to be proud of.

During my professional career, I also felt an unspoken clique-like attitude among the white guys on the set, a white camaraderie, a good-old-boy syndrome that did not include, no matter how liberal some of them might be, a black man. Whether or not it was real, I felt its presence. Often, when we discussed certain subjects, such as sports or politics, I had the distinct feeling that I had to watch every word I said.

For instance, I would hear "Look, Lou, we have a series with two more black people in it" or "Look at the number of black prop men on that set" or "Relax, Lou. See how many black actors are nominated this year." I would shake my head and smile, agreeing that progress was happening, but what I wanted to say was, "There is still an awful lot of work to do. Let's go deeper." Or "Look at how many successful films were made where not even the people on the streets in New York City or Detroit or Houston were black. Most people wouldn't notice it, but I sure did." If I said that, then the whole atmosphere would change. I'd feel the iciness rising, as if they were all saying, "Can't he just let it alone for once?" Or, during a discussion of O.J. Simpson, I wouldn't dare consider uttering the sentence "You know, there might be a chance that O.J. was really innocent and someone else killed Nicole and Ron." That would be the deal breaker. The door would be shut in my face.

Perhaps this was all psychological, purely in my own head, but whatever it was, all too often I felt that those in charge were telling me, "You should be grateful for the shot we just gave you." I was grateful, but, damn, I was also an equal, and I resented being ostracized from the white group for any remark or suggestion I might offer. Eventually, I got tired of playing the game of saying what others wanted to hear, rather than what I felt, and of always being the perfect gentleman. Rather than hang around the set and try to join the group and watch the other actors work, I got out of their way. I'd grab a headset and retreat into a corner and listen to music or go into my dressing room and wait to be called.

But back to *Diggstown* and my struggle to keep the beautiful black woman I'd married five years earlier in my real life. My role as Honey Roy Palmer, a middle-aged former boxer staging a comeback, required enormous physical exertion. I headed back into the gym for the first time in years and trained there for six hours a day, six days a week. I lost close to forty pounds, consuming little food but lots of vitamins. Because I needed to spend each day in three different gyms in L.A., making it back to Malibu every night was next to impossible.

But the training I received was phenomenal. My martial arts teacher, Benny the Jet, was the world champion kick boxer and martial arts choreographer who played the referee in the movie. Luis deFreitas, a former Mr. Olympia from Brazil and a colleague of Arnold Schwarzenegger, was the osteopath who performed the agonizing "rolfing" technique whenever I got a pulled muscle, physically stretching it back into shape with his hand, going right to the source to rub it, and building up my muscles and endurance. My yoga classes were necessary to keep both my body and my mind as strong as they needed to be for this role.

The master choreographer Jimmy Nickerson choreographed the ten fight scenes, which involved fighting ten different men. The bet in the movie had been that I could beat ten men in twenty-four hours. None of this was easy or painless, but I was determined to convince everyone that a fifty-five-year-old man could handle this role successfully.

Despite the hard work, I had to admit that I felt a sense of relief to be away from that house, where I never would have been able to concentrate on the movie, learn my lines, and keep up the physical routine. I understood how difficult it was for two people in the business to be married. During that movie, even though Cyndi had a small role in it, I was married to my art. We were on the set together for her scenes, but her role was nowhere as consuming as mine and she was not needed for any long periods of time. On my one day off every week, instead of heading home, I stayed in bed, regrouping my aching body for the coming week. I had hoped that Cyndi would understand that I was in harness as an actor, that I had slipped into another world for this all-encompassing role, just the way I had done for *Officer* and *Enemy Mine*, and that I had no choice but to be selfish with my time and spirit until the movie was finished. This, after all, was exactly what she would do when it was her turn to go to work. Sadly, at that time in our marriage, neither of us could understand what the other one was feeling.

This regimen continued for twelve weeks, until Cyndi called one night and said, "You're not coming home, are you?" and I said, reluctantly, "No." I filed for divorce as soon as the filming ended. Sadly, it turned out to be a nasty divorce, and she paid me back by taking our son with her. To Sharron, as well as to her, I was the villain. The two of them stayed in the house, and I went into an apartment until the trial was over and the judge said I could get my house back. I settled by writing a check for a down payment for a house of her own, along with child support.

I had to face the fact that Sharron and Cyndi were gone and that Satie was furious with me for losing the two of them. I also knew that at eighteen and about to graduate from Santa Monica High School, Satie needed a semester at a top prep school before he could gain acceptance into a major university like Syracuse. The fact that he was an excellent basketball player, as well as extremely bright, helped secure his admission to the elite Phillips Academy, far away in Andover, Massachusetts.

Once again, I was completely alone. And I understood that the demons I had worked hard to keep at bay were circling. Alone in my big house in Malibu, I knew that the toughest struggle of my life was lying in wait for me.

12

Dodging the Bullet

1992–1993

One of the first films I worked on after the divorce was *A Good Man in Africa*, for which I traveled to South Africa, the perfect place to try to put my life back together. In addition, work provided the best medicine for my personal problems. The political timing of the trip made it all the more exciting. I would be one of the first African American actors to be working in free South Africa. Because of apartheid, I had refused roles in films that were to be made there, but now I was ready to see the mood of the country.

I'd been impressed with the content of the book by William Boyd on which the film would be based; however, I didn't feel that the film was as faithful to the mood of the book as I'd hoped. The movie itself, which starred Sean Connery, Diana Rigg, and John Lithgow, as well as Joanne Whalley (Val Kilmer's beautiful wife), who played my wife, was one of the first to be produced in postapartheid South Africa. As a result, it was expected that there would be problems as an entire country acclimated to a new way of life.

The difficulties in integrating people in the schools seemed initially insurmountable, as did, initially, the integration of sports teams. When the 1995 Rugby World Cup championship was played in Johannesburg, however, Nelson Mandela made a significant step toward easing the problems of the transition when he appeared on the field wearing the South African Springboks' green number seven shirt. When the Springboks won, the entire country celebrated, hugging and dancing together in the streets. Sports, followed by the military, has always been ahead of the world, in regard to integration. In South Africa, at that time, innumerable rallies were also taking place, as hard-dying rivalries continued during the awkward transition.

Considering the adjustments that South Africans were making to this difficult postapartheid world, the production work on the movie revealed a minimum of conflict. Yet even though *A Good Man in Africa* was supposed to be a comedy, in which I played Professor Sam Adekunle, the next president of the fictional African country of Ninjana, I felt that the movie itself endorsed an outdated and colonial attitude about Africa. The most important aspect of the experience, however, was that although there were some problems, the crew of white South Africans and the black South Africans worked pretty well together.

When I returned a few years later to film *Inside*, with Arthur Penn of *Bonnie & Clyde* fame, I sensed that things were better in the country and in the working relations between the cast and the crew. I'd met Penn during *Golden Boy* and consider him one of the best directors I've been honored to work with. *Inside* paralleled the formation of the Truth Commission, conceived by Nelson Mandela, which was much like the Nuremburg Trials, so that South Africans could punish the guilty, bury the hatchet, and get on with it.

For my first postapartheid movie, I understood that there were people emerging in this new society who saw anyone sympathetic to the growth of South Africa as part of the threat to the status quo. Since the South African people and the whole country appeared to revere me because of my movie roles, the "obstructionists," or those who opposed the new postapartheid government, viewed me as an excellent vehicle to besmirch, in some way, these new leaders. As a matter of fact, I was convinced that I was being watched carefully by those who were looking for an opportunity to discredit my reputation in South Africa. Because this group was well aware of my drug problem, the perfect method to tarnish my name would be to lure me into their drug society. I had heard that they had tried to do the same with some other well-known Americans.

My dear friend Dali Tambo, the son of Adelaide and Oliver Tambo, the godfather of the African National Congress (ANC), who ran the congress while Mandela was imprisoned, kept a close eye on me during that first visit to South Africa. I'd met Dali years earlier when I'd been filming in Atlanta, and he'd interviewed me for his South African talk show. Now that all of the fine restaurants and discos in the country that had been closed to blacks during apartheid were open, Dali was delighted to show them off to me. As soon as we arrived at the designated place, the phones would ring with the message, "He's here," and the crowd would thicken. Naturally, we loved dining at these excellent restaurants and enjoying good music at the classy places in Johannesburg, many of which had become hot spots for both young blacks and whites. Still, I was made aware that antiapartheid people mingled in the crowds, many with cameras, hoping to get pictures of well-known blacks who appeared out of control.

In one instance, the press took a picture of me with someone they assumed was a party girl, whereas, in reality, she was the daughter of a South African minister. Another time, the friends I called had somehow managed to pull me into a party filled with revelers smoking crack. I knew the minute I walked in that I shouldn't be there, but it took a great deal of maneuvering for my friends to get me out of the room and into the dark Johannesburg streets, where I had a hard time finding a taxi to bring me back to my hotel. Photographs and gossip concerning that party were widely circulated. Despite the rumors spread by these obstructionists that I was exhibiting poor behavior, I would never voluntarily have done anything to harm the courageous work done by the ANC or Nelson Mandela. Yet I now humbly apologize for the fact that these rumors did exist at such a sensitive time in South African history, and I will spend the rest of my life making amends for them.

To this day, the moment I arrive at an airport in South Africa, I am met by a bodyguard, assigned not only to keep me away from danger but to make sure I am not made to look as if I am somehow causing trouble. There are certain streets and places in the country from which I would not return alive. Right now, the country is free and safe only in the history books. I understand all too well how recently the bonds of apartheid have been cut and that it will take a full generation or two for the new county to emerge successfully. I will always be grateful for these bodyguards, many of whom have become close personal friends.

Despite this protection in South Africa, I was just plain lucky to have escaped yet another attempt on my life there, one for which I had only my own impulsive nature to blame. When I returned in April 1993 to film *A Good Man in Africa*, I headed over to pay my respects to the family of Chris Hani, the charismatic black leader who had been tragically assassinated by a white supremacist at his Boksburg home a few days earlier. He had been in charge of the military part of the ANC and was the heir apparent to Mandela. I'd been raised with the Southern tradition of bringing flowers to pay my respects after a death, and that was the only thing in my mind that day as I had my driver and assistant Otis Harper deliver me to the Hani home in suburban Johannesburg. Devastated by Chris's assassination and temporarily oblivious to the ensuing South African political atmosphere, the two of us had driven straight into an impending bloody confrontation.

Almost at our destination, Otis and I were suddenly trapped in the car in the middle of a burgeoning demonstration between the oversize blue-eyed blond South African white police, with their tanks and guns and cannons, and the young, volatile, enraged black ANC members with their machetes and rocks. There was nowhere for our car to move, except perhaps to be overturned as angry mobs of blacks with machetes got ready to take on the white police and their armaments.

I took one look at Otis, a muscular former all-American football player, his previously tight Jheri curls now running wetly down his petrified face, and knew we were in serious trouble. I'm sure his fingerprints are still on the automobile's steering wheel. Finally, I decided that if I was going to die, I would not die in that car. So I picked up the enormous bouquet of multicolored flowers, opened the car door, and, with

Otis attached to my side, began to walk as steadily as possible toward the house. All around me, I saw a tableau of throngs of men, the smell of their violence seeping into my nostrils. Then something miraculous happened, and, almost like the Red Sea, the crowd parted. As Otis and I walked through a clear path to the house, both sides stared at us in amazement, as surprised as we were by what was happening.

We reached the Hani home, and I knocked on the door of the simple tract house. The door opened immediately, and Dali Tambo grabbed us. "You fools," he said, as he pulled the two of us in. "What are you doing here? You could have died out there. What are we going to do with you? You're stuck here now." I couldn't offer any explanation, just gave him a hug, which he warmly returned. When I entered the bedroom of the house, where mattresses covered the floor, Chris's widow, Limpho, wrapped in a bed sheet on a mattress, was surrounded by women. "These are for you," I told her, as I placed the flowers on the floor beside her.

"Thank you," she responded in a barely audible voice. I did not see her infant daughter, but I was certain she was being well cared for by these women. When I left the bedroom, I went back to the living room, which was filled with men drinking coffee, one of whom offered me a Coke. The aroma of the foods being prepared in the kitchen carried me back to my grandmother's house. Just as we had mourned her so many years earlier, this crowd was sitting around, laughing and discussing the past, while the women, who would later join them to eat the best food, were in the bedroom, painfully mourning. I didn't know it at the time, but that incident endeared me even more to the entire Tambo family. Oliver Tambo, who ironically died of complications of a stroke exactly two weeks after Chris's death, sat with me for a long time that afternoon. Yet that afternoon was not the last time I saw this extraordinary man. Just days before Oliver died, I stood beside him at a rally that consisted of around six thousand people. At the time, he continually put his hand in mine, an African sign of familial love.

That April day, however, I remained in the Hani home until just before the sun went down. The men had contemplated how to get me and Otis home safely, but with the crowds appearing to be close to rioting, this seemed an impossible task until Adelaide "Mama" Tambo, the godmother of the ANC, emerged from the house and spoke to the two sides of the crowd in Afrikaans and various tribal languages for almost forty-five minutes. When she came back inside, she told me simply, "I think you can go now."

Nearly four years later, on January 31, 1997, Adelaide Tambo called to talk to me from her Johannesburg home. I had not heard from her in all of those years. "You are my American son," she said, as I listened from my home in Malibu. "I am going away now, and I want you to look after my African son." When she finished that sentence, I knew what she meant. Twenty minutes later, she collapsed and died from natural causes. I thought about all that she and Oliver had done for me, how the two of them had made sure that my name was on the list for all of the inside receptions for the ANC, for Mandela, and for every important affair to which I had been invited. They had taken such good care of me. I will never forget either one of them. Yet on that April night when the crowds nearly enveloped me in their anger, it was Adelaide who had been my hero.

As Otis and I walked out the door, the tableau had changed a bit from when I had entered the house of mourning several hours earlier. On my left were the young black kids, who had obeyed Adelaide and were now sitting respectfully in lotus positions on the ground, their machetes by their sides.

On my right, the largest white men I had ever seen, looking like recruits to the NFL, leaned against their armored cars and cannons, their huge bodies draped in riot outfits, guns held facing downward in their huge hands. All I could think of then was the scene from Hitchcock's *The Birds*, when Rod Taylor and Tippi Hedren move ever so slowly from one place to another as the birds, perched above their heads and around their feet, scrutinize the couple with their beady little eyes, throngs of them ready at a moment's notice to attack their two victims with their sharp beaks. Only here, these were not birds staring at us, and no one was making a movie.

Otis and I got into the car in the near silence and took off, followed so closely by a car for half of our drive that it nearly crashed into us. An Afrikaaner police helicopter escort also flew low above our roof. Halfway to Johannesburg, the drivers must have received a commanding order to stop, because both the car and the helicopter suddenly turned around and abandoned us. By the time we got to my hotel, the riot had started, and five black kids had already died. I did not sleep that night, certain that at any minute there would be a knock on my door and I would be taken away, which would create an international incident that I would not survive. I learned later that at the same moment that I had been facing the crowd, Nelson Mandela was in a room with F. W. de Klerk, strategizing details on how to dismantle apartheid and getting ready for the election one year later. The next time I returned to the country, Mandela was its first black president.

Meanwhile, one year earlier, the streets were filled with bloody demonstrations as windows in downtown Johannesburg were smashed and cars overturned or hijacked, forcing Mandela to speak out. "Now is the time for all South Africans to stand together against those who, from any quarter, wish to destroy what Chris Hani gave his life for—the freedom of all of us." During that time, we continued our filming of *A Good Man in Africa*. I felt, more than ever before, as if the South Africans were claiming me, and I was more than willing to be claimed.

I remained mystified by exactly what had happened to me that afternoon when the crowd parted twice, to allow me to enter the Hani home as well as to leave it, until several years later when I returned to South Africa to be a judge for the Luries, awards for outstanding commercials. The plane had just landed when a 6'5" muscular white African linebacker-type approached my seat and told me to come with him. Oh, shit, I thought. I'm in big trouble. I'm being arrested. I should never have come back here.

I couldn't have been more wrong. The man was my personal bodyguard, and he had quite a story to tell me about my visit to Chris Hani's home. "I had you in the crosshairs of my rifle," he told me. "The reason you did not die that afternoon, sir, was because one of the chiefs yelled out, 'Hey, he's the guy from *An Officer and a Gentleman*. Leave him alone.' That movie is still popular here, and that's why no one would touch you. Now they all consider you a friend and will protect you just the way they do for the finest musicians and actors in the world. If I had not gotten that order, I would have shot you." Once again, I put another notch on my belt for all of the bullets I had, for some mysterious reason, miraculously eluded.

The diversity of my life in South Africa during the filming of these movies can best be illustrated by the other place where I spent some of my off time: the luxury South African casino and golf resort Sun City. Developed by hotel magnate Sol Kerzner in Bophuthatswana in 1979, this beautiful recreational oasis was a mere two-hour drive from Johannesburg. I'd visited Sun City for the first time as a judge, along with Vanessa Williams, for the Miss World contest. It had been exciting to see Miss South Africa, Palesa Jacqueline Mofokeng, chosen as the first runner-up in the contest. Jackie ended up with a role in *A Good Man in Africa*, but Vanessa and I had looked at each other the first day of the contest and understood it was a no-brainer. Miss Jamaica took your breath away; she was unquestionably Miss World. I didn't win any beauty contests, but I was always treated royally at Sun City by an old Brooklyn gumbah, Jerry Inzerella.

In Sun City, I met a beautiful light-skinned Zulu woman with exquisite blue-green eyes, and a whirlwind romance followed. She was part of the Chris Hani family. Although a part of me wanted nothing more than to marry this magnificent woman and spend the rest of my life in this country I loved so much, I knew it would not happen. I could hear my sons, from whom I would have to live a continent away, say disgustedly, "There he goes again. We've lost him again." Satie was with me for a while during the filming of *Good Man*, and, although he made many good friends as he always did wherever we went, such as Nelson Mandela's grandson Loiso, I knew he would never want to live there. I was working too hard to try to keep my two sons in my life to abandon them by marrying a South African woman and strengthening my ties with her country.

Several years later, back in the United States, I learned through the grapevine that this Zulu woman who had captured a piece of my heart was building a home in Cape Town for the two of us, waiting for me to return to live with her. When I'd left, I'd thought I'd made it clear that I was still recovering from my painful divorce and that it would not be fair to her, at that time, to continue our relationship. I'd obviously been frivolous in handling our affair, unaware that she expected me to return to her. I'd also been ignorant of the intrinsic belief among African women that when there was an attraction between a man and a woman that had been acted upon or turned into a relationship that moves in a positive way, it's sort of like an arranged marriage. Especially if you consummated a relationship, then there was no reason to look any further. Yet according to this culture, it was not necessary to have sex with the woman for her to claim you. I still get phone calls from three or four other women with whom I have spent time in Africa who want to make a home for me. One woman saw me at a public place and even now calls me frequently. Although it scares me somewhat to be approached by such persistent women, I am flattered by the attention from these beautiful, earthy, maternal women who want to make me their king and take care of me for the rest of my life.

I must admit that I do like that custom of the woman making the relationship permanent. Unfortunately, Western civilization seems to have invoked a multiple-choice institution where the list of possible lifetime relationships is far more complicated to maneuver for a man and a woman. Still, I will always feel sad when I think of this one particular beautiful woman and what might have happened had the timing been different for the two of us. When I returned to Capetown several years later, she was the owner of a silver mine, and a very lucky husband was now living in that house with her.

While it was not in the cards for me to live with one of these loving women, I often think of David Robinson, Jackie's son, who headed to Africa with a backpack more than twenty years ago and ended up in Tanzania. They liked him so much they assigned him a wife, and he has been living in the Tanzania bush ever since, running Sweet Unity Farms, a large cooperative with more than three hundred small coffee farms.

During that same visit when I met the beautiful Zulu woman, I traveled to an area where I could view Robben Island, off the coast of Capetown, where Nelson Mandela had spent eighteen of the twenty-seven years he had been imprisoned. I stood in

Llandudno, at the point where the Atlantic and Indian oceans collide, and could feel a thirty- to forty-degree drop in temperature. I could see Robben Island off to the right. As I thought of all that this great man had suffered, the beatings, the cattle prods, all forms of hideous torture, his hunger strikes, his Ghandi-like nature, I had an epiphany that affected the rest of my life. My own inconsequential complaints about any minor indignities to which I had been subjected in Hollywood began to wither away. How could I ever forget how Mandela had emerged from the gates of Victor-Verster Prison in Paarl holding Winnie's hand, and punching the air in a victory salute? The world had been frozen in place as South Africans, many of whom had already packed their luggage, stood still, their eyes glued to the television set as they waited to see the look on his face. His smile had been a giant vitamin pill for the country, which was restored and filled with hope as the entire world exhaled a collective sigh of relief.

Nor could I deny the fact that I had done more damage to myself through drugs and alcohol than racism or any other person ever had. As the anger and resentment and bitterness flew out of my body, I had no idea that I would undergo a similar experience some fifteen years later as I watched Barack Obama be sworn in as president of the United States. Yet now in Africa, I felt cleansed, ready to start my life anew, freed from the constraints I had imposed on myself. I also felt an overwhelming sympathy for the suffering of Winnie Mandela, who had lost her man for so many fruitful years of her life. Whoever played Winnie Mandela in the movie about her husband's life, I was certain, would have the role of a lifetime.

13

Six Months to Live

1993–2001

Back in the United States, my own newly established company, Logo Entertainment, which I named by combining the first two letters of my first and last names, allowed me an opportunity to produce some of my own television shows. The first one that my partner Peter Locke and I produced on NBC was *Father & Son: Dangerous Relations*, which earned top ratings in its time slot as one of the highest-rated shows of the week. The idea for this TV movie had come to me when I'd read a story in the *Los Angeles Times* about a father and son who'd been reunited in a maximum security prison. When the two of them were up for parole, the warden had decided to release them into each other's custody. It didn't take long for Peter and me to hire a writer to do the screenplay, along with directors, and get it into production. I played the father, and Blair Underwood played the son.

Physically, I found it a struggle to get through the film. I was working so hard to put together a new company that I felt exhausted all of the time, and the cocaine didn't help. Even though all of my life I had adored food, now I was forcing myself to eat, and the more I ate, the more weight I lost. It was scary to watch my weight slide to a new low. My personal life wasn't doing much better. I felt horribly guilty about the divorce, and my relationship with both of my boys was abysmal. I was too busy to spend any time with them or become involved in their lives. Everything about me seemed out of kilter as I tried, unsuccessfully, to focus on Logo and push everything else out of my mind. For *Diggstown*, I'd struggled to take off the weight, but for this movie, I couldn't manage to keep it on. Blair was an incredible actor, and it was a joy to work with him, but I could hear the scuttlebutt surrounding me: "He's using again." Yet I wasn't.

Despite my health problems, I was determined to continue to produce and act in insightful, relevant TV programs, and I tried to include, whenever possible, true historical details. In Showtime's *In His Father's Shoes*, which won a Daytime Emmy as Outstanding Children's Special, I played two characters, Frank and Richard Crosby, the father and the grandfather, in two different time spans. In this TV story, the boy, Clay Crosby, played masterfully by Robert Ri'chard, wears magical wingtip shoes that allow him to pass through time to be both the grandfather and the father and to understand what these two important men in his life were thinking and feeling.

In 1997, Logo Entertainment chose to produce the CBS pilot for *To Dance with Olivia*, set in the time of the beginning of Dr. King's marches. It was a television movie produced in association with Procter & Gamble, which would be the main sponsor, advertising its many products on the show. At that time, this pilot was the only Procter & Gamble–sponsored TV production, and we were delighted with the arrangement. So many of Procter & Gamble's products, Tide, Crest, Crisco, Ivory Soap, relied heavily on minority sales, so this was a natural fit. I was proud to be the executive producer, as well as the star, of *To Dance with Olivia*, an honest portrayal of one town's attempt to remove racial intolerance.

In the second episode, which sadly never made it to the screen, Dr. King was to visit the town just before his assassination. Procter & Gamble did all that it could to make the pilot succeed. The fact that audience polls showed the popularity of my films at that time being close to that of Barbra Streisand's and Robin Williams's movies was an impetus for Procter & Gamble to continue to throw its support behind our program. Lonette McKee was nominated for an Image Award for Outstanding Lead in a TV Movie for her magnificent portrayal of Olivia. Unfortunately, our placement opposite a Super Bowl did not help our ratings for the night the pilot aired.

Still anxious to forge ahead with new ideas, I became a part of *Love Songs*, a trilogy of love stories that aired on Showtime. Winning the prestigious Black Reel award for my directorial debut in a boxing-themed segment, "A Love Song for Champ," in which I also starred, renewed my energy and spirit.

One night during this period of my life when I was struggling to get my television pilots off the ground, I had a memorable encounter with a top producer in Hollywood who shall remain nameless. Coming out of a bathroom stall in a famous L.A.

restaurant, I noticed him doing cocaine at the sink. "Want some?" he asked me, obviously very high.

When I shook my head no, he stopped, placed his nose down on the line, took a deep breath, and stared at me for what seemed like a long time. "I know why you are not making it any further," he told me, as I washed my hands. "It's simple; you're a big black man and you're quite intimidating. Actually, I like you. I think you're a brilliant actor. But when you get too good, you put yourself into the crosshairs of too many rifles. You're too much of a threat now. You should have watched your steps all the time." He turned back to his coke lines. "And stay away from white women," he added, before he was lost again in the white powder. I knew there were a lot of people like that in the business, but it seemed to me that he put a face on the story.

I knew the man was stoned that night, but I also knew his words were filled with some kind of truth. They were only part of the reason I found myself succumbing to the frustration of receiving awards but no high salaries, no chance to call a shot. His words confirmed my belief that I was second class in this industry, that there had always been a limit to how far I could go. And whenever the rumors began to circulate that I was involved with drugs and alcohol again, these rumors had certain motives behind them.

Although I might have believed that I would always be second class, I was still working too hard and growing more fatigued with each new project that came my way. In addition, I was always concerned that I did not have enough time to concentrate on my recovery. As invigorated as I was by the work, I knew I needed to relax, sleep, and take care of myself, to stop working so hard. My health was suffering because food continued to go right through me, but there was simply no time to give in to these problems. I told myself I must have picked up some dysentery in Africa and that it would simply work itself out and go away. There was no time to visit a doctor, anyway. After all, the message from my managers was the same as always: "You gotta work." It seemed like a vicious cycle that I could not break. I would get a movie that would pay me $300,000, and once they took out 10 percent for the manager, 10 percent for the agent, a larger amount for the lawyer, and an even larger amount for the accountant, for taxes, and for my alimony payments, I'd have to go back to work within ten to twenty days to pay those bills. The responsibility and trappings of being a star, keeping my house together, and paying for a staff to do that often hung around my neck like a heavy chain. It kept getting more and more expensive to be a star. Nothing fruitful appeared to be happening inside the house that I was paying so much to keep together, and, nearly out of steam, I found it harder each day to keep my head above water and a smile on my face.

Yet I managed to rally my spirits and body when CBS gave us another shot with *For Love of Olivia*, the sequel to *To Dance with Olivia*. Once again, I played lawyer Daniel Stewart from the small Southern town of Silver Shade. In this episode, set in 1966, Stewart is a local congressman heading to Washington, a historical role that I hoped would continue. One of the best parts of that experience was the opportunity I had to work with Robert Urich, the outstanding actor who is probably best known for his roles as Spenser in *Spenser: For Hire* and as Dan Tanna in *Vega$*. I still miss him. I am convinced that had he not died of cancer in 2001, he would be a giant in the business.

For Love of Olivia did win in the ratings for its night but failed to break through the net that would have made the pilot into a continuing series. CBS offered yet another chance in 2000 with the made-for-TV movie *The Color of Love: Jacey's Story*. Gena Rowlands and I played the grandparents of a six-year-old biracial child named Jacey, the daughter of my son and her daughter, both killed in an automobile accident. The plot was set in the time of the beginning of Dr. King's marches. To watch Gena's character's inbred racism dissolve through her love for the child was to be privy to a superb performance by a world-class actress. She was rightfully nominated for an Emmy for Outstanding Lead Actress in a Miniseries or a Movie, and we both received nominations for the Golden Satellite Award for Best Performance by an Actress and Actor in a Motion Picture Made for Television. As always, I was stacking up the nominations and awards but not the dollar bills. And as my fatigue continued, frustration at the failure of any of my pilots to take off gnawed at my self-confidence.

While we were in Canada for the filming of *For Love of Olivia*, my health continued to deteriorate, so I hired an Asian cook who prepared healthy meals for me, making delicious sushi every day. It was soon obvious that many of my health problems stemmed from some sort of parasite I'd picked up years earlier while filming a movie, directed by George Miller, about AIDS in Pretoria. I remembered eating in a restaurant that was not ready to serve the public. That night, within forty-five minutes, the entire meal had gone through me. This marked the beginning of my problem with keeping food down, as something inside of me began to eat my food, almost the way a tapeworm attaches itself to the walls of one's intestines. This had to have been the beginning of my present condition of chronic dysentery, but I was hopeful that the healthy foods would help me overcome this condition.

One drawback to our filming in Toronto was that the Arizona Diamondbacks, a team in which I was a minority owner, were doing the impossible and playing the Yankees in the final game of the World Series. I tried my hardest to get from Toronto to Arizona in time for that game; however, the airline problems following September 11 made it even more impossible for me to reach Chase Field from Canada. It was enough of a miracle that the Diamondbacks won against Mariano Rivera, a Hall of Fame relief pitcher. So, I stood in front of a TV in Toronto— too nervous to sit down—as, bases loaded with the count of three and two, Gonzo (Luis Gonzalez) hit the ball over the head of Derek Jeter, who missed it by inches. Although it resembled a freeze frame, it was the real thing, and the ring I wear today is evidence that what happened that night was no fantasy.

Yet in the real world of my professional life, it was a constant struggle for me to remain sober, as well as to be independent and make enough money so that I could support my family well. Satie was at Syracuse University, where he married the beautiful Clemence, the co-ed he'd met during his first year there. I find it amazing that they have now been together almost twenty years. Unfortunately, I will always regret that I was too sick to be at their wedding. Clemence has gifted my son two of the most exquisite children I have ever seen. Satie and Clemence may well believe the children are theirs, but in truth, like all grandparents, I know they belong to me. Back then, Satie was, as always, understandably disappointed at the lack of time I was able to give him, arriving at the university only once a year for a too-short visit. As for my other son, Cyndi had arranged for Sharron to take some sort of electronics or computer classes in Philadelphia, about which I knew nothing, except the amount of the bill that I had to pay.

When I became ill on the set of one of my movies, for the first time too sick even to memorize my lines, an Asian doctor took a look at me. "I don't know exactly what's going on here," he said, "but I believe your vital organs are shutting down. If it continues, you will have about six months to a year to live. I would advise you to get examined as quickly as possible to find out." I was too stunned to do more than thank him for his time. I didn't follow his advice and consult another doctor. I was barely able to take in the impact of his devastating words and rest for a short time until I was strong enough finally to finish the film.

Outside the studio, times were rough in L.A. Since the Rodney King incident and the Watts riots in 1992, there was immense racial anger, not only in the black neighborhoods but moving toward the residential sections of Beverly Hills. It felt more like an insurrection than a riot, yet this climate possibly affected the work of proper programming. The powers that be in TV were now at a loss to figure out what program would appease the African American who was angry, not only the ones in the riots, but the average African American lawyers and doctors and teachers. They had all had enough of the separate-but-equal programs on TV, as well as in life. When the studios didn't know what to do with their black shows, they simply canceled many of them. The media were filled with stories about the anger, the police injustice in the ghettos, and the sad reality of life in various L.A. neighborhoods. Something needed to be done, and no one knew what that was. Physically, I knew I was in trouble too, but as with the world around me, I had no idea how to fix the problems.

14

No, Thanks

2001–2004

Inside my home, there was no denying that my health had reached a dangerous condition. Still plagued with dysentery and unable to stop losing weight, I could no longer hide the ill health that was evident on my face and on my body. Even after ten years, recovery was becoming more difficult to sustain, but I worked on it every day. Something strange was happening in my home in Malibu, but it took a while before I realized that this "something" was creeping in through a pipe underneath the ground through my door and settling into the walls, the carpets, and the floors. My cats had died, but all that I could come up with was that they had somehow been poisoned. The rumors that I was using drugs continued, but at that time, the rumors could not have been further from the truth. Over and over, I replayed in my mind the Chinese doctor's words that I had six months left to live. Was he right? Was I getting even sicker? Should I see another doctor? It took me some time to process what he had said, but before too long, I had accepted his prediction as the sad reality. There was no reason to see another doctor. For a long time now, I had suspected that I was deathly ill. Now I knew it was true: I was dying. And no drugs or alcohol could change that hard, cold fact. Cold sober, I had hit rock bottom.

Feeling isolated, with a death sentence over my head, I cared little about anyone or anything. I withdrew from any sort of personal life and used whatever energy that miraculously came to me on my TV work. I felt as if I were a mere observer of life. Away from the studio, I watched a steady stream of visitors who were somehow convinced that my house would be a safe place for drugs and alcohol take advantage of that idea and move through it. Desperately lonely, as I had done in the past I sought the company of people I should not have let into that house. Eventually, it came to a point where I would be lying on my couch, exhausted after working on a TV pilot, and in disbelief would see the people I had let in carrying camcorders, guitars, jewelry, and leather jackets out the door. This had happened to me once before. And just like the previous time, what could I do about it? Call the police and let them see what was happening in my house? To make matters even worse, I'd had some poor dealings with unethical accountants and found that whatever money I earned was not being managed capably. Because I knew I was dying, it made little sense for me to dwell on this problem, so I simply lay there, not caring at all.

Filming *Jasper, Texas*, which was based on a true story, was an enormous challenge for me. I felt awful, and my body was little more than skin and bones, which fit the description of the real-life mayor I portrayed. My dear friend Jon Voight was brilliant in his role as the chief of police, yet I saw little of him, because I spent all of my time between scenes out of the way, sleeping in my dressing room and rousing myself only when they called me for a scene. Looking at my gaunt body, little more than 170 pounds, some people commented that I was growing old gracefully. Most, however, were certain that I was using.

During *Lackawanna Blues* six months later, surprisingly I was still alive—but barely. The film was based on the acclaimed autobiographical one-man show by Ruben Santiago-Hudson, who wrote the adaptation and appears in the film, and was co-executive produced by Halle Berry. Ironically, they ended up cutting my death scene, perhaps because it looked terrifyingly real, as if I were saying good-bye to the world around me—which I was. That scene is in the DVD of the movie, and whenever I look at it, I remember exactly how painful that filming was for me. I gave whatever energy I could muster up to my role as the disturbed Ol' Lem Taylor, in this story of a remarkable woman who builds a community despite the boundaries of segregation. Even the one great dance scene with my beloved sounds of the rhythms and blues, the soul music that had always moved my own soul, had no effect on my lethargy as I sleepwalked through that role.

As sick as I was at the time, I suddenly found myself clinging to one ray of hope about my career that gave me a reason to get out of bed in the morning: my carefully thought-out plan for a Harlem Renaissance project. I had dreamed about this work for years, but as I grew sicker, I began to see it as my final statement. Once I saw this immense project come to life, I would be finished. Yet I would leave the world a happy man.

I was equally convinced that a certain particularly brilliant young writer, whom I'd met during one of my last few films, was the person who just might be at my side during its execution. I'd seen his energy and intelligence abound. I could visualize the two of us working together; I would be the executive producer, and he would be the producer and the writer. I was stimulated by the thought of being a mentor and passing my story on to the writers of the next generation. I might be almost out of steam, but this young man was just getting started.

The stars seemed aligned for the two of us to work together, when somehow, as unimaginable as it might seem, I was given the chance to be one of the guest performers in the Broadway production of *Chicago*, playing the coveted role of Billy, which, ironically, my old friend Richard Gere played with such aplomb in the award-winning movie. I knew my health was shattered, but, an actor through and through, I somehow still believed I could will myself to sing and dance my way through this glorious role. Sadly, I barely lasted the first days of rehearsals before I removed myself from the cast to enter a New York hospital for some minor surgery, aware that there was no way I could rejoin the cast when I was released. Yet the good news was that after the surgery, none of the doctors appeared to be convinced I was dying, and I felt a bit energized. I used whatever strength I could amass to meet with the young writer I was so anxious to talk to about my project, who was currently directing some theater in the city.

The moment I saw my young friend, I noted the same look he'd worn on his face the last time we were together, a look of dimmed hope that I'd seen on the faces of some other minority writers and actors and producers. A look that was part frustration, part sadness, it illuminated the fact that each of these people had not received the cornucopia he thought he'd earned. Instead, someone had thrown cold water on his dream, shattering the orgasmic joy of making that dream come true, of having the power, finally, to call the shots. I knew it well, because, despite the thrill of having played roles that moved me to the depths of my soul, I still came up lacking what I wanted most. But this writer, I'd believed from the first time we'd met a few years earlier, would be different. He'd won multiple awards for what he'd created but was not yet where he deserved to be. Yet someday, I was certain, he would be.

His road to success had not been easy, he explained sadly. "The powers in charge told me, 'We're going to let you in. You're going to be one of our exciting young playwrights.' As if I was lucky they were giving me any sort of a chance."

I nodded my head in agreement and listened quietly as he talked about his plans and discussed his frustration with the leaders of the industry. I knew so well how many young African American directors, producers, actors, and writers had ended up lost in the grist of this industry, their important stories absent from the screen. Oh, yes, there were always the stories of Nelson Mandela and Dr. King and a handful of others that would be told, but they were giants, too big to be ignored.

I told my talented young friend to be practical, to put first things first. He needed to make a lot of money and put it aside, never letting all of his income come from the industry. He had to declare his financial independence as soon as possible. Then after he'd made the money, he must live simply, always keeping his faith and his eyes on the prize. In his lifetime, things would break. When I finished talking to him, I joked, "And, most important, when you get famous and need to hire somebody, hire me."

Then I got down to business. I had a plan for the vehicle that would let him accomplish all of those goals. It would be a five-part, larger-than-*Roots* miniseries about the period of the Harlem Renaissance, that glorious time of African American life in Harlem in the 1920s that stretched through the Depression until World War II began, from 1915 to 1940, when the period began its demise as men left for the war. By the time they came back, it was gone. I envisioned the project involving five talented directors, each one working with a single aspect of this remarkable era. The first two-hour episode of the series would concentrate on the gangsters of the time, who were part of the experience of the Harlem Renaissance. They included Lucky Luciano, Al Capone, Dutch Schultz, and Bumpy Johnson, the notorious head of the black mafia, who staged a crime war against Schultz and was discussed as a mentor to Frank Lucas, the character portrayed by Denzel Washington in *American Gangster*. The first episode would also include politicians, such as Mayor Fiorello LaGuardia and Governor Thomas E. Dewey, who had ruled New York during that era. I could envision maybe Martin Scorsese directing that episode.

The second episode would feature Harlem Renaissance music and dance and show business, directed, I hoped, by Woody Allen. The third two-hour episode would revolve around the poets and the politics, featuring Langston Hughes and W. E. B. DuBois. I had several talented directors in mind for that section. The fourth part, ideally directed by Spike Lee, would be the black political movement, the *Amsterdam News*, the beginning of the NAACP, and the Back to Africa movement headed by Marcus Garvey and his famous friend, the Black Eagle.

The fifth and final part of the series, perhaps with a Taylor Hackford or an Oliver Stone type of director, would conclude with the beginning of World War II and would feature the churches, the Apollo Theatre, the Cotton Club, Adam Clayton Powell, and the unforgettable Easter Parade with Shirley Temple and Bill "Bojangles" Robinson dancing on a float all the way down Fifth Avenue.

It would be the type of miniseries one could pull off the shelf to reveal a chunk of important U.S. history that for too many years had remained untold. With an enthusiasm that came from deep within me, from the one place where my illnesses had not touched, I reveled in our discussion of our grand African American memorial. I already had received the cooperation of many of the Harlem churches. New York congressman Charlie Rangel had promised that during the filming, he would declare Easter Day a celebration of the Harlem Renaissance, reinstate the famous Easter Parade, and shut down Fifth Avenue to the end of Central Park, as, for one mile, everyone would march in their authentic finery and memorabilia, amid horses and buggies and antique cars, music platforms, and joyous bands.

I had even tied up the rights to *On Her Ground*, the story of the life of Madame C. J. Walker, an African American who was the first American female to become a millionaire by her own achievements. It was written by her great-great-granddaughter, A'Lelia Bundles. C. J. Walker's only child, A'Lelia Walker, dubbed the "joy goddess of Harlem's 1920s" by Langston Hughes, had hosted one of the most memorable salons of the Harlem Renaissance. It was in this salon, the Dark Tower, in her elegant New York townhouse, that she'd entertained Harlem and Greenwich Village writers, artists, and musicians, along with visiting African and European royalty. Whoopi Goldberg had already agreed to play Madame C. J. Walker, and Halle Berry was considering the equally powerful role of her daughter. My friend's excitement over my plan doubled mine, and although he warned me that finding the backing might be our brick wall, I left New York with his agreement to be part of the project.

Back in California, with so many pieces of the project set in place and feeling stronger than I had in many months, I was ready to set up an office to begin the work. Full of hope, with my appetite miraculously regenerated, I made the call to one of our top cable companies to begin the pitch for the series. Although my hat was off to this particular cable network for the many important groundbreaking shows it had already brought to the forefront, I still found it embarrassing to have to ask someone not of my race for a green light to do a relevant story about my culture and my history. I have always understood, of course, that it is presumptuous to ask anyone in that position to have sensitivity toward these subjects. The air of automatic assumption of superiority hangs heavy in the air, too often allowing the men who call the shots to sit back and deny support to brilliant young men such as my young writer friend. This makes all the less sense when you consider the fact that the white men who write these checks know that the African American dollar is the largest consumer dollar on the planet, money that rarely, if ever, makes its way back to the black neighborhoods that need it.

This project, however, was different. Who could not see the importance of this Harlem Renaissance memorial? The answer was quick and to the point. As degrading as it was, I was informed that there was no need for a face-to-face meeting. This phone call was as far as I would get. "No, thanks," I was told. "We're doing our own research with our own star. We're getting our facts from the archives. It's in development already. We'll do it on our own." I knew what that meant, and I was right: to this day it is still "in development" on the shelf, as "our own" work on it.

This man's answer reminded me how important it was that we do it on "our own," too, that African Americans have to be responsible and use their wherewithal to produce and put together productions about our own past and history, not unlike what Jews have done about their past. There are stories that must be told about the African Americans' rich history, messages that must be related to young African Americans and to everyone else, for that matter. We cannot rely on anyone else. We alone have to do it. The gauntlet had been flung. But I no longer had the energy to pick it up and run with it. Today things are slowly getting better. But not then.

15

Putting the Demons to Rest

JULY 4, 2004

As the Harlem Renaissance project fell apart, I could feel the last spurts of energy leaking out of me like air oozing from a torn balloon. When my agent somehow got me a part on *Cold Case*, I knew I was too sick to pass the physical. Rather than embarrass producer Jerry Bruckheimer and CBS head Les Moonves, for whom I had the utmost respect, I decided not to show up for the medical exam. I was completely sober at the time, but my agency, Paradigm, refused to accept that explanation and fired me on the spot.

I was finished with fighting. Profoundly empty, not surrendering but feeling defeated, I was certain that God was now ready to call me away from this world. I had placed my last phone call, pleaded my last case, endured my last embarrassment, received my last rejection. So weak I could barely get to the bathroom, I sat in my house, not living and not dying, unaware of the toxic mold growing around me, wreaking havoc on my already weakened body.

I concentrated my final reserve of energy on trying to figure out the right combination of drugs and alcohol to end what was left of my life, so that I could go out with a bang. Finally, after the mixture I meticulously created did not kill me, I waited a few more days and then, on July 4, 2004, cold sober, I called my sons, who were both living about twenty minutes away in L.A. I asked them to drive me to Promises, a private residential drug and alcohol rehab center. If I could not die, I'd have to figure out a way to live what was left of my life. Recovery at Promises seemed like the only possible solution. I will never forget the looks on my two sons' faces when they walked into the house and saw me. Their sadness and pain hurt me more than I had already hurt myself.

From the moment I arrived at Promises, I found it a tough adjustment. Some of the attendants giggled when they saw me; others cried. Yet I knew every time I looked at those faces that as low as I was, somehow I was miraculously beginning an unexpected resurrection. As it turned out, my delivery to the door of this recovery center saved my life, not only from the effects of drugs and alcohol, but from the insidious disease that was destroying the insides of my body. When my blood pressure became dangerously uncontrollable, I was rushed to the nearby Queen of Angels Hospital. By some miracle, there

I was seen by an Asian doctor who specialized in toxic mold. "Are you who I think you are?" she asked when she saw me.

I said, "Yeah," and she ordered me to stick out my tongue. She ran a few more tests to confirm her immediate diagnosis of toxic mold syndrome. She explained that toxic mold attacks the weakest parts of the body, in my case, my lungs, stomach, and kidneys, and said that she had never before seen such a concentration of the disease in one body. I now understood why my cats had died and why I had grown so devastatingly tired every time I walked into my house.

I could be cured, she assured me, but my house, which certainly no one would buy in its present condition, would have to be torn down to its basic structure. The professionals explained the year-long process to me. When the meters revealed that the mold was finally gone, the house would be rebuilt, its plumbing changed, its foundation restored, and the entire structure rewired and repainted, then imbued with a special substance that would prevent the mold from returning.

I saw an image of my house, infected at its innermost core with a barely detected disease, needing to be torn down to its very foundation, as being similar to what was happening to me. I, too, was being rebuilt, after so many years of being unaware of what was going on inside myself. Now, like this house, I was not destined to disappear, to be razed, to die. Now I wanted to live. Yet I knew it would be an enormous task to make myself whole and stronger than before. My wiring, my plumbing, my structure needed to be redone, and that would be a far more difficult job than rebuilding my house.

The cost for redoing the house, however, was staggering: $1.5 million, all of which would have to be paid for with a high-interest loan that I might well spend the rest of my life repaying. But I would do it, and I am still repaying it today. I had no choice. I was worth the price. The more I thought about it, I could recognize the parallel between the house breaking down and my own reconstruction. So many possessions that represented my old life, such as my guitars and camera collections, were already gone. They had vanished at the hands of strangers who'd easily removed them from my house, along with stealing my money and jewelry, as I'd watched helplessly from the couch. That entire lifestyle was gone, all of the trappings I no longer cared about.

Meanwhile, this capable doctor treated the toxic mold syndrome, while the equally phenomenal staff at Promises helped me combat my addictions. It was unquestionably the most difficult and painful month of my life as I stared down my devils and, once again, made the first crucial steps of the long, slow climb to recovery. It was not that different from the way new recruits are inducted into the Marine Corps: I was being taken apart and would now start from scratch as I made the move not into the world of the marines, but rather from the insane place to which I had descended, back to sanity. As my counselors told me over and over, I was no longer a father, a boyfriend, an actor, a friend. I was simply a man trying to build a better house, one brick at a time, in which to live my life. Only this time, the house I was building would have a stronger foundation than any other in which I might have lived. I heard the message clearly and was determined to follow it to fruition.

I understood that unlike ten years earlier, when I'd left Cyndi in charge of my family while I entered recovery, this was my final chance to make the necessary changes to get well. My body was too weakened by the effects of my alcohol and drug addiction and of toxic mold syndrome to survive another relapse. If I wanted to live, and now I certainly did, this time I had to make my recovery last.

From the beginning and long after I left Promises, my boys were part of this recovery, and our sessions together were often nearly unbearable. The onslaught of my sons' anger, some justified and some not, along with knowledge of the pain I had caused those I loved, was inestimable. There were times when I felt that I would never be strong enough to survive these attacks, but with the help of the staff and some painful soul searching, I did.

It had never been easy for my two boys to be my sons. Though Christina died from cancer some years later, in 2008, she had planted so much poison in Satie, feelings of anger that were certainly inflamed by all of the times I had not been around for him. And Sharron had his own unique set of problems, stemming from his early years and the adoption issue and made worse by my relationship with Cyndi. I will never forget the time a reporter came up to one of my sons during an award ceremony and said, "You must be so proud of your father, for all the good things he has done."

My son said nothing for a long minute and then finally responded. "Are you sure about that?" When the reporter related those words to me, the words were a cold knife in my heart. It was hard to believe that either the boy who had once fallen asleep on my shoulder, soothed by the songs I sang into his hot little ear, or the one who had followed me so trustingly back to L.A. could feel that way about me. But many years had passed since then, and many mistakes had been made. There had been just as many good times, but it was what I had not done or had done poorly that remained rooted in my sons' minds.

Many of my counselors were African Americans who had survived the nightmare I was now living. The patients ran the gamut of ages and lifestyles, but we shared a common disease and desire to cure ourselves. Liz Lopresti and Ted Snyder, who became my lifelong friends, were my two early lifesavers and gave their all to aid my recovery.

It took me a long time to get to the root of why I had abused my body and mind with alcohol and drugs. I searched back through my childhood and saw myself as a little boy, loving my father and all of my uncles, the strong men who had taught me how to play ball and lavished me with love and hugs. I watched them play ball together and was ecstatic when they gave me a chance to bat. They were so much fun, and I loved them so dearly. I watched them get drunk, but it always seemed to be a fun drunk. One of my uncles would start staggering, and they would all laugh, and so would I.

I was always entertaining my uncles. When I was around six, they took me to see Slim and Slam at the Apollo in Harlem, and I learned to sing and dance like those two stars. My uncles applauded and cheered me on as I performed for them. "Do the buck dance," they often told me before I went to bed, and I would do it and then drift off to sleep with the sounds of their laughter in my ears.

As I got older, things seemed to change. I saw that the men who came from the war were unhappy that they couldn't find jobs, while the white men they had served with obtained work easily. The parties seemed suddenly harsher, and an air of violence hung over them. I heard my aunts crying but was unable to understand what my uncles had done to upset them.

In high school, I had determined that I would be a doctor and help all of my relatives feel better. I also wanted to understand what was happening and why these men I loved so much were acting the way they did. At the beginning of college, when I had gravitated toward soft drugs like marijuana, I brought a little home to my father. "Try some of this, Dad," I told him. "It will help you relax, and you won't have to stagger."

He slapped me hard across the face, yelling, "How dare you bring this dirty stuff home!" Although alcohol might have been his drug of choice, he could not tolerate my using any soft or hard drugs at all.

The older I became, the more I sought out jazz musicians, many of whom were addicts and alcoholics. Perhaps they were a visceral link to the men I had loved so much in my childhood. Yet there was no way to forget that I had seen my father dying of alcoholism on the couch, and I came to accept that if I did not stop myself now, with my very last chance to get and stay sober, I would be doing the same thing to my own sons. I now understood how the disease of alcoholism had been deep inside me, years before I began to abuse alcohol.

When I left Promises, I was determined that I would never have to return. I settled into the guest house on my property while my house was being torn apart and slowly rebuilt into a home that was free of the deadly microorganism that had nearly killed me. I understood that I had to change, to take responsibility for my errors and to effect my own cure. There would be help, daily help that I would seek, but I would have to work hard not to lose everything I had achieved. I had to make sure that the foundation I was building was not made of paper, that, above all else, I made room for the spiritual in my life. I needed to humbly seek the help of a higher power, to make sure that this time I yielded *all* control of my life to it, that I didn't give some and then take some back, as I had in the past. My prayer would be a simple one: "Why am I on the planet? How can I be of service?"

The answer to that question propelled me to more introspection, to meditate, to eat and sleep properly, to reconsider my roles as father and grandfather and friend. If I needed a reason to remain in recovery and move forward, it should not be for another major movie role. Perhaps it would be to my advantage if Hollywood could not forgive my crime of addiction, with the "powers that be" deciding they were unable to erase the blemish beside my name the way they had for so many of my white counterparts. Perhaps my freedom from the industry would push me in another direction, one in which I had been unconsciously moving for many years. Someone needed me, but who that was I did not yet know. My sons, although they would always need me, were grown up with their own families now. And there was no woman waiting to build a new family with this sixty-eight-year-old man. Yet there were children; there had always been children.

Somehow, I was certain, I would find an avenue of self-less service and make myself into the type of person I always should have been in all of the relationships in my life, with my sons, with women, with the whole world. It was time to let in humility, to serve this higher power, to give away in order to keep, to make use of whatever gifts I might have accumulated these nearly seventy years. The stronger and healthier I grew, the more certain I became that I would find this purpose, wher-ever it might be.

16

Eracism

JANUARY 5, 2006

As I continued my soul-searching, the words "If you don't know where you come from, you can't know where you're going" kept repeating in my head. These words echoed, along with my conviction that the evils of racism could doom the planet on which we live, that all kinds of militarism, all wars, stemmed, in one way or another, from some form of racism, from our inability to communicate with one another and respect races and religions different from our own.

Then one day, as I was out walking, I happened to notice a T-shirt being hawked at a corner near my house. "E.ra.cism," it spelled out, separating the letters in dictionary format, "the removal of existence of the belief that one race is superior to another." I thought hard about this word *eracism*. I had seen it before in New Orleans and considered what a monumental task it would be to make that word a reality. Racism is even internal, within each race, reflected in black-on-black crime, white-on-white crime. It is not as if a person can simply wake up one day and say, "Today, I am no longer a racist." Racism is a disease, not unlike alcoholism or overeating. It takes deep introspection and self-examination to even begin to make the first step toward erasing it. Personally, I had to start with myself, to meditate and identify and erase any forms of racism to which I clung. The name "Eracism" was the easy part, but its goal was lofty and overreaching. Entire nations and the greatest minds had made little progress in erasing racism. Even the great historian W. E. B. DuBois had said that the main problem of the twentieth century would be the problem of race. But then again, I had arrived at a place where I now believed that nothing is impossible.

One morning as I lay in bed, half awake, half asleep, during that period when there's always time to hear a message that someone might be trying to send to you, the answer to my question arrived. I now knew why I had been placed on the planet and what I needed to do with the rest of my life: work with children, just as my mother had always done. If I was going to remove racism from the world, then, of course, I would have to start with the children, our most precious commodity. Children have to be taught by us. We can teach them good; we can teach them bad. Like that wonderful song from *South Pacific* tells us, "You've Got to Be Carefully Taught." The words from that song ran through my head until I sat up and began to sing them softly.

Once again, the gauntlet had been thrown down, but this time I was ready to pick it up. I would dedicate the rest of my life to eliminating the scourge of racism from the minds of all children with whom I came in contact, children at risk of falling into lives of violence, children in general, to give each and every one of them the tools to become decent, achieving adults who cared about one another and the universe. I was far from the first person to have such an idea. Certainly, other organizations have had the same lofty goals in mind as they reached out to boys and girls, providing them with a safe after-school place to play and learn, to keep them off the dangerous streets. Some examples are the Boys and Girls Clubs and the United Way—which I was an active member of and a spokesman for and which did so much for me in my youth—along with L.A.-based organizations that I so admire, such as the Challengers Boys and Girls Club. Yet the foundation I would create would go one step further than these wonderful organizations; it would use the concept of mentorship to enrich these children's lives and would follow a well-thought-out and precise curriculum. For there was so much I needed to imbue in these children: knowledge of their own unique history, physical fitness, hygiene, respect for their elders and the opposite sex, a dress code, and the ability to communicate with others in a civil manner. Most important, I wanted to provide the experiences that would eradicate racism. Overreaching, perhaps, but why not?

I'd never forgotten my first experience with helping kids some thirty years earlier in Tompkins Park Square, when we'd used the anti-poverty grant to introduce to the world of show business dozens of kids who'd formerly spent the summer breaking windows. We taught them how to act, dance, sing, build sets, and learn a craft. Never had I felt so exhilarated as when I'd traveled to the Berkshires with those kids or watched the shows they produced. Many of the kids had been well on their way to lives of crime, yet spending one summer in an organized program of theater had sent them in different, more positive directions.

Today, I wanted to reproduce that summer scene, only on a permanent basis, inside what we would call the Shamba Center. It would be named after the Swahili word for "farm," a place where you plant seeds. I visualized kids helping kids the way it used to be in our neighborhoods and in our families, with each of us taking care of one another before integration changed that, unwittingly shattering the concepts of cohesiveness and uniqueness, arriving as it did without the essential component of equality. The motto inside the Shamba Center would be the same words that had first sent me on this road: "Nothing is impossible." We would provide the tools, the seeds, to make each child plant that idea in his or her mind and believe those words. Maybe I would even find a vehicle to relate the important stories that I ached for minority children to hear, as I figured out the most opportune way to help them.

The idea of the Shamba Center came from my Jewish friends in Brooklyn, who had regularly disappeared into a synagogue or a yeshiva while we were growing up. At least 75 percent of them ultimately emerged into successful lives, not only professionally but, more important, in the personal sphere, as they raised their families with love and respect for learning and for one another. Their seeds of success, their sense of identity, had come not only from being Jewish but also from the extended multicultural neighborhood in which they were raised. Here in this melting pot of a predominantly Jewish neighborhood, everyone had something to do to keep the neighborhood strong, especially during the Depression when times were hard.

I remember one Christmas during those tough years, not with sadness or embarrassment, but rather with a sense of neighborhood unity. I must have been six or seven at holiday time.

Instead of eating with our relatives in our home or in one of their houses, we were all at the park, standing in line with our neighbors, waiting to receive a helping of some type of stew. I can visualize myself standing in the park with my bowl of stew, filled with some potatoes and lots of vegetables. I also recall that only children, not the parents, were allowed to have a second bowl. Yet I have no memory of feeling that my family was poor and needy. Instead, there was a sense of togetherness that made up for the fact that I had been very hungry. I have no idea how they did it, but the residents of our neighborhood erased the shame of needing a handout and replaced it with the attitude that we were all in this together and would never let one another go hungry for very long.

For me, Brooklyn had been an oasis of loving and learning, despite my family often being surrounded on all sides by riots, gangs, and crime of every sort. It was here, in this nurturing world where I had been raised, that certain seeds were firmly planted by forces beyond my front door: to value learning, to respect one's elders and oneself, to care for one's body and excel in sports, to push one's mind, to love and care for the neighborhood in which you lived. My parents had carefully chosen the place to raise me, but there were millions of kids who were not so lucky. In my neighborhood, we had passed the test of taking care of one another.

We had no need for cell phones then. Why would we have needed them when we had sentinels at the windows, those mothers and grandmothers who kept an eye on everything, making sure the children, always the children, were safe and headed in the right direction?

Personally, I felt as if I had no choice but to head out into the world and verify what I had learned in that neighborhood, to see whether it was true elsewhere. After all, that was what my cousins had guarded me for, so that I could leave this protected spot and test the waters beyond Brooklyn to see what I could discover. And not everything that I found matched what I had left behind.

There was no denying that most people can only dream about what happened to me. I was an oblivious Cinderella, never realizing how lucky I was. My prince came to me in so many different ways, while I continued on, blissfully unaware that these things did not happen to everybody. Broadway success arrived so easily that it never occurred to me that it was a stroke of extraordinary luck to be a teenager with a major role in a Broadway play. And how many black teens had won athletic and dramatic scholarships to New York University in the 1950s? In yet another stroke of incredible luck, although few, if any, blacks were playing on professional basketball teams, the Knicks offered me such an opportunity. Yes, there were problems waiting for me when I left the secure environment where this luck surrounded me. I was not, I understood, able to stay in one place and bask in my early success. I had to open the door and move away. That was not easy, nor would I have wanted it to be. For, as Hamlet says, "Ay, there's the rub." As I moved on with my life, problems were waiting for me, some of my own making, along with those I ultimately solved as well as I could.

Now that those years and tests are behind me, some that I came through with passing grades and others with the mark of failure, albeit hopefully not forever, I must consider other people who did not have such opportunities when they were young. What could be more wonderful than establishing a place, a physical building, the Shamba Center, where everything I had received as a child would be given to other kids? My high school alone, Abraham Lincoln High School, had generated famous musicians, authors, politicians, journalists, judges, playwrights, and athletes, along with three Nobel Peace Prize winners.

All of these people, as students, had been encouraged to be the best they could possibly be. Here was evidence that early childhood nurturing really paid off. So much talent, so much brilliance had somehow developed inside this unique neighborhood. Whatever was created there could also occur in a Shamba Center, where we would try to replicate that homogeneous neighborhood, with kids growing up together as we reached out to them with our program. The end result would be that when these kids matured and became chiefs of police, lawyers, teachers, doctors, artists, carpenters, or whatever, as well as mothers and fathers, racism would simply not be in the picture. These children would have been "carefully taught" to see the beauty in a brown-skinned Mexican child or to appreciate the expressive dark eyes in a black face or the unique splendor in a white or an Asian face, to celebrate the difference in each and every one of them—to erase from their consciousness the evil of racism and the concept that one race is superior to another.

After my years of frustration, my illness and recovery, and my conscious decision to live a selfless life, and prompted by this early-morning dream and the memory of that *South Pacific* song—whose words that you have to be taught to hate rarely left my thoughts—I officially established the Eracism Foundation on January 5, 2006. Its goals were noble yet, in my mind, achievable: to eradicate the impact of all forms of racism by providing programs that foster cultural diversity, historical enrichment, education, and antiviolence initiatives. It would be an all-out conscious offensive against racism, violence, and ignorance. Certainly, I would have to accept the fact that racism may never completely disappear, but it should be much less prevalent in the world than love is.

My energy had never been greater as I contemplated the specifics of tackling the new mountain in front of me. Each detail, large or small, consumed my attention. Attendance would be compulsory, but that would be no problem because the children would want to come to the Shamba Center every day, to arrive directly from school and stay until seven o'clock, when their parents or guardians would pick them up. Its doors would remain open all weekend and every day in the summer.

There were so many minds to tap for the work of my foundation, each leading to another person equally as brilliant and anxious to be involved. As I spread the word and mentioned Eracism in every interview, speech, or discussion, my phone began to ring. At the beginning, I found that some people, sadly, saw my grand plan as their own private way to make money for themselves. This hurt me but did not destroy my resolve to make my dream a reality. I spent my time watching videos and documentaries of similar programs, visiting other groups, talking to children, and meeting with educators and businessmen.

My resolve remained strong in part because I couldn't put out of my mind a scene that had played out before me three years earlier when I was in Atlanta, acting the role of Willie in Tyler Perry's wonderful film *Daddy's Little Girls*. What happened away from the lights one evening was equally as significant as what I did in front of the lights. That night I was sitting in a chair, reading a book and waiting for my scene, when a group of black kids, maybe ten of them, between the ages of eight and twelve, walked up to me. They'd been watching us work there on Auburn Avenue, in their neighborhood, just a block away from 501 Auburn Avenue, the National Historic Site that marked the house where Martin Luther King Jr. had been born. The kids all had the classic gang-banger look, with the stocking skull cap, oversize pants hanging down to reveal the cracks in their butts, shirttails out, untied sneakers on their feet, and money in their pockets. I knew their story.

Too young to go to jail, these drug runners would be sent to Juvenile Hall instead, so the drug seller used them to distribute crack in the neighborhood. "Whatcha reading, Mr. Gossett?" one of the kids asked me.

I pointed to the cover of my book, *Black, Red and Deadly: Black and Indian Gunfighters of the Indian Territory, 1870–1907*, by Art Burton, and said, "A story about Bass Reeves. You guys ever heard of Wyatt Earp and Bat Masterson?"

"Sure," one of them answered right away. They all started to talk, letting me know they'd seen Kurt Russell and Kevin Costner play those big cowboy roles.

"Well, look at this guy," I told them, pointing to the picture of the black man with the big thick mustache on the back cover of the book. "Do you know who he is?" They all shook their heads. "Well, this guy was the most successful marshal in the West," I said. "More powerful than Wyatt Earp and Bat Masterson put together. The greatest manhunter of the West."

They looked at me like I was nuts. "No way," one of them said, and they all laughed.

It was time for my scene, so I didn't have a chance to say anything else. I closed the book and left it on my chair and smiled at the kids. "See you later," I said, as I got up and walked away.

When I came back an hour or so later, the kids and my book were gone. No surprise. "Those kids stole your book," the assistant director told me.

"Yeah, I know," I said. I also knew those kids were dying to hear a story about a powerful black man, an Old West marshal yet. I was thrilled that they had stolen my book and was determined to get more stories about black heroes into their hands and heads and hearts. This was the only ammunition I could think of to prevent those kids from spending the rest of their lives in prison, until the age of twenty-five, when it would be all over for them. Tragically, I understood that the ambition of these typical gangbangers, who proudly displayed their bullet and knife scars, was to die in prison by that age. For the young black women who associated with them, the plan, all too often, was to have a couple of kids with different fathers and become welfare moms. I could imagine those Auburn Avenue boys, right at that moment, sitting behind a dark staircase with a flashlight or a cigarette lighter, reading that book, and grasping a fleeting moment of pride, their low self-esteem boosted by the little-known fact that black men could be just as heroic as white men.

I had to get these stories out to the kids, in movies, in documentaries, in any way I could. Some of the plans for the Shamba Center were simple. Once the children arrived there, they would put on a T-shirt with the name Eracism, along with a hat and shorts or pants and shoes, ready to play sports. The first thing they would do would be to celebrate their existence in some sort of moment of prayer or meditation, then move on to their lessons. Like children in a family, they would make use of and become mentors, reaching back to help those who were younger. There would be field trips to baseball, basketball, and football games and to the theater, movies, and museums. They would get to know their own neighborhoods, to celebrate their own cities.

This vital connection to such opportunities and to their own past would inspire and equip children to embark on a positive future. For those who had already fallen into the hands of violence, we would design intensive antiviolence initiatives and forums. The foundation would also address my fears about our planet and the harm we cause it daily. Because we cannot give our children a dying planet, we must teach them to take care of the one where we live, so that like them, like a tree, it will replenish itself and grow, eventually feeding all of us. Here in the Shamba Center, much like an Israeli kibbutz or a gathering place in ancient African civilizations, we would all work together to care for the young.

The Eracism Board would be the most crucial element of the foundation. These would be the men and women whose vision and conviction would make Eracism a reality and keep it growing long after I was no longer there. My plan has always been to create the foundation, to see the Shamba Center at work, and then to let those we'd carefully selected to be in charge take over. The first few members of my board came quickly and enthusiastically: Father Clements, an African American Catholic priest and a social activist of national renown, whose famous motto, "Each one, teach one," mirrored mine; my friend and mentor Azime Fancy, an African-born Indian and a brilliant businessman, who taught me Swahili and the importance of having a road map, along with the concept and name of the Shamba Center; another mentor, Xerona Clayton, Dr. King's personal secretary and the founder of the Trumpet Awards; and Bernice King, Dr. King's youngest daughter.

I have had the honor of meeting the Obamas several times. I first saw Barack Obama when I was the master of ceremonies for a Congressional Black Caucus in Washington, D.C., and he was a new senator. Before that event, I had received an award from Alpha Phi Alpha, the oldest black fraternity in the country. When I had a few minutes to relax between events, I stepped into another conference room and took a deep breath with some friends. I was holding a can of soda when five or six young black men, each of whose appearance alone seemed to spell the word *brilliant*, approached me. One of the men pointed out another man to me and said, "This is Barack Obama, and he is going to run for president."

I looked at this handsome, tall, lean young man who came forward to shake my hand, and I said, "Sure. Anything you need from me, you've got." He smiled broadly and took off to shake another hand. Not in my lifetime, I told myself, will a man who looks like him and sounds like him, with a name like Barack Hussein Obama, become president of the United States of America.

From then on, however, I heard and learned a great deal about this remarkable man, ultimately watching him at the Democratic National Convention in Colorado, where his miracle began its journey to reality. I studied him carefully and proudly from the third row of the Kodak Theater during his debates with Hillary Clinton, where CNN had invited me to sit. I worked for him in Arizona and North and South Carolina and wherever else I went on my own speaking tours. Although I did not get the opportunity to introduce him one night when he spoke in Orange County, he did hug me gratefully when I arrived.

Five weeks after the election that brought this extraordinary man to the highest position of power in our country, I dodged yet another bullet that came close to ending my life. Ironically, this happened on the night I was to receive the 2008 Mary Pickford Award for Outstanding Contribution to the Entertainment Industry at the 13th Annual Satellite Awards. I was the thirteenth recipient of the award, following such luminaries as Kathy Bates, Susan Sarandon, Francis Ford Coppola, Maximilian Schell, Jodie Foster, and Rod Steiger. And, most important, I was the first African American chosen by the International Press Academy for this illustrious award. The Academy had also cited me "as a philanthropist and humanitarian . . . as the founder of the nonprofit Eracism Foundation aimed at creating entertainment that helps bring awareness and education to issues such as racism, ignorance, and societal apathy." I was deeply grateful for this award and eagerly anticipated that December evening.

God, however, had other plans for me that night. Suddenly overwhelmed by an acute exacerbation of chronic obstructive pulmonary disease with early respiratory failure, I arrived at UCLA Medical Center in the predawn hours, barely able to breathe, never mind walk or talk. As the medical team worked vigorously on me, I could feel myself slipping away. Aware of only the smallest snippets of the conversation around me, I somehow understood that the situation was dire, that the doctors were ready to put me on life support, which would be irreversible, and I would never be able to breathe on my own again. But that was okay. I was ready to leave. I could feel myself slipping into a place far away from these voices. Now I was moving down a tunnel, unable to stop, and everything was soft and gentle, and I felt loved and protected. Then another voice broke through, and it was louder than the humming sounds of the doctors around me. This voice was deep and firm. "Go back," it said. "It is not your turn."

Whether this was all the result of the medication or my feverish mind was playing tricks on me, I had no idea, but I could feel myself begin to relax as a mask was placed over my face. Now I could breathe, at first in tiny gasps, but gradually in deep, satisfying breaths. Then I fell asleep, a heavy, restful sleep that was giving me life, not taking it away.

For days to come, like a baby who was totally dependent on others, I lay in my bed, surrounded by the most caring and capable team of human beings, all dedicated to the one goal of saving my life. They were from every walk of life, all colors and nationalities, nurses, doctors, aides, each offering me the loving care that brought me back from near death. They fed me, clothed me, and fussed over me, adjusting my breathing machines and intravenous medications, washing me clean when

I could not take care of my bodily functions. They took care of me, asking nothing in return. To each of these selfless and talented human beings, I was simply a patient, one who would not die on their watch.

So, that is who they were, my most special team. But who was I? Who was this patient, this 220-pound mass of weakened bones and ailing flesh on which their hands ceaselessly worked? I was an aging actor who had recently fretted about the current state of his career, who worried about being "blacklisted," about Hollywood scuttlebutt, about roles not given and decent, fair salaries never paid. But astonishingly, to these miracle workers, I was someone they felt they knew. At some time during the last nearly sixty years, I had brought each of them a moment of pleasure, either in their dens or in the theater. And, as one so beautifully explained to me, they were thanking me for that gift. So they healed me and sent me home, whole and renewed, ready to face life with a strong body and an unbowed spirit. This was my Oscar; they had given it to me.

Sadly, but not unexpectedly, a small spot of ugliness tried to tarnish my epiphany. But I was used to it and threw it off with the same lack of fanfare that my loving team had shown when removing my soiled bedclothes. Because I had been unable to breathe on the night of the Satellite Awards and had ended up so seriously ill in the hospital, I had missed the special ceremony for which I had meticulously and joyously prepared.

Word on the street was hideous. The rumor mills circulated the news, "He is using again," certain that I had slipped back into my former state of drug dependency. "We know what happened," they continued to whisper. "It's the result of what he did in the past." Once again, as had happened far too many times during the last fifty years, they were wrong. But that was okay. It didn't matter.

They would have no way of knowing, nor would they find it interesting or newsworthy, that I was home now, growing stronger every day, thanks to the heroics of my team. Here I was celebrating Christmas in a hospital bed in my living room, surrounded by my two beautiful sons and their families. It is these two sons who are the accomplishment of which I am most proud, these two grown men now, neither of whom I expected to father or raise, these two sons whom I may have disappointed more than once, but whom I never, for one moment, stopped loving. Yet real life is much stranger than the world I inhabit in front of a camera or an audience, and my role as a father was never scripted or filmed.

Nor would I have ever believed that a month after my hospitalization I would be watching, with a joy akin to euphoria some fifty yards above the podium, while Barack Obama was sworn in as our forty-fourth president of the United States of America. Cicely Tyson was beside me, standing on a chair, as the oath of office was administered. The moment this handsome black man said, "Amen," and took his hand off the bible, I felt Cicely begin to collapse. As she slipped off her chair, she made a deep, unintelligible, primeval sound, which was repeated by my lips, as the two of us sank onto the grass, heaving uncontrollable sobs, close to unconsciousness. When we regained control of ourselves, we sat up and hugged each other, repeating over and over, "He made it. He made it."

From that moment on, it was as if all of the anger and sadness swarmed out of my body. I let go of all of the bad things that had happened to me, being chained to a tree, dirty dressing rooms, closed restaurants and hotels, racist comments, the inability to create my own projects, the drugs, along with the visions of attack dogs, the hoses, the lynchings. As all of that ugliness seeped out of my consciousness, I understood that there was no longer any reason to feel negative, to blame anyone for any failures I might face. All that I felt was happiness and a new calm. Today that feeling is still with me, for although I am not a weakling and will always stand up for justice, I believe that any excuse for rage at being discriminated against is unacceptable. This election proved that there is no such thing as second class.

From that day on, I felt myself going through a transition in which I am settling into another level, a more solid, spiritual place. Here, at this later stage of my life, I feel open to meaningful relationships with both men and women that I must not have had enough time or energy to develop in my younger years. Now, I am speaking to people for whom I have had great respect, using our moments together to exchange experiences, hope, and strength. More frequently, I come upon generous people both in my industry, top actors and directors, as well as those in every day society, who take the time to congratulate and thank me for my body of work. For so many years I felt as if I was in the periphery because my value system wrongly judged everything by the money, the importance of the character and the project, and the attention I got in respect to the white actors with whom I worked. I want to thank everyone who has come out of the woodwork to tell me they enjoy my work. It is a liberating feeling to know that I am no longer a victim of any circumstances.

More than ever before, I feel the rightness of Eracism, God's way of showing me that I am finally, at long last, on the right track. The most crucial aspect of Eracism, I have always understood, is to make certain that every teacher who works at the Shamba Center is well suited to the task. They must all be master teachers, the finest we can find, educators who have always dreamed of teaching in a place like our Shamba Center. And they must be well paid, as I believe all teachers should be. Their extensive screening and training program will make certain that their outlooks are positive and free of racism. We cannot take the risk of any negatives being transmitted to our children.

The teacher's job will be facilitated by a highly structured and well-thought-out curriculum created by the education department of a major university. It is through this curriculum, a program of learning the main elements of what might normally be learned in a functional family, that the rich African American history, as well as the equally unknown and vibrant histories of other minorities, will finally come to life. Lessons about hygiene and respect for the opposite sex and elders and one another will be a crucial part of this extensive curriculum.

My initial idea is to test the children every six months on all of these subjects to measure their progress. They will be questioned about history and the subjects we have taught them, not to be graded but rather to see how well we have been teaching.

They will also be asked to write essays on what they think about the world and how we can save our planet, so that we can learn from their bright young minds. I have no doubt whatsoever that their knowledge will be vastly improved, even after the first six months.

An enormous source of support to me has been L.A. mayor Antonio Villaraigosa, the first Latino mayor of the city in more than 125 years, and his top staff, all of whom aspire to make L.A. the first successful city of diversity in the United States. Although our plan is to establish a Shamba Center in every major U.S. city, we hope to open our first center in an existing building in L.A., where we would showcase our program. Within these walls will be rooms or learning stations, one for computer use, one with large screens in which to watch documentaries and plays, along with cameras to create the kids' own interactive videos. A well-stocked kitchen, a large gym with (at my personal insistence) a full basketball court, as well as yoga mats and weights and machines, will fill out the remaining space. Here I can visualize children of all races, exercising, eating healthy snacks and meals, meditating, and creating, all the while being educated and entertained at the same time.

My dream comes, of course, with a hefty price tag, which I believe can be paid for with private contributions, rather than with state, federal, or local funds. Even in today's economy, I am convinced that the money is there. What better investment can any individual or company find than our children? Nothing, we all now know, is impossible. These words are our motto and will be spoken many times every day that our doors are open. Right now, those who know so much more about grants than I do are applying for them, as well as appealing to businesses, such as Nike, Adidas, Sony, General Electric, Mitsubishi, and others. A partnership with Google is presently being explored. Even the neighborhood churches in many U.S. cities have already agreed to cooperate in any way they can.

A large carrot to entice the children, whose attendance must be mandatory, is the promise of visits from athletes and celebrities, along with politicians and businessmen, who would grace the center with their presence as often as possible, lecturing, laughing, playing ball, and teaching values. This is my time to call in favors from so many of the talented and famous people whose paths have crossed mine. I firmly believe that once these prominent men and women see what lies inside each Shamba Center, they will be honored to be part of these children's lives. But first, let's create one center that we can then replicate to prove the point.

Recently, when I excitedly blabbed on and on about the foundation to a counselor who had worked for many years in an organization that helps children, she listened respectfully and, when I was finished, said simply, "Fat chance. Good luck." I understood that her heart had been broken too many times before, and she had lost hope. Still, everyone had said the same thing about the first African American president, and we saw how that turned out. Certainly, I expect skeptics to shake their heads in disbelief as I move forward with my foundation, but I prefer to take my inspiration from Bernice King, who believes we've climbed to the mountain top and are now in the exact Promised Land that her father glimpsed. Here, we all understand, the work really starts.

For now this project is my life, 24/7. Wherever I speak, as I did to a group of two thousand teachers in Dallas, Texas, or at the Wheelock College graduation, or when I receive an award, such as the Distinguished Humanitarian Award from the Huntington's Disease Society, I spread the word and seek contributions to the Eracism Foundation. With my sons wonderfully married now and their beautiful children all a crucial part of my life, I am free to put my energies into a needier cause. This, apart from my family, is my legacy.

My phone continues to ring. Never have I felt so full of energy, so determined to accomplish my goals. There isn't a day that goes by that I am not grateful for all I have been able to accomplish in my life. Even though I might have faltered along the way, I do not look back but rather focus on today. To know that somehow I managed to help a child lead a better life would be the greatest reward I could ever imagine. To erase racism from the lives of these children, I fully realize, will be a gargantuan task. But for an exemplary black man who fell down and then learned how to stand up even taller than a marine drill sergeant, it is within reach.

It took hours to get into this reptilian costume to play the Drac Jerry in *Enemy Mine* (1985), and the contact lenses in my eyes caused often unbearable pain for nearly every hour of the day.

Sharron, age nine, is standing next to Jesse Jackson with me behind him in the Operation Push March on Washington to bring to light the plight of the homeless. That was in 1986 when Jesse was getting ready for a run for the presidency.

Here I am as air force colonel Charles "Chappy" Sinclair
standing beside his plane in one of the four *Iron Eagle*
movies, a series that spanned from 1986 to 1995 and did
some of its filming in Israel using Israeli fighter jets.

Fiddler looks quite handsome, hugging his fiddle, outside the plantation house in *Roots: The Gift*, a 1988 ABC-TV movie.

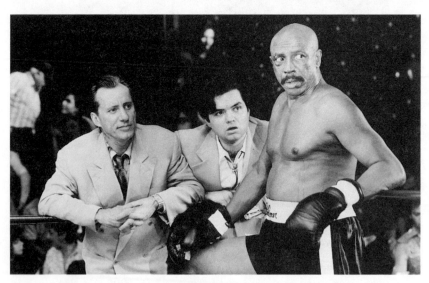

In *Diggstown*, a 1992 MGM film with Bruce Dern and James Woods, I played boxer Honey Roy Palmer, a forty-eight-year-old ex-heavyweight fighter coaxed out of retirement by scam artist Woods to fight ten opponents in one day. (Left, James Woods; right, Oliver Platt)

I got a chance to work with my dear friend Jon Voight in *Return to Lonesome Dove*, a 1993 TV miniseries, which we filmed in Montana.

Satie was around fifteen when he came with me to Billings, Montana, to film the miniseries *Return to Lonesome Dove*. I loved having him on the set.

It was a joy to work with the beautiful and talented Lonette McKee, who played Olivia in *To Dance with Olivia* in 1997 and again in *For Love of Olivia* in 2001.

Shaquille "Shaq" O'Neal, my grandson Malcolm, and I delivered toys on Christmas in 2003 to the LA Challenger Clubs for Boys and Girls. Shaq pulled up with an eighteen-wheeler loaded with toys for the kids. His heart was as big as the truck.

Here I am with Ossie Davis at the 27th Annual Kennedy Center
Awards in 2004, honoring Ossie and his wife, Ruby Dee. Ossie died
two months later. What a loss for the entertainment world, but an
unimaginable heartbreak for Ruby, his devoted wife for fifty-six
years.

Every time I am with my most special friend Ruby Dee, I am
reminded how much I adore her and how much I miss her cherished
husband, Ossie Davis.

Here's Pau Pau with his favorite four Gossetts. Malcolm (in front of me, left) and Olivia (far right) are Satie's two children. Brionne (next to me, right), who accompanied me to the 2009 Academy Awards, and Micah (middle) are Sharron's two children.

Here's my restored 1986 Corniche II. Years ago, I kept getting pulled over by the police, who wanted to know why that black man was driving a Rolls. Today, I'm friends with most of those policemen, who recognize me when I drive that beautiful car.

In this photo, I am leaving Africa in 2008, surrounded by members of the Masai tribe, after filming *Eyes on Kenya*, about African orphans.

PHOTO CREDITS

INDEX

Page numbers in *italics* refer to illustrations.

Abraham Lincoln High School, 33, 35, 276

Actors Studio, 2, 74–79, 92

alcoholism, 26, 29–31, 67–68, 71, 73–74, 204–205, 219–220

Ali, Mohammed (Cassius Clay), *109,* 182

Allen, Steve, 60

Allentuck, Max, 46

Anastasia, Albert, 35

Anderson, Maxwell, 51

Andrews, Mary, 34

Angelle, Bobby, 153–155, 158

Anthony, Sharron. *See* Gossett, Sharron (son)

Asagai, Joseph, 88

Ashby, Hal, 98, 158

Austin, Lynn, 46

Baker, Josephine, 160, 228

Belafonte, Harry, 84, 104, 121, 160

Berry, Halle, 257, 261

Bertha (great-grandmother), 7–8, 26

Big Story, The, 91

Blackberry (horse), 162

Blackboard Jungle, 4

Black Death, 204–205

Black Drought, 22

Blacks, The (Genet), 96–98, 101

Blanco (cat), 178

Blood Knot, 110–111

Blum, Gus, 41–42, 44, 54, 226

Bondy, Ed, 3, 15, 112, 186, 199, 230

Booth, Shirley, 62, 65–66

Box, John, 139

Boyd, William, 236

Brand, Edward, 193

Brando, Marlon, 76, 78, 99

Bridges, Beau, 158–159

Britt, May, 120

Broadway Show Softball League, 91–93

Brubaker, Tony, 143
Buck, Alan, 31
Burton, Art, 279
Burton, LeVar, 179–180
Bushbaby, 133–142, 147–148, 160
bush grass, 141–142

Cambridge, Godfrey, 96
Campbell, Stan, 92
Carruthers, Ben, 75, 77, 144
chronic obstructive pulmonary
    disease, 283–285
Circle in the Square Theatre, 81
Clayton, Xerona, 114, 281
Clements, Father, 281
Closer, The, 25
Coleman, Willie Lea, 182–183,
    207–208, 217, 218–219, 221
"comets," 79
Companions in Nightmare, 1–5,
    15–18, 189
Connors, Chuck, 144–148, 180
Cowboy in Africa, 144–148

Daddy's Little Girls, 278
Daniels, Billy, 2, 118–119
Davis, Ossie, 89, *295*
Davis, Sammy, Jr., 2, 111–115,
    117–118, 119–120, 122,
    124–125
Dean, James, 49, 77–79
DeCarle, John, 206
Dee, Ruby, 2, 83, 90, 98, *296*
Desk Set, The, 4, 62, 64–67
Diamondbacks, 252–253

Dick, Melvyn, 31, 61
Diggstown, 229, 232–233, *292*
Dixon, Ivan, 84–85
domestic violence, 67–68
Don't Look Back, 185, 197, *211*
Douglas, Melvyn, 4, 16–17
Dunham, Katherine, 161
DuPont, Penny, 65

Effrat, John, 91–92
Elkins, Hilly, 111–115, 120–121,
    125, 230
Elliot, "Mama" Cass, 96, 144
Enemy Mine, 201–209, *290*
Eracism Foundation, 114, 132,
    272, 277–289
Eyes on Kenya, 298

Fancy, Azime, 281
Father & Son, 247–248
Feuri, Sidney, 222
Feury, Peggy, 46, 74
Firemen's Fund, 208–209
Fleisher, Ruthie, 33
For Love of Olivia, 251–252, *294*
Foxx, Redd, 101

Gathering of Old Men, A, 220
Gere, Richard, 187–191, 258
Gideon Oliver, 155, 157
Glascoe, Hattie, 116–117,
    122, 127
Golden Boy, 2, 111–115, 125
Good Man in Africa, A, 235–236,
    239, 243

Good Morning America, 214–215

Gossett, Brionne (granddaughter), *297*

Gossett, Clemence (daughter-in-law), 253

Gossett, Hellen Wray (mother), 24, 31–32, 34, 52, 66–67, *106,* 113–114
   biographical information, 26–27
   illness of, 164–165, 167–168
   on race issues, 12, 15, 16, 63

Gossett, Lacey (grandfather), 28, 51

Gossett, Louis, Jr., *106–109, 210–213, 290–298*
   Academy Awards and, 194–195, 196, 198, *212*
   actor training, 2, 46, 60, 74–79
   as child actor, 44–54
   drug allegations against, 193–194
   drug rehabilitation of, 201, 221–222, 264–270
   drug use by, 68–71, 126, 141–142, 150, 168, 177, 185, 190, 201, 207, 219–220, 228, 237, 238
   education of, 28, 31–33, 56–61, 79–80, 83
   Eracism Foundation, 114, 132, 272, 277–289
   extended family of, 19–31, 37–38, 218–219 (*See also individual names of family members*)

Gossett Academy of Dramatic Arts (GADA), 128–132
   health issues of, 206–207, 209, 247–254, 255–256, 283–285
   homes of, 20, 35–37, 142, 151, 165–166, 171, 181–182, 201
   marriages of, 116–117, 122, 127, 170, 172–177, 193–194, 221–234
   on music, 71–73, 94–95, 132, 151, 170, 229
   non-acting jobs of, 44, 93–94
   producing by, 197, 247, 249–252, 257–263
   Shamba Center, 274, 276–278, 280–281
   on spirituality, 194, 286
   on sports, 32, 59, 83, 91–93, 100–101, 171, 252–253
   views on Coney Island, 20, 32–35, 42, 43–44, 57, 274–275
   See also individual names of films, plays, television shows

Gossett, Louis, Sr. (father), 12, 15, 16, 20, 24–25, 27, 43, 66–67, 73–74, *106,* 172

Gossett, Malcolm (grandson), *294, 297*

Gossett, Micah (granddaughter), *297*

Gossett, Olivia (granddaughter), *297*

Gossett, Robert (cousin), 25

Gossett, Satie Bertrand (son), *210,* 226, 233–234, 244, *293*
  birth of, 174–175
  childhood of, 176–179, 180–183, 184–185, 192–194, 198, 199, 201, 207–208, 216
  education of, 192, 253
  father's recovery and, 264, 266–267
  marriage of, 253
Gossett, Sharron (son), 215–219, 221, 226–228, 227, 228, 233–234, 253, 264, 266–267, *290*
Gossett, Timothy (uncle), 25
Gossett Academy of Dramatic Arts (GADA), 128–132
Grant, Lee, 158–159
Greene, Lorne, 180
Griffin, Merv, 60
Guvnor (uncle), 20–21, 23, 63–64, *106*

Hackford, Taylor, 188, 189
Hallums, Eugene, 38
"Handsome Johnny" (Havens, Gossett), 151
Hani, Chris, 239–243
Hani, Limpho, 240
Hansberry, Lorraine, 89–90
Happy Felton Knothole Gang, 57
Hardin, Tim, 150
Harlem Renaissance project, 257–263
Harlem Youth Act, 128

Harper, Otis, 191, 239–240, 241
Harry O, 143
Hartman, David, 215
Hatful of Rain, A, 75
Havens, Richie, 95, 116, 129, 151
Helen (aunt), 25, 226
Hellen Wray Gossett Child Care Center, 52, 164
Helfgott family, 27
Helmsley, Estelle, 49
Hendrix, Jimi, 167
Herzog, Wendy, 175
Hodges, Adele, 187
Hoffman, Dustin, 99–100
homelessness, 215–217

Inside, 237
insurance, for actors, 208–209
interracial romantic relationships, 101–105, 112, 159, 163–164, 166–167, 230–231, 250. *See also* race relations
Iron Eagle, 199, 201, 222–226, *291*
It Rained All Night the Day I Left, 224

Jackson, Jesse, 217, *290*
Jan Hus House, 61–62
Janssen, David, 143
Jasper, Texas, 257
Jones, Ike, 179
Jones, James Earl, 56–57, 98, 111, 130, 220
Josephine Baker Story, The (HBO), 228–229

Kennedy, John F., 122, 128
Kennedy, Robert, 122, 123
Kerzner, Sol, 243
Kikuyu, 134, 140
King, Bernice, 281, 289
King, Coretta Scott, 114
King, Martin Luther, Jr.,
    114–115, 116, 122, 197,
    249, 252, 278
Kyle, Golden, 105
Kyle, Lillian, 104–105, *109,*
    167–168

Lackawanna Blues, 257
Landlord, The, 86, 98, 158–159
Last Poets, 132
Lawman without a Gun, 181
Lazarus Syndrome, The, 181
Lear, Norman, 181
Lee Strasburg Acting Studio,
    46–47, 50
LeNoir, Rosetta, 61
Lindstrom, Pia, 214, 215
Little, Rich, 229
Lloyd, Norman, 3, 16
Locke, Peter, 247–248
Logo Entertainment, 247, 249
Loncraine, Richard, 202,
    203–204, 205
Lopresti, Liz, 267
Lortel, Lucille, 130, 131
Lost in the Stars (Anderson), 51
Love Songs, 249
Lovey (dog), 178
Lyceum Theatre, 51–54, 75

Mafia, 32, 35, 124
Malcolm X, 115, 117, 122
Manatis, Janine, 74–75
Mandela, Nelson, 236, 237, 242,
    245–246
Mangosing, Christina, 170,
    172–177, 193–194, 217
Marathon Man, 99–100
marijuana, 69–71, 150
Mark Twain Junior High
    School, 35
Masai, 134, 140
McClintock, Ernie, 130
McDaniel, Hattie, 156, 195
McKee, Lonette, 249, *294*
McNeil, Claudia, 88–89, 98
Meilziner, Jo, 46
Merchant of Venice, The, 130–131
"meteors," 79
Mofokeng, Palesa Jacqueline, 244
Monroe, Marilyn, 76–77, 122
Morrow, Vic, 4, 179–180
Murderous Angels, 159–161

Nathan's, 44
Negro Actors Guild, 91–93
Negro Ensemble Company, 130
Neil, Fred, 95
Neville Brothers, 220
New England Café, 62–67
Newman, Paul, 86, 92
New York University, 28, 56–61,
    79–80, 83
Nickerson, Jimmy, 232
Nixon, Richard, 132

Nkrumah, Kwame, 160
Noyes, Thomas, 46
Nurses, The, 134–135

Obama, Barack, 24, 53, 246,
    281–282, 285
Officer and a Gentleman, An,
    186–191, 194–195, *212*
Olivier, Laurence, 48, 99–100
O'Neal, Frederick, 46, 49
O'Neal, Patrick, 4, 17
O'Neal, Shaquille "Shaq," *294*
On Her Ground, 261
Original Five Blind Boys, 71–72
Ostrin, Norman, 31

Paige, Satchel, 185
Palance, Jack, 50, 78
Pappalardi, Felix, 73
Paradigm, 264
Patterson, Floyd, 39–40
Pendleton, Camp, 186–187
Penn, Arthur, 111–112, 237
Peter, Paul, and Mary, 82, 150
Peterson, Wolfgang, 202, 204,
    205–206
Petrie, Daniel, 98
Plummer, Christopher, 100
Poitier, Sidney, 2, 4, 74, 76, 92,
    104, 121
  awards to, 195
  in *A Raisin in the Sun,* 83–85,
    88–89, 98
poker, 86–88
Police Story, 154

Powers of Matthew Star, The, 182
Procter & Gamble, 249
Promises, 264–268
Pryor, Richard, 69, *109,* 129
P.S. 187, 20
Punisher, The, 227

Quaid, Dennis, 201, 205

race relations, 72–73, 125, 285
  Academy Awards and, 195
  African Americans in major
    roles, 156–157, 181
  black nationalism and,
    116–117, 122
  civil rights movement and,
    114–117
  Cowboy in Africa and,
    144–148
  in Europe, 166–167
  Gossett's personal experience
    with, 5–8, 9–15, 62–67,
    190–191
  income of actors and, 150, 153,
    183, 199, 221, 250
  interracial romantic relationships
    and, 101–105, 112, 159,
    163–164, 166–167,
    230–231, 250
  Jewish/African American
    relations, 32–35
  land reclamation issues and,
    23–24
  race riots, 37, 44, 254
  See also Eracism Foundation

Raisin in the Sun, A (Hansberry), 1,
    83–90, 93, 98, 101
Randall, Jason, 189
Rangel, Charlie, 25
Redfield, William, 17
Reece, Cyndi James, 221,
    226–228, 229–234, 253
Reed, Robert, 180
Return to Lonesome Dove, 293
Rhodes, George, 120
Rhodes, Shirley, 120–121
Richards, Beah, 75, 89
Rill, Eli, 74–75
Ritchie, Michael, 230
Roberts, Doris, 66
Robinson, Bumper, 207–208
Robinson, David, 245
Robinson, Jackie, 57, 160, 245
Robinson, Sugar Ray, 31, 32
Roots, 125, 146–147, *292*
Ross, Stanley Ralph, 58–59,
    117–118
Ruben (great uncle), 23

Sackheim, Bill, 157
Sadat, 191–192, *213,* 224
Sands, Diana, 74, 79, 83, 85–86,
    89, 98–99, 158
Santiago-Hudson, Ruben, 257
Scott, Doyle, 33
Scott, George C., 81, 92, 185
Sebastian, John, Jr., 95
Shamba Center, 274, 276–278,
    280–281
Shimkus, Joanna, 104

Sib (aunt), 23
Silvera, Frank, 2, 49–50, 75, 76
Sinatra, Frank, 124
Skin Game, 160
Smalls, Charlie, 60, 87
Smith, Bessie, 22
Smith, Henry, 152
Smith, Maggie, 165, 166
Smith, Mimi, 152
Smyrl, David Langston, 128–130
Snyder, Ted, 267
Sorvino, Paul, 130
Springboks, 236
Stanley, Kim, 17–18
Stapleton, Maureen, 46
Steers, Helen, 27, 41
Steinberg, Paul, 36
Stix, John, 46, 48
Stookey, Noel "Paul," 73, 150
Storik, Barry, 31
Strasberg, Lee, 74
Strojan, Al, 43
Sugar Rays, 32
Susskind, David, 60, 91
Sylvester, Rocco, *106*

Take a Giant Step, 45–48,
    51–54, 61–62, 74, 77, *108,*
    113, 163
Tambo, Adelaide "Mama,"
    237, 241
Tambo, Dali, 237, 240
Tambo, Oliver, 237, 240
Tate, Sharon, 144
Terra, Georgie, 12, 20

3rd Battalion, 502nd Infantry
    Regiment, 225
Tiger (cousin), 179, 199, 201
Tim (uncle), *107*
To Dance with Olivia, 249
Torres, Liz, 129
toxic mold syndrome, 255–256,
    264–266
Travel Channel, 230
Travels with My Aunt, 165, 166
Trent, John, 133, 135–142
Turner, Sandi, 33
Tyson, Cicely, 285

Underwood, Blair, 248
Universal, 5–8, 16, 143
Urich, Robert, 251
U.S. Army Signal Corps, 12
U.S. Marine Corps Recruitment
    Division (MCRD), 186–187

Villaraigosa, Antonio, 287
Voight, Jon, 257

Walker, A'Lelia, 261
Walker, Madame C. J., 261
Washington, Lamont, 119
White, Jane, *108*
White Dawn, 173–174
William Morris Talent Agency, 3
Winger, Debra, 188
Wolf, Dick, 157
Woody (uncle), *107*
Wray, Etta B. (grandmother),
    26–27, *107*
Wray, Tenny (grandfather),
    26–27
Wynter, Dana, 17

Yellin, Sue, 33
You Can't Take It with You, 44
Young, Gig, 17
Young Rebels, The, 153
Yunnie (uncle), 28
Yvonne (cousin), 179, 199, 201

Zulu and Zayda, The, 3, 118, 129